BUILDING
SUCCESSFUL
MULTICULTURAL
ORGANIZATIONS

BUILDING SUCCESSFUL MULTICULTURAL ORGANIZATIONS

CHALLENGES AND OPPORTUNITIES

Marlene G. Fine

Q

QUORUM BOOKS
Westport, Connecticut • London

Library of Congress Cataloging-in-Publication Data

Fine, Marlene Gail.
    Building successful multicultural organizations : challenges and
opportunities / Marlene G. Fine.
        p.   cm.
    Includes bibliographical references and index.
    ISBN 0-89930-681-0 (alk. paper)
    1. Multiculturalism.   2. Personnel management.   3. Organizational
effectiveness.   I. Title.
HF5549.5.M5F56   1995
658.3'041—dc20

British Library Cataloguing in Publication Data is available.

Library of Congress Catalog Card Number: 94-39345
ISBN: 0-89930-681-0

First published in 1995

Quorum Books, 88 Post Road West, Westport, CT 06881
An imprint of Greenwood Publishing Group, Inc.

Printed in the United States of America

The paper used in this book complies with the
Permanent Paper Standard issued by the National
Information Standards Organization (Z39.48-1984).

10 9 8 7 6 5 4 3 2

DEDICATION

For my sons, William Fine and Julius Johnson,
and my partner, Fern Johnson,
who give meaning and purpose to my work,
and bring joy to my life.

CONTENTS

ACKNOWLEDGMENTS

I am indebted to the many women and men who shared their organizational experiences with me; their stories inspired me to write this book. I am especially grateful to Connie Griffin and Patricia Hynes for encouraging me to do diversity work in organizations and for giving me the opportunity to do so at the Environmental Protection Agency. Donna Bivens taught me how to listen to the voices of people of color in organizations and enriched my understanding of their lives. Stephen Haas of the University of Massachusetts Boston library ably assisted me in my research efforts. Janice Raymond and Carolyn Anderson have been my intellectual role models and friends for many years; their advice about the process of writing a book got me started and kept me going. Tom Gannon, who is now retired from Quorum Books, suggested that I write this book and was confident that I could do it. Eric Valentine, my publisher, showed enormous patience through several missed deadlines. Most of all, I thank Fern Johnson—mentor, friend, and life's companion—who spent endless hours discussing ideas, sharing her expertise in communication and culture, and commenting on my drafts, and whose encouragement and support inspire and sustain me every day.

INTRODUCTION

By the year 2000, the work force as we know it will be extinct: Over the next decade, the majority of people entering the U.S. labor force will comprise women, people of color, and immigrants. This book addresses the organizational issues created by the changing demographics of the U.S. work force. As increasing numbers of women, African Americans, Hispanics, Asians, Native Americans, and other racial and ethnic minority groups enter the work force,[1] organizations must confront cultural difference as the norm in organizational life. The purpose of this book is to give organizational leaders a framework for understanding cultural diversity and to suggest strategies for creating organizations that develop the full productivity of a multicultural work force.

"Cultural diversity" tends to be broadly defined in its current use in organizations to include a variety of races, genders, ages, ethnicities, classes, sexual preferences, physical abilities, and religions. For the purposes of this book, I am limiting my analysis primarily to issues of race, ethnicity, and gender. My analysis is cultural; I believe that people of different cultural backgrounds share particular patterns of interpreting experience and interacting with others. Social scientists have documented the different cultural assumptions of, for example, gays and lesbians, the differently abled, and members of different social classes. No one book, however, can address the cultural assumptions of all groups. The theoretical analysis I present here is applicable to cultural categories other than race, ethnicity, and gender. My decision to limit the discussion of cultural diversity in this book to race, ethnicity, and gender is not intended to be exclusionary in re-visioning[2] organizations. A truly multicultural organization must value, respect, and recognize all employees, regardless of race, gender, class, ethnicity, age, sexual preference, physical ability, or religion.

The idea for writing this book emerged from my experiences talking and working with employees in a variety of organizations, large and small, public and private. Many of these experiences were through research and consulting activities. My research interests have always been in exploring the impact of race and gender differences on organizations and the people in them. Both as an organizational member myself and as a consultant look-ing into organizations, I have been struck by the ways that people of differ-ent gender, race, and ethnic backgrounds interact with each other, and, often even more strikingly, perceive the world around them. In my earlier research studies, I discovered that people, both men and women, white and of color, bring different assumptions, values, and behaviors with them into the workplace. Furthermore, those assumptions, values, and behav-iors shape how they are perceived and responded to by their co-workers, how they respond to organizational situations, and how they interact with other people. I have sat through numerous painful meetings in which mem-bers of different groups or cultures have talked past each other, never truly hearing the other's voice or acknowledging the truthfulness of the other's position. These meetings rarely produce productive outcomes for anyone. Even when there appears to be surface consensus on an issue, some mem-bers of the group leave angry, frustrated, or just defeated.

This book is intended to help people in organizations better understand multicultural interactions in the workplace. It is not, however, a how-to book of rules for managing a culturally diverse work force. I have no quick fixes or recipes to offer executives who want to create a productive multicultural work force. Bringing our own cultural assumptions into our awareness and learning to recognize the cultural assumptions of others is a difficult and sometimes painful process. Working together to create a multicultural community within an organization requires patience, hard work, and an organization-wide commitment to change.

Organization-wide commitment and willingness to change are critical. This book does not take the perspective that executives in organizations should learn how to manage diversity; such a perspective assumes that the power dynamics in organizations will remain the same and that managers simply need to learn how to control and use people who are different from themselves. Instead I believe that people in organizations must work to-gether to create new organizations with new assumptions and values about people, their behavior, and how work gets accomplished.

My perspective is transformational: The multicultural work force of the twenty-first century will transform U.S. organizations in ways that we can-not yet imagine. This transformation is critical for two reasons. First, the viability of organizations in the twenty-first century will depend on their ability to be multicultural. The demographic trends in the United States are clear: During the next decades, significantly more children will be born to nonwhites (primarily Hispanics and African Americans) than to whites, large numbers of immigrants (primarily Asians and Hispanics) will enter the United States, and women will continue to join the work force in record numbers. The work force of the future will, of necessity, be multicultural, since neither public nor private organizations will have sufficient numbers of young white men to hire. If organizations cannot transform themselves in ways that will allow and encourage people from vastly different cultural backgrounds to work together productively, they will not be able to achieve their organizational goals. Second, cultural diversity has the potential to strengthen organizations by adding new ways of understanding organizational problems. In recent years, we have seen numerous examples of how U.S. industry has been hampered by its inability to see beyond an ethnocentric vision of how to do business. U.S. companies have frequently failed to understand, develop, and adopt new ideas that would keep them competitive in the contemporary marketplace, whether those ideas involved developing new consumer products and marketing campaigns for particular consumer groups or envisioning new inventory systems, work schedules, quality control systems, and ways of organizing production-line work.

Organizational leaders can choose to ignore the imperatives created by the changing demographics of the work force. They can continue to manage their organizations based on the assumption that all employees share the same "patterned ways of thinking, acting, feeling, and interpreting" (Ting-Toomey, 1985, p. 75) or, that if they don't, the differences can be suppressed by the dominant culture within the organization. Or they can begin now to grapple with the implications of bringing together people who do not share the same cultural assumptions but must work together to accomplish the goals of their organizations. We have the opportunity now to transform organizational life and to participate in making that transformation productive and positive for all employees, regardless of race, gender, class, ethnicity, age, sexual preference, physical ability, or religion.

This book is divided into seven chapters. Chapter 1 describes the current demographic changes in the U.S. work force. Chapter 2 provides a critique of current organizational theory and offers an alternative theoretical perspective for understanding cultural differences in organizations. Chapter 3 reviews the literature on cultural differences, focusing on the patterned ways of thinking, acting, feeling, and interpreting of particular cultural groups, including Asians, Hispanics, African Americans, and Women. Chapter 4 looks specifically at how cultural differences are manifested in the workplace and the implications of those differences for all employees. Chapter 5 describes strategies and programs that have been used by public and private sector organizations to address cultural diversity issues. Chapter 6 focuses on strategies for helping individuals improve their interpersonal relationships in the workplace. Chapter 7 focuses on strategies for helping organizations re-vision organizational assumptions and practices that preclude women and people of color from participating fully in organizational life.

NOTES

1. Naming these various ethnic, racial, and cultural groups presents complex choices for several reasons. First, each group includes a range of ethnicities and identities. African Americans include blacks born and raised in the United States and those who have emigrated here from the Caribbean and African countries. Native Americans represent many different Indian tribes indigenous to the United States, Eskimos, and Aleuts. Hispanics comprise a wide range of backgrounds and ethnicities, including Mexican American, Puerto Rican, Cuban, Dominican, and Central and South American. Asian Americans are even more diverse; including those with ancestry that is Chinese, Japanese, Korean, Thai, Vietnamese, Cambodian, Laotian, Malaysian, Indian, Filipino, and so forth. Second, naming is a personal and political act. Some Hispanics prefer the term Latino because it "better reflects their roots in and connection with the peoples and cultures of Latin America as well as their blend of indigenous, African, and European influences" (Ferdman & Cortes, 1992, p. 273), while others with Mexican roots prefer Chicano or Chicana. Using the same reasoning, many blacks in the United States prefer the term African American because it reflects their connection with the peoples and cultures of Africa. Some American Indians use the term Original Americans to refer to themselves in order to highlight the fact that they lived here before other groups arrived on our shores.

My naming choices throughout this book generally reflect the most widely used and understood terms. I use the term Hispanic to refer to all Latin American cultural groups in the United States, although I also sometimes use Latino. Hispanic avoids the patriarchal implications of Latino. I use the term African American to refer to black Americans whose cultural roots are in both Africa and the United States; African Americans are a distinct cultural group within the larger racial category of blacks. In most instances, I follow the convention of not capitalizing "black" or "white" when the terms refer to either racial group, except when the reference appears with the name of a cultural group that is capitalized. I refer to nonwhites as people of color rather than minorities in order to highlight the racial and cultural differences among them. The term is also technically more appropriate since nonwhites are no longer a minority in some parts of the United States. As a white woman, I am sensitive to the political implications of my naming others. The lack of unanimity about names among the diverse groups represented in each of the cultural communities about which I am writing, however, forces me to do so. Keep in mind throughout the book, therefore, that individual members of these cultural groups may prefer different names.

2. My use of the verb "re-visioning" (or sometimes "re-vision") here and elsewhere throughout this book is deliberate and purposeful. By re-visioning I mean to

see something that is known in an entirely new way. The term is drawn from "to vision," which means to see as in a revelation. Re-visioning is the act or action of going back to see something revealed in a new way. The word is not meant to imply "revise," which means to look carefully over with a view toward correcting. Revise suggests tinkering or making minor changes; re-vision suggests transformation of the whole through the act of seeing the whole in a new way.

1

THE CHANGING DEMOGRAPHICS OF THE WORKPLACE

Shortly after the middle of the next century, non-Hispanic whites will no longer be the majority cultural group in the United States. For many Americans, who were raised, as I was, in all-white or nearly all-white communities, the vision of a multicolored, multicultural nation is incomprehensible. For some who grew up believing that the American way is the white way and the only way, that vision is disturbing and frightening.

This chapter provides a brief overview of the changing demographics of the U.S. population and the ways in which those changes will affect the work force in the twenty-first century. The purpose of the chapter is to provide a context for understanding why organizations need to address issues of cultural diversity in the workplace, and to demystify the plethora of numbers and projections about demographic changes that is bandied about in the popular press.

OUR CHANGING COLOR AND ETHNICITY

Although projections about the changing racial and ethnic make-up of the U.S. population now seem to appear everywhere, the Bureau of the Census only recently began collecting data on race and ethnicity. The Federal government had no particular reason to collect statistics on race until the Civil Rights Act of 1964 was passed. Even then, there were no standard definitions of race or procedures for collecting data on race until the 1970s. By then, the explosive growth of the multiracial Hispanic population in the United States had created a need to collect data not only by race but also by ethnicity.

In 1980, the Office of Management and Budget issued a policy directive (OMB Statistical Policy Directive No. 15, "Race and Ethnic Standards for Federal Statistics and Administrative Reporting") that established a government-wide policy for all federal agencies for collecting, reporting, and maintaining data on race and ethnicity. Policy Directive No. 15 defines four racial groups and two ethnic groups, each of which is "based on geographical or cultural, rather than scientific distinctions" (*Federal Data Collection*, Dec. 1992, p. 2). The racial groups include: (1) White; (2) Black; (3) American Indian, Eskimo, and Aleut; and (4) Asian and Pacific Islander.[1] Ethnicity, in contrast to race, is defined by two broad categories: Hispanic and non-Hispanic origin. Both Hispanics and non-Hispanics can be of any race. These racial and ethnic categories create eight possible cultural groups for the purposes of collecting data on race and ethnicity. Although the policy directive does not establish a preferred method for categorizing people in these groups, the Bureau of the Census, except in special instances in which an individual leaves a question blank, uses self-identification rather than observer-identification to establish an individual's race and ethnicity. The closest the policy directive comes to establishing how an individual's racial identity should be defined is in the directions for reporting the racial identity of persons of mixed racial and/or ethnic origins. Persons of mixed racial and/or ethnic origins should use the category "which most closely reflects the individual's recognition in his community" (*Federal Data Collection*, Dec. 1992, p.10).[2]

It is important to be aware of these racial and ethnic categories and how people are identified as members of them because there are many misconceptions about demographic trends in the United States based on misunderstandings about how the data are collected and analyzed. First, many people mistakenly believe that race is a scientific category based on genetic background and established through some set percentage of ancestral blood. It is not. Race is defined primarily through skin color and geographic origin. For example, Asians come from a diverse range of Asian countries and the Pacific Islands, including Cambodia, China, Japan, Korea, and Hawaii, among numerous other places. Second, many people confuse race with ethnicity and believe that Hispanics are a racial category. This misconception is especially problematic in understanding demographic projections in the United States.

I began this chapter by saying that "shortly after the middle of the next century, non-Hispanic whites will no longer be the majority cultural group in the United States." I chose this wording quite carefully. Numerous articles on cultural diversity in the United States herald that the United States will be a nation of color by that time. We will be a nation of much more color than we are now, but the demographic projections still show the U.S.

population as primarily white through most of the next century. Hispanics, however, will be the largest ethnic group in the country, and that demographic shift presages a radical cultural change. Understanding the difference between whites and non-Hispanic whites is essential to understanding the population and work force changes that we can anticipate in the future.

Population Growth

The Bureau of the Census predicts that the population in the United States may reach 276 million by the year 2000; by 2050, it may increase another 50 percent to 392 million (Day, 1993). The rate of population growth during the next century, however, will be much slower than the growth we are experiencing now. The United States is presently experiencing the second largest decade-long growth spurt in its history (second only to the post-war baby boom of the 1950s), but that growth will begin to moderate by the turn of the century as the last group of baby boomers moves out of childbearing age and into middle age.

As our population growth moderates over the next several decades, however, the distribution of racial and ethnic groups within the population will shift dramatically. Since 1970, the white non-Hispanic population has grown at a significantly slower rate than the minority group population in the United States. Non-Hispanic whites accounted for 83.5 percent of the total U.S. resident population in 1970; by 1990, they accounted for only 75.6 percent (*Census Reform*, Jan. 1993). The white population in the United States, especially the non-Hispanic white population, will continue to decrease as a proportion of the total population. In fact, by 2031, the Bureau of the Census predicts that the non-Hispanic white population in the United States will stop growing; after that point, any increase in the white population in the United States will be the result of increases in the population of white Hispanics (Day, 1993).

While the growth of non-Hispanic whites is about to end, racial and ethnic minority groups are dramatically increasing their numbers. In 1990, Blacks, Asians, and American Indians were 15.8 percent of the total U.S. population, and Hispanics of all races were 9.0 percent. The Bureau of the Census predicts that by 2050, nearly half of the population will be Hispanic, Black, American Indian, or Asian (*Census Reform*, Jan. 1993). Table 1 shows the predicted change in the percent distribution of the population from 1990 to 2050.

Although each of these minority groups is growing and will continue to grow rapidly, their individual growth rates vary widely (see Day, 1993, for a complete set of projections and analyses of population growth in the United States based on data from the 1990 Census). The black population will increase 200 percent, to 62 million, by the middle of the next century,

Table 1
Percent Distribution of Population by Race and Hispanic Origin

	1990	2050
White*	75.7	52.5
Black*	11.8	14.4
American Indian*	0.7	0.9
Asian*	2.8	9.7
Hispanic**	9.0	22.5

*Persons not of Hispanic origin.
**Persons of Hispanic origin may be of any race.

Source: Data taken from Day, 1993.

growing at twice the rate of change of the white population. After 2012, more blacks will be added to the U.S. population each year than whites.

Asians are the fastest growing cultural group in the country. The Asian population in the United States more than doubled (108%) during the 1980s, increasing more than 40 percent in every state except Hawaii, where Asians and Pacific Islanders already represent 61.8 percent of the population. In California, the Asian population increased a whopping 127 percent during this time period ("Race and Hispanic Origin," June 1991). The explosive growth of the Asian population is expected to continue, with annual growth rates in excess of four percent during the 1990s. From 2008 on, Asians are expected to add greater numbers each year than non-Hispanic whites.

Although Asians are the fastest growing group, after 1996, Hispanics will add more people to the population each year than any other racial or ethnic group. Hispanics are adding so many new people to the total population each year that they may become the second largest cultural group in the country as early as 2010.

These demographic changes, although dramatic, are not visible everywhere in the United States. The distribution of minority groups is much more concentrated than the overall population distribution in the United States ("Race and Hispanic Origin," June 1991). Since 1970 the distribution of blacks has remained fairly stable, with 53 percent living in the South and only nine percent in the West. Only three states have more than two million blacks (New York, California, and Texas), and six of the ten states with the largest black populations are in the South. The four nonsouthern states with large black populations (California, New York, Michigan, and Illinois) contain large urban centers to which southern blacks migrated in large numbers starting in the 1940s and ending by the late 1960s. All ten states with the highest percentage of blacks in the total state population are southern.

The West has the greatest racial and Hispanic diversity of any region in the United States, with the largest share of the total American Indian (48%), Asian (56%), and Hispanic (45%) populations. By the turn of the century, California could have a "minority majority," and in Los Angeles county, Blacks, Asians, and Hispanics already compose 59 percent of the population (Farney, Dec. 2, 1992, p. A4).

The distribution of Asians and Hispanics is much more concentrated than the population in general. The majority of Asians live in only three states: California, New York, and Hawaii. The Hispanic population has been even more concentrated, with the majority living in either California or Texas. In the 1980s, however, Massachusetts (104%), Florida (83%), and Washington (79%) experienced the highest Hispanic population growth rates among the states. The highest percentage of Hispanics as a proportion of the state population live in five contiguous southwestern states: Texas, New Mexico, Colorado, Arizona, and California.

Reasons for the Changing Demographics

Three factors are responsible for the changing racial and ethnic mix in the United States: (1) different fertility rates, (2) net immigration, and (3) age distribution (Day, 1993). These factors are generally well known and frequently discussed in accounts of diversity issues in the United States; those discussions, however, are often based on misunderstandings about the complexity and interrelatedness of the factors. Popular press accounts of diversity would lead one to believe that there is both a rising tide of immigration in the United States and burgeoning fertility among black and Hispanic women. Both beliefs are inaccurate.

Immigration in the United States was the highest from about 1840 through 1930, although it peaked from 1901 through 1910, with nearly nine million immigrants arriving on our shores. From World War II on, immigration remained relatively small, although the numbers grew slowly each decade, from one million in the 1940s to nearly six million in the 1980s. The number of immigrants relative to our total population, however, has remained relatively stable and is much smaller than it was at the height of immigration in the early part of the century. From 1901 to 1910, there were 10.4 immigrants for every 1000 residents; by the 1980s, that rate had dropped to 2.7 immigrants per 1000 residents (U.S. Bureau of the Census, 1991).

In the 1990 Census, 7.9 percent of the population reported being born outside of the United States. The Bureau of the Census population projections from the 1990 Census suggest that net immigration (the number of immigrants to the United States minus the number of emigrants from the United States to other countries) over the next decade will average 880,000 people per year (Day, 1993). Approximately two-thirds of the immigrants who arrive each year are either Asian or Hispanic.

Immigration has had the greatest effect on the Asian population, both in terms of overall population growth and in the mix of cultures represented in the Asian population. The growth in the Asian population, which is the fastest growing racial or ethnic group in the United States, is primarily the result of net immigration. Census projections suggest that the number of Asian immigrants will be larger than the number of Asian births for the next 25 years (Day, 1993). Immigration has also changed the face of the Asian population in the United States. Asians and Pacific Islanders are not a homogeneous group; the category represents numerous countries of origin that differ in language, culture, and recency of immigration. For example, most Japanese and Chinese families in the United States are native-born and have been here for many generations. Most Pacific Islanders, although newer to our shores, were also born here. Most Hawaiians are, of course, native to the United States. The most recent Asian immigrants tend to be Vietnamese and Cambodian.

Recency of immigration is important in understanding population growth because the fertility rates of women born outside of the United States tend to be higher than the fertility rates of women born in the United States. Asians now have higher fertility rates than either whites or blacks in the United States (Table 2 lists the fertility rates for White, Black, Asian, and Hispanic women), but their fertility rates are expected to decline over time as a larger share of Asian fertility will be from Asian women born in the United States (Day, 1993).

While the Asian population is growing rapidly through immigration, the growth in the Hispanic population is due to both immigration and high fertility rates. In fact, although many Americans believe that the growth in the Hispanic population is the result of large scale immigration, especially illegal immigration from south of our border, 1990 Census data suggest that the growth in the Hispanic population is affected more by the birth rate than by immigration (Day, 1993). Hispanic fertility rates are the highest of any racial or ethnic group; in 1993, there were 2900 births for every 1000 Hispanic women (Day, 1993). Just as the Asian fertility rate is expected

Table 2
Fertility Rates* by Race and Hispanic Origin

White	1973
Black	2470
Asian	2514
Hispanic**	2900

*Represents births per 1000 women of childbearing age.
**Persons of Hispanic origin may be of any race.

Source: Data taken from Day, 1993.

Table 3
Median Age by Race and Hispanic Origin

White	33.9 years
Asian	30.4 years
Black	28.0 years
Hispanic*	26.2 years

*Persons of Hispanic origin may be of any race.
Source: Data taken from Bennett, 1992a; 1992b.

to decline as a greater proportion of the Asian population is native-born, the fertility rate for Hispanic women should also decline.

Many people also have misconceptions about the growth in the black population in the United States. Although the black population is growing more quickly than the non-Hispanic white population, the growth differential between them is not because black women are having more and more babies each year. Although black women have slightly higher fertility rates than white women (2469.5 births per 1000 black women; 1972.7 births per 1000 white women), the major difference between the two groups is not how many babies each has but when they have their children. White women tend to have their children a few years later than black women (Day, 1993). Popular mythology to the contrary, fertility rates for black women remained stable throughout the 1980s and have declined since 1960 (Bennett, 1992b).

The contributing factor that has the most serious implications both for population growth and work force composition is the difference in age distribution among the different racial and ethnic groups. See Table 3 for a summary of the median ages of the White, Black, Asian, and Hispanic populations. The non-Hispanic white population in the United States is aging. At one end of the age spectrum, the aging of the white population means that more whites are dying each year. At the other end, fewer women are entering their childbearing years. As I said earlier, although non-Hispanic whites presently account for 75 percent of the U.S. population, declining birth rates and aging mean that they will make no net contribution to the total population by 2030, and that their proportion of the population will decline to 53 percent by 2050. By 2030, non-Hispanic whites will account for three-quarters of the U.S. population aged 65 and older, but less than half of the population under 18 (Day, 1993). This age distribution means that fewer whites will be coming into the work force while many more will be dependent upon it.

The black population in the United States, which is primarily a native-born population whose ancestry dates to slavery or earlier, is also aging, but blacks are younger than whites. Approximately 33 percent of blacks are under 18, and eight percent are 65 and over; in contrast, 25 percent of whites are under 18 and 13 percent are 65 and over (Bennett, 1992b). The Asian population (median age = 30.4 years), although slightly older than the black population (median age = 28.0 years), is younger than the white population (median age = 33.9 years) (Bennett, 1992a; 1992b). The Hispanic population is the youngest among the racial and ethnic groups, with a median age of 26.2 years (Garcia & Montgomery, 1991b). The relative youth of the Black, Hispanic, and Asian populations, coupled with their higher birth rates, means that they will contribute a growing share to the overall growth rate of the U.S. population, while non-Hispanic whites will contribute less.

It is important to note here that although the black population is increasing both numerically and in proportion to the white population, the annual growth rate of blacks has declined by over one-third since 1960. The Asian and Hispanic populations are growing much faster than the black population, and Hispanics will shortly pass blacks as the second largest racial or ethnic group in the United States. Many people in the United States identify cultural diversity issues as synonymous with racial tensions between blacks and whites. They are not. Cultural diversity issues encompass numerous cultural groups that are now, or will be in the future, represented in the U.S. population, but that are currently marginalized in American public life. Cultural diversity issues are not just between whites and minorities, but also among the many groups that have been designated as racial or ethnic minorities.

GENDER, RACE, AND ETHNICITY IN THE WORK FORCE

The United States is experiencing a long-term decline in the growth of its labor force. From 1975–1980, the labor force grew at an average annual rate of 2.8 percent; from 1990–1995, that growth rate was expected to decline by nearly two-thirds, to one percent per year (Sternlieb & Hughes, 1988). The age distribution of the population means that there will be some loss of people 55 and older from the work force and relatively little gain from those under 18. Most of the current and future growth in the labor force will be the result of new entrants who are between 25 and 54 years of age, which puts the work force at the height of its productivity for the remainder of this century (Sternlieb & Hughes, 1988). The vast majority of those new entrants will be racial and ethnic minorities and women. *Workforce 2000*, the Hudson Institute's landmark study of work force trends, predicted that five-sixths of the net additions to the work force between 1985 and 2000 would be nonwhites, women, and immigrants (Johnston & Packer, 1987).

Because the work force is both aging and growing less quickly, the effects of the demographic changes in the population in general will be intensified in the work force. At the beginning of the 1990s, over one-fifth of the U.S. labor force was composed of racial and ethnic minorities; 10.8 percent was Black, 7.5 percent Hispanic, and 2.6 percent Asian (Bennett, 1992a; 1992b; Garcia & Montgomery, 1991a). By the turn of the century, all three groups will increase their representation in the labor force, but Hispanics (10.1%) will begin to catch up to Blacks (11.7 %) (U.S. Bureau of the Census, 1991), and shortly after the year 2000, they will surpass them, becoming the second largest group in the labor force.

The most dramatic change in the composition of the work force, however, is the large scale entry of women. In 1970, there were 31.5 million women in the U.S. work force; by 2000, there will be 66.8 million. In 1970, 43.3 percent of women in the United States worked outside of the home; by 2000, 62.6 percent will work outside of the home. Even more telling, the percentage of women aged 25 to 34 who work outside of the home will jump from 45.0 percent to 82.4 percent in the same time period (U.S. Bureau of the Census, 1991). This increase in the number of women working outside of the home holds across all racial and ethnic groups; the labor force participation rates of White women, Black women, Asian women, and Hispanic women are roughly equivalent.

At the same time that women are increasing their labor force participation rates, the rate for men is declining slightly; from 1975 to 1995, the labor force participation rates for men went from 77.9 percent to 75.3 percent (Sternlieb & Hughes, 1988). The decline in the labor force participation rate for men is primarily the result of the aging of the white and black population in the United States. The number of men who are retiring and leaving the work force (or dying) is greater than the number who are coming of age as workers. The dramatic increase in the labor force participation rate for women, on the other hand, is the result of economic and social changes. Since 1969, average weekly real earnings have decreased over 12 percent (Commission on the Skills of the American Workforce, 1990). As real income has steadily declined over the last two decades, more and more families have been forced to have two adults working fulltime (and, in some instances, more than fulltime) to cover food, housing, health care, and educational expenses. The skyrocketing divorce rate during that same time period also forced many women into the labor force to support themselves and their children. In addition, the Women's Movement in the late 1960s and early 1970s made it increasingly acceptable for women to work outside of the home, and many women, especially younger ones, decided to do so.

Implications of a Changing Work Force

The changing color, gender, and ethnicity of the work force open new windows of opportunity for women and people of color. At the same time, these changes create numerous challenges to both public and private sector organizations. Real opportunity, of course, depends on having access to well-paying and meaningful jobs. The first challenge organizations will face is to provide opportunities for people of color to move up the organizational ladder. Although the changes in the composition of the work force will give people of color new opportunities for entry-level employment, organizations will need to work diligently to ensure that people of color will be able to move beyond those positions.

This challenge will be made even more difficult by the shifting numbers of Asians and Hispanics relative to blacks in the population generally and the work force specifically. As the Hispanic population begins to surpass the black population numerically, blacks may feel increasingly alienated from American society. Because most African Americans have family roots in the United States that go back many generations, some of them resent the attention given to members of newer immigrant groups. Some interpret the rejection of affirmative action programs and the embrace of cultural diversity initiatives as racist because it displaces African American concerns. These feelings are understandable. We have seen increasing evidence of African American resentment and alienation in the racial tensions between Blacks and Asians, and Blacks and Hispanics.

The increasing representation of women in the work force, especially those with children or of childbearing age, creates a second challenge for organizations. Employers need to develop "family friendly" policies and practices that ensure the health and well-being of children and aging parents. As our population ages, more families will need help in caring for elderly parents and other relatives. And as our labor force ages, children will become an even more precious resource. The nation's failure to increase productivity over the last 20 years can be blamed, in some part, on our lack of attention to the health and education of our youth.

The major challenge created by the changing color, gender, and ethnicity of the work force, however, will be transforming the white male culture of U.S. organizations into a multicultural culture that nurtures and sustains all of its workers. In the next chapter I explore the characteristics of the white male culture prevalent in U.S. organizations and show how that culture excludes women and people of color, sometimes intentionally and often tacitly.

NOTES

1. In the interest of brevity, throughout the remainder of the book, I will use "Asians" to refer to Asians and Pacific Islanders, and "American Indians" to refer to American Indians, Eskimos, and Aleuts.

2. The issue of how to categorize and count persons of mixed-race ancestry has become controversial. In the 1980 Census, mixed-race individuals who did not self-identify their race were categorized according to the race of their fathers. In the 1990 Census, the practice was reversed, and mixed-race individuals who did not

self-identify their race were categorized according to the race of their mothers. Switching the method of counting, of course, makes it impossible to compare the data on mixed-race persons from the 1980 Census and the 1990 Census. More importantly, however, switching the method points to a fundamental problem with the definition of race for purposes of demographic data collection. Is an individual's race determined genetically or culturally? If race is genetic, then what constitutes the cut-off point for racial identity: 100 percent? 75 percent? 51 percent? If race is culturally determined, then what culture do mixed-race children claim? In some cases, the answer is very clear. For example, non-Hispanic children of one black and one white parent almost always are identified as black by others, and they generally self-identify as part of the black community, where they are more likely to be welcomed than in the white community. But for increasing numbers of mixed-race families, their cultural identity is not fully with either community represented by family members. Instead, they are forging new cultural identities based on their unique situations. After the 1990 Census, the Bureau of the Census received numerous requests from mixed-race individuals to add at least one mixed-race category to the 2000 Census form. The Bureau is presently exploring the issue.

2

DIFFERENCES IN THE WORKPLACE: A THEORETICAL PERSPECTIVE

I grew up in a traditional American family. My father went off to work each morning (and most evenings and weekends, as he struggled to make ends meet) and my mother stayed at home to raise the children and manage the household. When I was a teenager, my mother went to work, ostensibly because she was bored, but, in truth, because we needed the money to help pay the cost of sending two children to college. My mother never considered her work a career and she promptly left the work force when my younger brother finished his education.

That particular reality of my life—a father who worked fulltime outside of the home and a mother who worked fulltime inside of the home—was mirrored in the television shows I watched, the textbooks I studied, the movies I saw, the books I read, and in the lives of most of my friends. That my family and the families of my friends were white made the reflection seem even more accurate. There were, of course, subtle differences between my family and its television counterpart on *The Donna Reed Show*. We were Jewish; my father held neither a professional nor a managerial position; and our problems never seemed to get resolved in 30 minutes. But the essential rightness of the vision of white men going off to run the country's businesses pervaded my understanding of the world in which I lived.

The rightness of that vision also pervaded the literature on management, where discussions of who managed the nation's companies and how they managed them were dominated by images of white men in pinstriped suits who made rational decisions based on logical thinking and solid data, and communicated their ideas assertively, clearly, unemotionally, and un-equivocally. Although the description of how white men manage is dis-torted by our cultural stereotypes (we all know men who are not logical, assertive, clear, unemotional, or unequivocal), the fact is that most manag-ers were, and still are, white men. So it is not surprising that management scholars developed theories and perspectives on management that were based on the experiences of white men.[1]

This chapter includes three major sections. First, I will describe the de-velopment of current organizational theory, which was built on the assump-tion of an homogeneous (i.e., white male) work force. Second, I will cri-tique current organizational theory by looking specifically at how it shaped management practice as significant numbers of women and people of color began to enter the work force. Finally, I will develop a framework for un-derstanding cultural diversity in organizations that is based on the assump-tion of a heterogeneous work force.

ORGANIZATIONAL THEORIES FOR WHITE MEN

Theories are abstract, intellectual constructs that explain and predict phe-nomena in the real world. Organizational theory comprises a set of propo-sitions that attempt to explain or predict how groups and individuals be-have in different organizational structures and circumstances; it is concerned with the ways in which people form social units to achieve organizational and personal goals (Shafritz & Ott, 1987). The term *organizational theory* does not refer to a single theory of organizations. There are myriad theo-ries about organizational phenomena, some of which are related to and build upon one another, while others are radical philosophical departures from previous work. *Organizational theory* as I use it throughout this book refers to the predominant assumptions that underlie mainstream research and practice in management.

Several factors in the development of organizational theory and research created and reinforced its emphasis on understanding the experiences of white men. First, organizational theory has always been about the *manag-ing* of organizations. Organizational theory is deeply rooted in highly prag-matic concerns about accomplishing organizational purposes, whether those purposes are ruling nations, winning wars, or producing goods and services.

The earliest treatises on organizational theory emphasize hierarchy and leadership as key elements in the successful accomplishment of those pur-poses. Several important works from our earliest recorded history state that hierarchical organization, division of labor, and leadership are central principles of organizational theory (Shafritz & Ott, 1987). In Chapter 18 of Exodus (1491 B.C.), Moses' father-in-law, Jethro, warns Moses that he will wear himself out if he continues to be solely responsible for adjudicating disputes among and teaching God's statutes to the people of Israel. Jethro tells Moses to delegate authority along hierarchical lines. In 370 B.C., Xenophon described a Greek shoe factory, and provided the first known description of the advantages of the division of labor. In *The Discourses*, Machiavelli (1513) stated the principle of unity of command, advising that it is better to have one person of average competence in charge than two leaders of exceptional ability (Shafritz & Ott, 1987).

The longstanding emphasis on the people and the activities at the top of the organization created a managerial bias in organizational theory and research that has focused attention on the white men who have held, and continue to hold, those positions at the top of virtually all organizations in the western world. Although historically women have dominated the pink-collar ranks and people of color have often been employed in blue-collar positions, organizational theory has generally ignored their presence because it has focused on managers and their concerns. To the extent that workers have been featured at all, it has been as objects on which management can experiment, as in Elton Mayo's famous studies in the 1920s of Western Electric's Hawthorne plant. We see this focus today as both researchers and practitioners seek strategies for managing the increasing cultural diversity of the work force.

The second factor that has focused interest on white men has been the financial support of the military for research in organizational theory. Many of the early research studies in this century were funded by the military and were done in military organizations using military personnel. Until the 1970s and the creation of the volunteer Army, Navy, Air Force, and Marines, military organizations were dominated by white males. Even today, although African Americans comprise 20 percent of the military services (a significantly larger percentage than in the general population in the United States), they represent only seven percent of the officers (Will, Feb. 11, 1991). Research questions generally reflect the needs of funders and research findings reflect those same funders' assumptions. It is not surprising, therefore, that the management studies funded by the military continued to study and validate the social, psychological, and behavioral attributes of white men.

Finally, just as the managerial ranks of corporations and the military were dominated by white men, so, too, were the academic ranks of the universities where most organizational research was done. Thus, not only were the subjects of research studies white males, the researchers themselves were white and male. The reproduction of the male authority pattern (patriarchy) in the academy has shaped the research agenda across the disciplines of the academy and has profoundly affected our understanding of the world around us. *Patriarchy* is a male-dominated system of social relations, a society manufactured and controlled by males (Daly, 1987, with Caputi). The dominance of men within the social system has led to the suppression of women's experiences and the silencing of women's voices. Feminist theory seeks to understand the causes of women's oppression and to radically restructure patriarchal social relationships. Feminist theorists in the arts, humanities, physical and biological sciences, and social sciences recently have begun to question the patriarchal research agenda and have begun to reshape our understanding of diverse issues, including what constitutes science (Keller, 1985), how people "know" (Belenky, Clinchy, Goldberger, & Tarule, 1986), how children develop moral judgment (Gilligan, 1982), and the nature and functions of bureaucracy (Ferguson, 1984).

Until very recently, however, those voices and their re-visions of experience were not heard in organizations. The unquestioned assumption of the normative nature of white male behavior in organizations was reinforced by the basic assumptions of the larger culture in which organizations were situated. Basic assumptions about the societal roles of men and women, about the division of labor, and about the necessity for hierarchy were deeply ingrained in the American psyche, and were simultaneously reflected and reinforced in what we saw in organizations and in what researchers found when they studied organizations. Because basic cultural assumptions are taken for granted and operate at a preconscious level, they are "non-confrontable and non-debatable" (Schein, 1985/1987, p. 392). Thus, researchers rarely questioned their assumptions about the normative nature of white male attitudes and behavior, even when they discovered that other attitudes and behaviors in the organization were different.

For example, Hatfield and Huseman (1982), in a study of the relationship between job satisfaction and congruence between superior/subordinate communication, concluded that communication congruence (i.e., the degree to which superiors and subordinates share similar perceptions of their communication with each other) significantly affects job satisfaction. A closer look at their data, however, reveals that the relationship is weaker for women, and, in fact, is very weak for black employees. Despite their statement that for blacks "congruence . . . may not be as important as the subordinate's own perception of factors affecting the superior-subordinate relationship" (Hatfield & Huseman, 1982, p. 356), they suggested that future research should identify ways to enhance the congruence between superiors' and subordinates' communication in order to improve job satisfaction. In this case, even though the researchers found differences, they suppressed those differences in favor of conclusions based on white male norms. The Hatfield and Huseman study is not atypical. The academic literature in organizational theory generally does not acknowledge cultural differences among employees, despite the presence of women and people of color in organizational life for the last two decades. The prevailing assumption in the organizational literature is that these newcomers would either behave in the same way as white males or assimilate into white male patterns.

WOMEN AND PEOPLE OF COLOR ENTER
THE THEORETICAL DOMAIN

Women

Throughout the 1970s, increasing numbers of women joined the work force. The 1970 census reported that 40 percent of the labor force was female (Gordon & Strober, 1975, p. 1); by 1980, women were 43 percent of the work force (Loden & Rosener, 1991). Several converging economic, social, and cultural changes created a climate that brought white women out of the house and into the workplace.[2]

Although many people credit the Women's Movement with the social changes that underlie the large-scale entry of women into the work force, those changes were propelled by concurrent economic changes. As economic growth slowed and consumerism escalated in the United States, families found it harder to maintain their lifestyles on one income. My mother's entry into the work force to help pay for her children's college education was not unusual. As the cost of housing, education, food, and other essentials increased, wages failed to keep pace, and as more luxuries were redefined as necessities, more women went to work. The divorce rate also skyrocketed, forcing many women to become the sole supporters of their children. The changing mores of U.S. men and women made it easier for women to make the move out of the house, and economic necessity changed our attitudes about women's roles and appropriate family lifestyles.

Regardless of why women went to work, the reality is that they did. And as they did, both women and the organizations that employed them sought some understanding of women's new place in society. The study of women in the work force focused primarily on issues related to the status of women in management. Although pink-collar workers focused attention on the low salaries and poor working conditions of secretaries, and numerous economic studies showed that women at all occupational levels earned less than men in similar jobs, most academics and organizational theorists were interested in why women weren't being promoted to managerial positions.

In an early study of attitudes toward women in management, Basil (1972) surveyed 300 organizations, asking the highest ranking woman and highest ranking man to whom a woman reported about their attitudes toward women managers. Their responses were strongly negative: The highest ranking men and women believed that women lack the qualifications for management, the motivation for success, and the ability to withstand the pressure; that women are unable to relocate; and that women are less educated than men. Basil also reviewed the available literature about women in management and concluded that the literature painted a picture of women as "temperamentally unfit" to be managers: "Women are not as rational as men, cannot be as objective, are inclined to jealousy and to make decisions based on emotionalism" (Basil, 1972, p. 14). His conclusion about the image of women in the literature echoed the comments of male executives in an earlier *Harvard Business Review* (Bowman, Worthy, & Greyser, July/Aug., 1965) survey.

The pervasiveness of negative attitudes toward and stereotypes about women managers led to numerous studies that compared men and women on a number of dimensions related to managerial ability. In an exhaustive survey of the psychological literature on sex differences, Jacklin and Maccoby (1975) found few psychological differences between the sexes in areas germane to management, such as leadership, task persistence, achievement motivation, and intellectual abilities; they concluded that "Women are not psychologically handicapped for promotions in management" (p. 37). Larwood and Wood (1977) published a series of studies that presented evidence about whether women are fit to be managers. Although Larwood and Wood asked readers to draw their own conclusions from the evidence, they admitted their own bias in favor of women's abilities led them to conclude that women and men had similar abilities to manage.

That bias was not shared by others, however. In the late 1970s, several major academic and popular press books told women that they were different from men, and that their differences made them deficient as managers. Most of these writers espoused what has been termed a "new deficit" position (Johnson, 1983) for interpreting women's skills in the workplace, arguing that because women have limited experiences in male environments, they have never developed the skills appropriate to those environments.[3]

In 1976, Margaret Hennig and Anne Jardim published *The Managerial Woman: The Survival Manual for Women in Business*. Called "required reading" by the *New York Times*, the book asserted that women managers share similar problems "because a common heritage of beliefs and assumptions shapes our concept of ourselves" (p. 68). Hennig and Jardim argued that the socialization of women made them dependent, uncertain, lacking in self-esteem, seekers of security, and poor team members. Men, in contrast, were seen as flexible, "more alert to cues and signals which women may neither hear nor see" (1976, p. 50), team players, planners, and influencers. Although Hennig and Jardim said that they did not place a value judgment on these differences, they nonetheless advised women to learn men's ways:

The issue is, if you want a career, how do you help yourself achieve it in organizations made up predominantly of men? How must you be seen and heard? Given the culture and its masculine codes, what must you downplay if you don't want to be seen as foreign to the system? (Hennig & Jardim, 1976, p. 206)

Popular writers echoed this advice. Betty Harragan (1977), in one of the most popular advice books ever written for working women, *Games Mother*

Never Taught You, argued that "working is a game women never learned to play" (p. 34). Harragan presented a series of case histories of working women and concluded that these women lacked "elementary conceptual knowledge about the working environment" (1977, p. 21). She advised women to learn the rules (including how to talk about football at the water cooler on Monday morning) if they wanted to be successful in business. Kate Rand Lloyd, then editor-in-chief of *Working Woman*, blamed the way women are raised, saying it has "programmed us at many levels to fail" (Catalyst Staff, 1981, p. xviii). She told women that all is not lost, however, for "it's not in our genes. . . . We may need retraining or additional education" (Catalyst Staff, 1981, p. xviii).

The emphasis on training pervaded not only the literature but also organizations. Many companies began to offer special management training programs just for women that focused on skills women allegedly lacked. These programs included training in assertiveness, communication skills, problem-solving, planning and organizing, and time management. Private consultants who offered such training outside of the corporation flourished.

Several premises are central to the new deficit position. The first is that women and men think and act in different ways because they have been socialized in different ways and in different environments. The second is that women's attitudes, behaviors, and skills in the workplace are inferior to men's (because white, European, heterosexual men manage most businesses, their behavior has become normative for the business environment, and, by traditional social science standards, behavior that deviates from the norm is deficient). The third is that women must change their behaviors and attitudes and improve their skills if they are to succeed in organizational life.

Among the early writers on women and management, only a few who claimed there were gender differences in managerial style argued that those differences did not imply that women's skills were inferior to men's. Some, like Arjay Miller, then Dean of the Stanford Graduate School of Business, thought that women's socialization made them better interpersonal communicators and, therefore, better managers (introduction to Gordon & Strober, 1975). A very few believed that there was no need to compare managerial skills because both men and women could perform managerial jobs in acceptable ways. Basil (1972) suggested that social science research on leadership traits supported the conclusion that "there's no one way to be successful as a manager" (p. 109). He said that this conclusion raised "the possibility that women could determine their leadership patterns to suit their own personalities and strengths and not have to compete with men on the basis of male strengths" (Basil, 1972, p. 109). Basil, however, accepted traditional stereotypes about feminine behavior and he suggested that women should be able to "be feminine and even seductive . . . to achieve success in a managerial career" (1972, p. 111). That suggestion doesn't seem all that odd when you consider that he asked Edith Head, Hollywood's premier fashion designer in the 1960s, to write the foreword to his book!

The publication of Rosabeth Moss Kanter's *Men and Women of the Corporation* (1977) appeared to mark a major theoretical shift in the organizational literature. Kanter examined the roles that men and women play in organizations and how those roles constrain and shape behavior. She identified three primary roles—managers, secretaries, and wives. Kanter's work was noteworthy primarily because it painstakingly detailed the genderized nature of roles in organizations; Kanter identified organizations as patriarchal systems that reproduce within themselves the sex role stereotypes and sex role relations of the larger society. Thus, women primarily occupy marginalized and largely invisible roles as secretaries and wives, serving men behind the scenes. As managers they face serious obstacles to success because they are stereotyped as having feminine qualities, such as being too emotional, that are considered inappropriate for managers.

Kanter's analysis differed from others, however, in that she attributed gender bias in organizations not to women's different life experiences and the "deficient" behavior that results from those experiences, but to structural problems in organizations. For example, she argued that men are perceived as winners in organizations because they have access to power resources to which women do not have access. Since powerless leaders are perceived as autocratic by their subordinates, women managers are viewed negatively by those who work for them. That perception is further reinforced by women's behavior. Often promoted into new positions for which they do not have adequate training and experience, women (according to Kanter) adopt authoritarian leadership styles.

Kanter also developed a perspective on understanding the managerial behavior of women that was based on their status as tokens in organizations. According to Kanter, tokens exist when groups are skewed in number such that the dominants in the group control the group. Kanter identifies three consequences of token status. First, tokens are more visible, which creates enormous pressure on tokens to perform their jobs better than everyone else. Second, tokens are seen in contrast to dominants and so their differences from dominants are heightened. Third, tokens are forced to assimilate into the dominant culture. Kanter believed that once the numbers of women and men in managerial positions was more balanced, organizations "would be more tolerant of the differences among them" (1977, p. 283). Other theorists also shared Kanter's belief that increasing the numbers of women in predominantly male roles would lead to greater acceptance of women because they would be seen as individuals rather than as representatives of a group (see, for example, Epstein, 1975).

At the core of Kanter's analysis is the assumption that real gender differences in the ability to manage do not exist. Her theoretical position is based on the assumption of homogeneity: If organizations change the structural determinants of behavior and increase the number of women in managerial positions, women and men will manage in relatively similar ways, and organizations will become gender blind. Although Kanter's perspective appeared to suggest a radical change in organizational theory and workplace practice, the transformation was superficial. Rather than restructuring the workplace, Kanter's approach changed only the determinants of women's behavior by offering them the same opportunities as men. Her analysis cannot be enlarged to account for the cultural differences of the new work force in the United States because the analysis is based on denying the existence of such differences.

In addition, Kanter's analysis is confined to the organization per se; Kanter fails to take into account the historical and sociocultural issues related to the status of women. The analysis of the token status of women, for example, presumes that the power differentials between women and men are based solely on the numerical imbalance in the organization. A brief look at the history of the status of women in the United States would suggest that the power differentials exist in virtually all contexts, even when women are not represented only by tokens. In fact, studies of organizational contexts in which men have token status, such as nursing, indicate that despite their token status, men do not experience the same social isolation, performance pressure, or role conflict that female tokens experience (Fairhurst & Snavely, 1983a; 1983b; Snavely & Fairhurst, 1984). Clearly male tokens have an external source of power that is greater than the loss of power they experience by being numerically underrepresented. Anyone who has attended public school in the United States is well aware of the phenomenon. Although most public school teachers at both the elementary and secondary level are women, virtually all principals and superintendents are men.

The experience of women in management over the last two decades also belies Kanter's analysis of tokens. Despite the fact that women have moved into entry-level and middle-management positions in large numbers, few women have achieved executive status (Fierman, July 30, 1990). Sutton and Moore (Sept./Oct. 1985) replicated the famous 1965 *Harvard Business Review* survey that found that most corporate executives in the United States believed that women were emotionally unfit to be managers. Although they concluded that executives' attitudes toward women were now somewhat more favorable, they still found "much resistance to female managers," and almost half of the women in the survey said they believed "that women will never be completely accepted as executives in corporate America" (Sutton & Moore, Sept./Oct. 1985, p. 66). Kanter said that women feel performance pressure in their positions because of their token status. Yet Sutton and Moore found that women continue to believe that they "must be exceptional to succeed in business" (Sept./Oct. 1985, p. 66).

Researchers who have investigated the status of women in corporations often refer to the "glass ceiling," or the threshhold beyond which women in organizations are not promoted. The token theory of women in organizations suggests that when the numbers are sufficient, women will break through the glass ceiling and move into executive positions. Yet as the overall number of women in corporate life has increased, the number of women in senior positions has not. The glass ceiling has remained unbroken, with large numbers of women clustered just below it. In fact, a 1991 Labor Department study revealed that the glass ceiling is even lower than researchers expected, with many fewer women being promoted into middle-management positions than had been predicted (Sehgal, Aug. 9, 1991).

People of Color

Although many consider the United States to be a country comprised of diverse peoples, historically most of that diversity has been ethnic rather than racial. Until recently, nonwhites have accounted for only a small percentage of the total population: The 1970 census showed only 10.7 percent of the U.S. population as nonwhite (Dickens & Dickens, 1982). Immigration patterns, coupled with a declining birth rate among whites, especially in relation to the birth rates among nonwhites, are beginning to change the population mix. During the next two decades, people of color will account for 87 percent of the growth in the U.S. population (Loden & Rosener, 1991). During that same time period, 29 percent of new entrants into the labor force will be nonwhites, making them 15.5 percent of the total work force in the year 2000 (Johnston & Packer, 1987).

Throughout the 1970s, largely through the efforts of affirmative action policies, nonwhite workers, particularly African Americans, began to make some inroads into organizational life. Although affirmative action policies were to a large extent the result of the Civil Rights struggles of the 1950s and 1960s, they served, in most cases, to make women rather than blacks more visible in organizations. As the largest racial minority in the United States at the time, African Americans, however, did begin to see some results from affirmative action policies.

As they did when women began to enter the work force in significant numbers, organizational theorists and practitioners launched their analysis of African American workers by focusing on issues related to managerial skills and the reasons why blacks had difficulty being promoted to managerial positions. There was much less literature about black managers, however, than about white women. This fact is not surprising. Women as a group comprised a larger percentage of the total population than did black men and women. Thus, they provided more potential readers for trade books. Their numbers also made them more immediately visible and important to employers, and therefore, to academic researchers. Further, although the academic ranks in management schools were (and still are) heavily male and white, there have always been significantly more women management faculty than faculty of color.

These reasons, however, provide only a superficial understanding of the relative invisibility of blacks in organizational research. At a deeper level, it was much easier for the dominant culture to focus on the entry of white women into the workforce rather than black men and women for three reasons.

First, white men and women live together. When white men leave the public world of work, they return to their private worlds at home—and those private worlds most often include women. They could not ignore the entry of women into public life and then face them privately. White men, on the other hand, could ignore black men and women. Racial segregation in our private lives has long been the norm in U.S. culture. Most white men do not live next door to black men and women. White women may be different, but not so different from white men that they avoid social contact with each other. In fact, the differences between women and men are celebrated in the culture as reasons for interacting socially with one another. Racial differences are usually unmistakable and permeate our public and private worlds. Unlike gender differences, racial differences appear in our cultural mythology as reasons for separation. Few people, black or white, who have grown up in the United States have not been told that "blacks belong with blacks and whites belong with whites."

Second, the black analysis of the barriers to black progress in the corporate world was more radical, and, therefore, more potentially dangerous than the analysis of the barriers women faced. Fernandez (1975) compared the careers, attitudes, and opinions of black and white, male and female managers at all levels in eight organizations and concluded that racism was the primary factor precluding black managers from participating fully in organizations. He identified two types of racism: (1) Neoracism, which is individual white attitudes towards blacks; and (2) institutional racism, which comprises the exclusionary procedures, rules, and regulations of organizations. Fernandez reported that black managers said that the advice they would give to young blacks in their organizations was to "stand up for what you believe is right—be your own person," and to counteract the racist idea of conforming to "white standards of appearance, values and attitudes" (1975, p. 209).

Rather than taking the position that blacks should learn white ways of doing business if they want to succeed, black writers challenged the dominant white culture, charging it with racism. Black writers acknowledged that many blacks found organizations to be hostile and unknown territories. Davis and Watson (1982) introduced their book, *Black Life in Corporate America*, as their "report on the human side of the story of men and women operating in foreign social space with unfamiliar protocol, with habits, manners, values and styles of thinking that until recently were very new to them" (p. 1). But unlike the writers who advised women, black writers told black managers that they should not assimilate into the dominant white male culture. Instead, they argued that the dominant culture had to change, had to become more inclusive of others (Davis & Watson, 1982; Dickens & Dickens, 1982; Fernandez, 1981). This transformation was critical not only to protect the integrity of black culture but also to create better organizations. Fernandez (1981), for example, wrote that a "homogeneous managerial force tends to replenish itself with noncritical 'yes men' who concern themselves with driving independent and original minds out of the company" (p. 288).

Finally, women were more likely than African Americans to accept the advice that they should learn to fit into white male organizations by adopting white male modes of being and behaving. The pervasiveness of sex role stereotypes throughout the culture, especially male-defined concepts of femininity, suggests that sexist assumptions, values, and beliefs are not simply imposed on women, but are internalized by women. This makes sex role stereotypes powerful shapers of women's behavior. Without a strong, independent sense of self and a recognition of the existence and value of a separate women's culture, women were easily persuaded that they were inadequately prepared for the world of work.

This analysis is not meant to suggest that African Americans are not also subject to white constructions of their identity and the racism that is the result of judgments based on stereotypes of "blackness." But African Americans do have a unique culture, which is shared and celebrated by blacks and is acknowledged by nonblacks, and which gives them an identity apart from the identity that is imposed on them by others. Despite concerns that some black sociologists and others have about the assimilation of middle-class blacks into mainstream white society, blacks in organizations are less likely than white women to accept the premise that they should be like white men in order to succeed in organizational life because white ways of doing things are better than black ways. Although blacks suffer the same psychological consequences as do women of trying to "pass" in organizations, when they return to their communities after work, they return to places where they can reaffirm their worth and where they can identify whites as the "other." With the exception of some lesbians and feminist women, women return to homes where they live with men and reaffirm their feminine worth.[4]

The analysis of workplace issues for blacks differed in two additional ways from the analysis for women. Black writers did not focus their analyses entirely, or even primarily, at the micro-level. Although they were concerned with neoracism, they were more concerned with institutional racism. Analyses of the black experience in the workplace suggested greater political sophistication on the part of black analysts and a more complex understanding of the institutional barriers to the advancement of people of color. In addition to the recognition of the importance of institutional racism, black analysts also recognized that since organizations are a microcosm of the larger society (Dickens & Dickens, 1982), all of the problems blacks experience in the workplace cannot be solved within the corporate context. Instead, society as a whole has a responsibility to deal with its racism and sexism (Fernandez, 1975).

CULTURAL DIVERSITY IN THE UNITED STATES IS COOPTED

After the flurry of initial interest during the 1970s and early 1980s in the entry of women and blacks into the workforce, few articles appeared in the major academic journals. Apart from more specialized outlets such as *Working Woman* or *Ebony*, even the popular press generally ignored the changing demographics of the U.S. work force. By the late 1980s, academic researchers appeared to tire of research studies on gender differences in management. In an exhaustive review of the literature, Powell (1990) said that he found no actual differences between male and female managers and he concluded that "companies should not act as if there are" (p. 71). The emphasis in the literature on women and management was on perceived rather than actual differences (Noe, 1988; Powell, 1990), and researchers called for efforts by organizations to overcome stereotypes and create gender-blind evaluation techniques. A few studies of the experiences of people of color in the workplace revealed that they had been rewarded less often and less well and that they were generally more dissatisfied with their experiences than white employees (Fine, Johnson, & Ryan, 1990; Greenhaus, Parasuraman, & Wormley, 1990).

Sporadic articles on creating multicultural organizations appeared (Cox, 1991; Cox & Blake, 1991), and academics showed some interest in responding to the demographic trends forecast in *Workforce 2000: Work and Workers for the 21st Century* (Johnston & Packer, 1987). The primary focus on issues of cultural diversity, however, shifted from domestic concerns to globalization and the multinational workforce. Several factors led to this shift in focus.

First, the academic response to affirmative action shifted as the political climate changed. Throughout the 1980s, affirmative action programs and policies were systematically dismantled, through both lack of support by the executive and legislative branches and Supreme Court interpretation. Although those who are outside of academic life often refer to academics as living in an ivory tower that is isolated from the political realities of everyday life, historically, academic research has tended to reflect the prevailing political positions. The sociolinguistic research on Black English Vernacular (BEV, the particular dialect of standard English that is spoken by some African Americans) provides an example of the relationship between politics and academic research. The early research on black English focused on examining the ways in which the dialect failed to conform to the rules of standard English. Based on their findings, researchers concluded that the dialect was a deficient linguistic form—a research finding that was compatible with the political, economic, and social status of blacks in the United States. As the Civil Rights movement gained political and social prominence and credibility, the research on BEV shifted dramatically. Researchers now began with the assumption that the dialect had a complete grammatical, lexical, and phonological system. Their research focused on describing that system and the features of it that make the dialect unique from other dialects of standard English. Based on this line of research, academics suggested that Black English Vernacular was different, but not deficient.

As did the literature on BEV, the literature on diversity in the workplace reflected the country's political agenda. As affirmative action policies and programs came under increasing fire in the public arena, the academic literature began to shift to a critique of affirmative action. Affirmative action programs became synonymous with quotas and hiring and promoting less qualified people.

The critique is interesting both linguistically and strategically. The term "affirmative action" was originally created to emphasize acting in positive ways by reaching out to minority communities. It was intended to let employers know that their responsibility in matters of equal employment opportunity went beyond saying "No women or minorities applied for the job," or "We tried to hire a woman or black but found no one with the qualifications." By redefining the term to mean setting quotas that resulted in hiring unqualified women and people of color, those opposed to affirmative action shifted the grounds of the debate about affirmative action policy from corporate responsibility to individual qualifications.

The new grounds created an untenable position for affirmative action proponents. First, the prevailing philosophy (or, some would argue, myth) in management is that the workplace is a meritocracy where workers are rewarded for their competence, not their sex or skin color. If affirmative action means hiring those who are less qualified, then affirmative action policies destroy the image of the organization as a meritocracy. Second, as long as organizations evaluated job qualifications and performance according to white male standards, most women and people of color would be judged unqualified. Critics of affirmative action, therefore, could almost always point to ways in which affirmative action candidates were inferior to white males.

Politics has also made discussions about multicultural organizations suspect in academic circles. Again the issue is one of definition. Colleges and universities were among the first organizations in the United States to respond positively to the principles of affirmative action. Throughout the 1970s and 1980s, institutions of higher education actively pursued faculty and students of color, especially African Americans. Although most schools met with relatively little success in recruiting faculty of color,[5] they were able to bring students of color to campuses in numbers sufficient to create a minority voice among students. This presence was enlarged during the 1980s when the number of college age people began to decline, forcing colleges to broaden their client base by recruiting heavily among nontraditional student populations, especially foreign students.

To go along with their recruiting efforts off-campus, some higher education administrators have begun working on-campus to create environments that are inclusive of these new students and curricula that prepare all students for living in a world that includes diverse peoples. The initial efforts to broaden the academic curriculum beyond the study of western culture (which is represented most often by the words and deeds of white men) were labeled "diversity" or "pluralism." As academics began to refine the terminology in the debate over the curriculum, the emphasis moved toward an emphasis on culture and the inclusion of different cultural perspectives in the curriculum. Multiculturalism is the term now used to refer to campus initiatives to broaden the curriculum to include multiple cultures. These curricular changes are intended to reflect more accurately the lives of all students on campus and to prepare them to live and work in an increasingly diverse and global society.

Critics, however, have again shifted the grounds of the public debate by redefining the term: Multiculturalism is identified as a strategy of left-wing faculty and sympathetic administrators who are attempting to impose their ideological position on everyone else. Critics of multiculturalism have even coopted the terminology of the radical left. The term "politically correct," originally coined by those inside radical movements as a form of self-critique and a way of laughing at their own excesses, is now applied by the right as a blanket criticism of behavior that is in opposition to the left. Thus the right claims the moral high ground by misappropriating and misapplying the critique to itself. By labeling its own behavior *"not* politically correct," the right is able to prove that its ideas are being suppressed by the left. The debate about multiculturalism, then, shifts the focus to ideological issues, while ignoring the demographic reality of U.S. life.

The public debates over affirmative action policies and multiculturalism aside, another potent force has emerged both on campuses and in organizations to divert attention from the changing demographics of the workplace. Issues of cultural diversity in the U.S. work force have been supplanted by concerns about the trend toward globalization and the ability of the United States to compete in the global marketplace.

It is not surprising that concerns about globalization have generally coopted concerns about diversity in the domestic work force. For one thing, the international arena is more glamorous. Whether organizations are preparing executives to work abroad or colleges are developing courses to train students to compete for overseas assignments, the issues appear more exciting than do the issues involved in developing ways to create a productive work force of culturally diverse employees here in the United States. Perhaps more importantly, internationalization is an immediate issue. The United States has already lost much economic ground to other countries because of our ethnocentric approach to business. Corporations are beginning to realize the strategic importance of opening new markets in other countries, and they are realizing that they need to acquire an understanding of those cultures to move into their markets. And now that many U.S. businesses operate some or all of their manufacturing operations overseas, they have an immediate need to understand how to manage employees in other countries. Management schools, in particular, have pushed very hard to internationalize their curricula; even the American Assembly of Collegiate Schools of Business, the accrediting society for business schools, has added a curriculum standard related to international business issues. Few management schools, however, offer courses (or even scant coverage within existing courses) on topics related to cultural diversity in the U.S. work force. Although some corporations have created special positions such as Manager of Cultural Diversity, few are developing substantial diversity initiatives that are integrated into the company's overall business strategy. In most companies, cultural diversity is simply the new rubric for the old affirmative action programs.

The emphasis on globalization in academic research has resulted in much literature that is useful in understanding cultural differences in the U.S. work force, especially studies of intercultural communication and comparative studies of business beliefs and practices in different cultures. I will discuss some of that literature in subsequent chapters of this book. The danger, however, is that some organizational theorists believe that issues of cultural diversity in the United States can be subsumed by the literature on globalization issues. The theoretical framework that guides intercultural research and theory building, however, is not appropriate to understanding cultural diversity within the United States.

Although the intercultural perspective that is taken in most international business studies recognizes that the way business is conducted in the United States is particular only to the United States and that cultural values, beliefs, and behaviors shape business practices across different cultures, the intercultural perspective assumes that there is a host culture to which visitors from other cultures adapt. The central assumption of intercultural preparation for business people is "when in Rome, do as the Romans do." U.S. workers who are assigned abroad are urged to learn the ways of their hosts and to assimilate into the host culture, at least on a short-term basis (Brislin, 1989; Storti, 1990).

Conceptually, assimilation into the host culture is problematic in understanding cultural diversity in the U.S. work force. As I have already discussed, the host culture in most organizations is white male culture, a culture that is not hospitable to those who are different. White male culture also no longer represents much of the work force, and in only a few years, it will not represent most of the work force. Although we may not like the analogy, clinging to the traditional assumptions of the workplace creates a "South Africa dilemma" for the United States. Unless we change our assumptions, we will have a minority white faction that suppresses and oppresses the majority faction, comprising people of color. As the demographics of the work force and the general population in the United States change, U.S. culture is in flux. We can no longer talk about a melting pot nation in which assimilated peoples share the same history, language, and personal and political values.

Pragmatically, assimilation is a strategy that has had serious negative consequences for individuals in organizations and the organizations themselves. The woman or person of color who assimilates into white male organizational culture pays an enormous psychological price. Those who assimilate are denied the ability to express their genuine selves in the workplace; they are forced to repress significant parts of their lives within a social context that frames a large part of their daily encounters with other people. Even when people are successful in performing their jobs, the coping strategies that they adopt often lead to physical and psychological stress, "ranging from inhibition of self-expression to feelings of inadequacy and, perhaps, self-hatred" (Kanter, 1977). For some, the stress is so great that they cannot successfully do their jobs.

The organizational costs of assimilation are equally high. Beyond the opportunity costs of limiting the organizational vision, organizations suffer productivity losses. People who must spend significant amounts of energy coping with an alien environment have less energy left to do their jobs. People who are forced to keep a part of themselves hidden from others only bring a part of themselves to work each day. Workers who are angry, lack self-esteem, feel constant stress, and are socially isolated are less productive. Assimilation not only creates a situation in which people who are different are likely to fail, it also decreases the productivity of organizations.

Faced with a shrinking work force overall in the future and an increasing number of workers who are different by virtue of their race, gender, age, or cultural and linguistic background, organizations will confront even more serious problems regarding productivity. Organizations must begin now to confront those problems by developing new organizational theories and practices that are based on multicultural assumptions rather than

the cultural assumptions of a single dominant culture, especially a dominant culture that will not represent the majority of U.S. workers in the next
century. These new theories and practices should be framed by a perspective that recognizes, understands, values, and encourages rather than suppresses differences in the workplace.

A THEORETICAL PERSPECTIVE ON MULTICULTURAL ORGANIZATIONS

I use the term "multicultural organizations" to characterize the organizational response to demographic changes in the work force in order to focus
attention on the need to create organizations that reflect multicultural rather
than monocultural assumptions. Cultural diversity in the workplace, on
the other hand, implies differences among people in the work force, but
does not necessarily include any cultural transformation of organizations.
A cultural transformation is imperative, however, if the United States hopes
to avoid creating a kind of organizational apartheid.

Definition

A multicultural organization is an organization that:

1. Values, encourages, and affirms diverse cultural modes of being and interacting;
2. creates an organizational dialogue in which no one cultural perspective is presumed to be more valid than other perspectives;
3. empowers all cultural voices to participate fully in setting goals and making
   decisions.

This definition considerably broadens the focus of the dominant definitions of multicultural organizations.[6] Although most of the current work
on multicultural organizations recognizes the importance of the first criterion—valuing, encouraging, and affirming diverse cultural modes of being and interacting—it rarely acknowledges the impossibility of organizational transformation occurring without the other two criteria. In fact, the
underlying assumption of most work on diversity in organizations is that
business will proceed as usual; the only difference is that the people who
do the work will no longer be only white and male. The level of analysis
tends to be interpersonal, effectively ignoring the need for a radical restructuring of the workplace.

The vast majority of cultural diversity initiatives within U.S. organizations focus almost exclusively on the first criterion of valuing diversity
(see Chapter 5 for a description of diversity initiatives in some major U.S.

organizations). The assumption behind these initiatives is that if we can learn about each other interpersonally, we will learn to work together productively. Little emphasis in these initiatives is given to rethinking *how* people work together and the ways in which our concepts of working together are culturally biased.

It is not surprising that management practitioners and academics have not focused on the need to re-vision organizations in order to adapt to a multicultural workforce. The theoretical perspective that shapes most research in organizations blinds us to the need for such changes. However, newer theories, based on a different perspective, are emerging. This perspective, called the "interpretive perspective," provides a theoretical frame that I believe can accommodate my conception of a multicultural organization.

Interpretive Perspective

The scientific method, which is "the controlled and objective study of the relations among phenomena" (Kerlinger, 1964, p. viii), has been the dominant research method in the physical, biological, and social sciences during this century. Over the last several decades, social scientists have begun debating the utility of framing theory and research about human behavior within the paradigm of the scientific method. Although management theorists have been slower to join the debate than those in other social science fields,[7] an increasing number of critiques and re-visionings of management theory have appeared in academic books and journals. These re-visionings most often are based on interpretive theories of human behavior.

My definition of multicultural organizations is grounded in organizational theories that grow out of an interpretive perspective. The interpretive perspective starts with the theoretical assumption that individuals create and shape their own reality through communication (Krone, Jablin, & Putnam, 1987); "interpretivists focus on the subjective, intersubjective, and socially constructed meanings of organizational actors" (Putnam, 1983, p. 34). Organizations are defined as social constructions created through discourse (Mumby, 1987) and organizational communication is defined as how people in organizations make sense of their activities.

The interpretive perspective has not been the prevailing perspective in organizational theory. The functionalist perspective, which comprises a variety of research traditions that embrace the assumptions of logical positivism to different degrees (Putnam, 1983), has dominated the research in organizational behavior, including intercultural interaction. Logical positivism is the philosophy that underlies the scientific method in research. Research that is based on the principles of logical positivism is characterized by four central features: (1) The search for causality; (2) the assumption of reductionism; (3) the goal of prediction; and (4) the desire to generalize (Tucker, Weaver, & Berryman-Fink, 1981). Functionalists study the relationship between organizational variables (e.g., organizational structure, leadership styles, race or gender of employees, or channels of communication) and organizational outcomes in order to predict and control those outcomes.

The functionalist and interpretive perspectives approach understanding cultural diversity in the workplace in fundamentally different ways.[8] The functionalist perspective assumes that cultural categories, such as race and gender, can be reduced to stable, independent variables. These variables then can be manipulated to create different organizational outcomes (i.e., the dependent variables in organizational research). For example, the concept of managing diversity emerges from the functionalist perspective. Managing diversity assumes that researchers can develop techniques that will allow managers to use workers of different cultural backgrounds in ways that will improve organizational productivity. The assumption is that these techniques can be learned and applied to all individuals and organizations.

The interpretive perspective, on the other hand, sees cultural categories as social constructions created through social interaction and discourse. Each cultural category has its own discourse communities. Cultural diversity in the workplace represents a situation in which different discourse communities, each with its own set of assumptions, values, beliefs, expectations, and experiences, are situated together. Despite their common location (the workplace) and overarching purpose (to work), they do not necessarily experience the same reality, because their interpretations of reality are constructed through their cultural discourses. The interpretive perspective is grounded in a variety of symbolic theories, which posit that human beings are unique because of their capacity to create and use symbols, and thus, to create reality. Examining cultural and organizational symbols and symbol-making processes, therefore, is central to understanding organizational experience—which is not experienced in the same way by all members of an organization.

A variety of studies of gender and race in organizations point to the different experiences of white men, white women, and men and women of color (see, for example, Fernandez, 1981; Fine, Johnson, & Ryan, 1990; Fine, Morrow, & Quaglieri, 1990; Greenhaus, Parasuraman, & Wormley, 1990). These studies strongly suggest that white men, white women, and women and men of color experience different realities even within the same organizations. For example, in a study of a regional office of a large federal agency, Fine, Morrow, and Quaglieri (1990) found that women, white men, and people of color each believed that the organization had a different set of criteria for promoting people to management positions; white men had markedly different perceptions of how much emphasis the agency did and should place on gender and race issues in the organization; and white women and men reported significantly higher levels of satisfaction with the organization than did women and men of color.

Cultural Level of Analysis

The different realities experienced by different cultural groups point to the significance of the level of analysis in my definition of multicultural organizations. Most of the work on diversity in organizations focuses on the interpersonal level. That focus is apparent in several different approaches. Some perspectives begin their analyses at the interpersonal level, broadly defining diversity in terms of individual differences. Even though the definition of diversity includes groups that could be defined as cultural categories, for example, gays and lesbians or the differently-abled, they are defined more narrowly, as individuals who have a particular lifestyle or physical impairment. Other approaches use cultural examples in defining and discussing diversity (these examples are most often used in reference to racial differences), but do not continue to work at the cultural level in analyzing organizational behavior and culture. All of these approaches to cultural diversity focus primarily on interpersonal interaction; the proponents of these approaches advise organizations and their employees to work to ensure that individuals become more sensitive to the interaction styles of others.

Focusing on the cultural level of analysis does not preclude developing interpersonal sensitivity; in fact, such sensitivity is critical in helping employees begin the process of transforming organizations. It does, however, direct our attention to the cultural influences that shape both individual and group behavior, and to the ways in which organizations are culturally created, and therefore, culturally biased. In taking this perspective, I do not mean to deny the importance of individual psychological differences, but rather to highlight the importance of cultural differences.

Working with culture as the unit of analysis also provides a way to construct a theoretical perspective on organizations and organizing that can accommodate a multicultural work force. Ting-Toomey (1985) defines the cultural variable as patterned ways of thinking, acting, feeling, and interpreting. The definition of multicultural organizations that I have presented directs us to examine those patterned ways of thinking, acting, feeling, and interpreting for the different cultural groups represented in the work force so that we can better understand each other. Further, the definition allows us to create a pattern of thinking, acting, feeling, and interpreting that is multicultural rather than monocultural. A multicultural cultural perspective would be open to diverse ways of understanding the world, and would frame organizational processes in terms of difference rather than similarity. Such a multicultural culture is critical to creating organizations in which all employees can fully realize their own potentials and ensure that their organizations are fully productive.

Transformational Outcomes

My definition of multicultural organizations leads to a transforming perspective on cultural diversity in the workplace. The definition includes full participation by all cultural voices in setting organizational goals and making organizational decisions—the particular processes through which individuals construct organizations. Including new voices and empowering all voices in the discourse that creates organizations will, by definition, cause change; thus, the perspective is transformative.

What this transformation will look like is problematic. We can anticipate only the broad outlines. Multicultural organizations will not have a white, masculine bias that pervades their structures, policies, procedures, and discourses. Multicultural organizations will expect all employees to be bicultural—to be able to think and act within more than one cultural perspective. Traditionally, most minority employees in organizations have always been bicultural; they could not have survived organizational life unless they were able to live in the dominant culture, and they could not have retained their personal identities and psychological health unless they could also return to their own cultures. Members of the dominant culture, however, have rarely experienced the need to view the world through other cultural lenses. Multicultural organizations will reflect difference as their central construct. Employees will differ from each other and their means of achieving organizational goals will also differ. Organizational policies and procedures will incorporate and reflect those differences.

Multicultural organizations are the ends in process. As we learn to respect, value, and reward different cultural modes; as we learn to respect and hear all cultural voices; as we ensure that all cultural voices participate in setting goals and making decisions, we will create multicultural organizations. The transformation is continuous and has no end point: The product is the process.

The transformative nature of this definition of multicultural organizations may be difficult for many executives and organizational theorists to deal with on a daily basis. The status quo is always more comfortable. When the world around us is constructed as a representation of our own belief system, it is not only a hospitable environment, but also one that appears to have no anomalies—at least not to those who share the same world view. To those outside the dominant culture, however, the environment is hostile and filled with inconsistencies.

Even for those who recognize the constraints and narrow vision of a monocultural view, transformation is difficult to envision. We are all locked into our own visions of how organizations should look and how people should interact in those organizations. Imagining entirely new enactments that are based on a multicultural perspective is virtually impossible. We will unlock those visions as we allow other voices to join in the organizational dialogue. This perspective on cultural diversity cannot tell you what a multicultural organization will look like; it can only provide an argument for change and a general way to begin to approach change. U.S. management theories rely heavily on the concrete rather than the abstract, on quantifiable results rather than qualitative judgments, on product rather than process. A theoretical perspective that posits that "the ends are the means in process" and that "we'll know where we're going when we get there" is antithetical to current management theory. Yet, I believe that organizations need such a perspective to grapple with the problems and potentials of a culturally diverse work force.

NOTES

1. Although I refer to white men throughout this analysis as if they are an homogeneous group, I recognize that there is a range of ethnicities and other cultural differences among white men. The white male culture that is created and sustained in organizations closely approximates White male Anglo Saxon Protestant, or WASP, culture. Because homogeneity has been a central construct in organizational theory, ethnicity has been systematically suppressed in organizational life. Non-WASP men have been expected to assimilate into the dominant culture in order to be accepted in organizations.

2. It is important to note that these trends, particularly the social and cultural changes, most affected white women rather than women of color. African American women often deride the Women's Movement of the 1960s and 1970s as the political awakening of privileged white middle-class women who had the time and money to agonize about the meaning of having numerous material possessions but empty lives, what Betty Friedan (1963) called the "problem that has no name" (p. 15). Historically, African American women have always had to work to support their families. With the historical legacy of slavery and racism, and current high unemployment rates among black males (young African American men have an unemployment rate that is double the rate for young white men), African American women have always been and continue to be a part of the U.S. work force (albeit a forgotten and often invisible part) who are paid significantly less than their white counterparts, both male and female.

3. The original "deficit" position stated that women were inherently inferior to men. While some people may continue to believe this, few were willing to say so publicly by the 1970s. The theoretical shift from biological determinants of behavior to social/psychological determinants was consistent with a trend throughout the academic world as the social sciences gained prominence.

4. Although the analytical approach I am taking throughout this chapter separates gender and race identities (and other cultural identities such as class, ethnicity, sexual preference, and so forth) into discrete categories, that separation is an artifi-

cial one that is useful only for heuristic purposes. The complexity of the bound-aries of our primary identities becomes obvious when you consider women of color. Although some scholars attempt to establish the primacy of either race or gender for women of color, such arguments serve no purpose in understanding their lives. Our individual identities are never one cultural identity or the other; they are, in-stead, some unique blending of our various cultural identities. On the other hand, identifying the tensions that are generated at the intersections of different cultural identities (e.g., race and gender for women of color) can suggest important insights about people's lives.

5. Several factors have led to the lack of success in hiring and retaining faculty of color. First, the pool of potential candidates of color is limited by the number of minorities in the United States who receive doctorates each year. Most four-year institutions of higher education require faculty to have a Ph.D. in a field appropri-ate to the subject they teach. The percentage of doctorates awarded in the United States to minorities is minuscule in contrast to those awarded to whites. The num-bers are particularly small in the sciences and management.

Second, the hiring process is tightly controlled by the faculty, not by the admin-istration. Faculty members set the standards by which their potential colleagues are judged, and those standards usually conform to the standards that were, or that they believe were in force when they were hired. The reward system at universities tends to foster conservatism among faculty; risk-taking in research and teaching usually is not rewarded, and, in fact, is often punished. Faculty are thus encour-aged by the system not to take risks in any endeavor, even in instances when the administration would want them to try something new, such as in hiring women and faculty of color. Women and faculty of color often do not have credentials that are similar to the white males who have dominated higher education. For example, women often have spent several years raising children, during which time they taught parttime and published few articles; in management, people of color often hold the Ed.D. degree rather than the Ph.D. because some schools of education have made a determined effort to recruit students of color into graduate programs. Faculty are generally unwilling to risk hiring people whose academic backgrounds are different, and whose potential as teachers and researchers, therefore, is unknown. This situation has made university faculty particularly susceptible to the argument that affirmative action means hiring people who are less qualified.

Finally, even when universities have been successful in hiring women and fac-ulty of color, they have often been unable to retain them. Because they are so few in number, women and faculty of color are forced to take on enormous student advis-ing and university service obligations. Women students and students of color who are searching for role models, seek them out in large numbers for academic and personal advice. They are asked to serve on many university committees so that the minority voice is represented. With so much time and energy devoted to their service and teaching obligations, few have the resources left to devote to the kind of research effort that would result in a positive tenure recommendation. Thus, many burn out long before the tenure process begins.

6. A few writers have recently begun to articulate definitions of multicultural organizations that focus on the need to create new organizational assumptions and norms. For example, Taylor Cox, Jr. (1991) offers a definition that is similar to mine: "The multicultural organization is characterized by pluralism, full integration of

minority-culture members both formally and informally, an absence of prejudice and discrimination, and low levels of inter-group conflict" (p. 47). Cox recognizes that the majority culture cannot remain privileged over minority cultures, and that members of the majority culture bear some responsibility for change. Marilyn Loden and Judy Rosener (1991) describe a "culture of diversity" that should characterize the organizations of the future. A culture of diversity is an *"institutional environment built on the values of fairness, diversity, mutual respect, understanding, and cooperation; where shared goals, rewards, performance standards, operating norms, and a common vision of the future guide the efforts of every employee and manager"* (p. 196). Loden and Rosener recognize the importance of transforming the dominant organizational culture, but their analysis focuses on interpersonal rather than cultural issues.

7. As one of the newest social sciences, management has been particularly self-conscious about its adherence to social science orthodoxy. New academic disciplines frequently are subject to charges that they are not legitimate areas of study. One of the ways that academic disciplines respond to such charges is by demonstrating that their research theories and methods comprise a coherent, focused perspective. Disciplines that are forced to prove such coherence are often intolerant of alternative perspectives for generating theory and research. More established disciplines tend to be secure enough in their place in the academy that they will consider new theoretical approaches. For example, the physical and biological sciences, rather than the social sciences, have been the leaders in developing new theoretical paradigms. It is not surprising, therefore, that management has lagged behind the other social sciences in generating and adopting new ways of thinking about research.

8. Putnam (1983) offers a succinct overview of the functionalist and interpretive perspectives in organizational communication research. For a review of the shortcomings of logical positivism in social science research, see Berger and Luckmann (1967), Harré and Secord (1973), and Pearce and Cronen (1980). Despite more than 20 years of serious critique in the social sciences, logical positivism has remained the dominant research perspective in management. The recent interest in studies of organizational culture indicates a move away from the functionalist perspective, although some of the research on organizational culture emerges out of the functionalist perspective. Smircich and Calas (1987) argue cogently that "'culture' has been incorporated into the positivist, technical interest as part of the 'traditional organizational literature'" (p. 229). To the extent that culture is defined as something that organizations "have" that can be manipulated and controlled, culture is reified as a static structure rather than being viewed as a socially constructed enactment of what an organization "is," as the interpretive perspective would view it.

3

CULTURAL IDENTITY AND PERFORMANCE

"Culture" is a term that is used often by both academics and practitioners in discussions of organizational theory and behavior. Because it is so commonplace, however, the term carries a variety of meanings, most of which serve to confuse rather than clarify issues of cultural diversity in the workplace.

ORGANIZATIONAL CULTURE

The study of organizational culture became popular during the late 1970s and early 1980s (see, for example, Deal & Kennedy, 1982; Frost et al., 1985; Peters & Waterman, 1982; Schein, 1985/1987) for a variety of reasons. The social sciences were moving away from traditional, neo-positivist approaches to understanding human behavior generally, and some researchers were embracing new approaches grounded in symbolic perspectives, or interpretive theories of human behavior. The study of organizational culture fits easily into these theories.

Although the concept of organizational cultures appeared in the organizational literature much earlier (Louis, 1983), the newer organizational studies that were emerging from the shift to interpretive theories of human behavior were significant because of their focus on culture as an anthropological concept. The earlier work on organizational cultures viewed culture variously as organizational climate, character, ideology, and image, each emphasizing the notion of the "indigenous feel of a place and its caste"

(Louis, 1983). The change to interpretive theories of human behavior focused attention on the symbol-making and symbol-using capacity of humans, thus shifting the definition of organizations to social constructions created through discourse, and the definition of organizational communication to how people in organizations make sense of their activities. This focus on the social construction of community in and through symbols is quite consistent with the anthropological concept of culture. Organizational scholars began to play with the concept of culture to see if it would yield useful insights into organizational life.

At the same time that this theoretical shift was occurring in the academic world, events in the corporate world set the stage for the introduction of organizational culture analyses. The mergers and acquisitions of the 1970s and 1980s saw the melding of disparate corporate organizations, and organizational consultants saw the opportunity to introduce another academic concept to the real world. The concept of organizational culture was loosely applied in these analyses and generally did not focus on the intersubjective meanings of organizational members. The analyses focused instead on "the indigenous feel" of organizations with the intent of helping people understand why some mergers were more difficult than others and why some just didn't work. The definition of culture was imprecise and generally superficial, resulting in a spate of popular press articles about the jeans culture of new high-tech companies or the suit-and-tie culture of IBM.

Neither the imprecise use of culture in organizational applications nor the anthropological metaphor in academic research is helpful in understanding cultural diversity in the workplace. Although the anthropological approach is theoretically sound and provides a deeper analysis than simply examining the "feel" of an organization, both approaches suffer from the same flaw. In each approach, the organization is seen as a fixed container in which the members of the organization share a common organizational culture. The culture of the organization is superordinate to the cultural identities that members bring with them into the organization.

Identifying organizational culture as the unifying construct in people's work lives may have had some validity in the past. To the extent that organizational studies focused on the experience of white males in organizations, organizational culture in general and specific organizational cultures in particular did reflect either a common set of lived experiences, or, as in the case of ethnic white males whose cultural identities were suppressed in their work lives, a common set of desired experiences. We would expect that workers, especially at professional and managerial levels, shared a set of experiences in the United States as white males, and brought to the workplace similar meanings about work and its role in their lives. Their experience in the workplace, then, became another set of shared experiences that further extended their common bonds.

This model works nicely until you begin to introduce people who differ from the "organizational man" into organizations. Several years ago I was doing a values clarification exercise with some of my MBA students. To do the exercise students first rank-ordered ten concepts in terms of each concept's importance in making decisions in their work lives. Then they formed small groups and were instructed to achieve consensus on the relative importance of the concepts. One small group had several U.S. students and one woman from Pakistan. The group members began arguing loudly almost as soon as the group discussion began, and I was finally forced to intervene. The conflict was both simple and profound. One of the concepts that students had to rank was religion. Not surprisingly, all of the students from the United States placed religion at the bottom of their lists, saying that religion had no influence on their business decisions. The student from Pakistan, on the other hand, ranked religion first and said that all of her business decisions were determined by her religious beliefs. The U.S. students not only were astounded by her statement, they also refused to believe her, even after she provided several examples. The examples, in fact, only served to heighten the U.S. students' disbelief.

This story points to the problems that occur when people from different cultural backgrounds come together to work. Not only do the participants bring different assumptions and meanings to their work, they also tend to deny the validity of other cultural assumptions and meanings. Focusing on organizational culture per se glosses over specific cultural differences among members of the organization and perpetuates the ethnocentric assumptions embedded in particular cultural perspectives.[1] Although individual organizations in the United States may vary along a number of cultural dimensions, most of them reflect white male cultural assumptions. For example, organizational cultures may be more or less formal, but still use masculine standards for evaluating organizational competence. Examining organizational culture highlights superficial differences among organizations and keeps hidden the deeper cultural assumptions that cut across organizations.

CULTURAL DIVERSITY

My analysis of workplace diversity focuses on the cultural backgrounds of the individual members of the organization. Any discussion of cultural diversity in the workplace must begin with an understanding of the general concept of culture and an acknowledgment of the integrity of different cultural perspectives. A conceptual understanding of c
tegrity of different cultures is central to my analysis. Tl
U.S. work force is not fixed; over time, the particular m
change, and those changes are not completely predict
tures themselves are not static, they, too, change over tin

not predictable. None of us knows everything there is to know about every culture that is now represented in the U.S. work force, or that will be in the future. Working within a culturally diverse work force, therefore, requires a conceptual understanding of culture and cultural integrity so that we will be both able to recognize and open to learn about new cultures as we encounter them.

This chapter is divided into five sections. The first section provides a definition of culture and an overview of the relationship between culture, identity, and behavior. The remaining sections examine that relationship in greater depth for four specific cultural groups: Asians, Hispanics, African Americans, and Women. My analysis in each section is necessarily brief; each of these topics deserves book length treatment and, in fact, numerous books have been written about each. My purpose, however, is not to treat each topic exhaustively, but rather to provide enough detail to show the importance of culture in the lives of members of each group, and to lay the foundation for showing how cultural differences can and do manifest themselves in the workplace.

DEFINITION OF CULTURE

Ting-Toomey (1985) offers a simple definition of culture, saying that it is the "patterned ways of thinking, acting, feeling, and interpreting" of particular groups (p. 75). Culture guides our understanding and behavior: It shapes how we approach the world.

Eva Hoffman (1989) provides a vivid example of how culture informs our perceptions of the world around us and guides our actions. Hoffman, born in Cracow, Poland, emigrated with her family to Canada in 1959, when she was 13 years old. In her autobiography, she describes how her best friend passed around a journal to her schoolmates to "write appropriate words of goodbye" (Hoffman, 1989, p. 78) before she left Poland. Her Polish friends wrote:

Melancholy verses in which life is figured as a vale of tears or a river of suffering, or a journey of pain on which we are embarking. This tone of sadness is something we all enjoy. It makes us feel the gravity of life, and it is gratifying to have a truly tragic event—a parting forever—to give vent to such romantic feelings. (Hoffman, 1989, p. 78)

Two years later she spent a month traveling with a group of American teenagers. When they said goodbye, they, too, passed around journals to be signed, but their inscriptions to each other differed markedly from those written by Hoffman's Polish friends: "It was great fun knowing you! . . . Don't ever lose your friendly personality! Keep cheerful, and nothing can harm you." Hoffman compares the journals and concludes, "I know that, even though they're so close to each other in time, I've indeed come to another country" (1989, p. 78).

Culture comprises four elements: Norms, values, beliefs, and expressive symbols (Peterson, 1979). The study of culture has historically focused on the norms, values, and beliefs of different cultures, but in recent years, consistent with the general shift in the social sciences to symbolic perspectives, the new focus in the study of culture is on "expressive symbols as portraying fundamental beliefs" (Peterson, 1979, p. 137). This new focus changes the researcher's approach to studying culture from identifying the norms, values, and beliefs of particular cultures to understanding how members of a particular culture create meaning. Johnson (1989) rearranges the elements of culture to reflect more clearly this new focus on meaning. She says that culture includes "three interrelated and co-equal systems of meaning: (1) Language and communication; (2) artifacts; and (3) abstractions" (p. 305). The system of language and communication includes "the verbal and nonverbal patterns that characterize the expressions" (Johnson, 1989, p. 305) of a particular cultural group. Artifacts are the "unique products" created by members of a cultural group that both reflect and create the experiences of the group, such as music, art, clothing, literature, and rituals. Abstractions guide behavior and shape both communication and artifacts; they include "values, morals, ethics, logic, philosophical orientations, laws, and religious beliefs held by a people" (Johnson, 1989, p. 308). These three systems provide "the publicly available symbolic forms through which people experience and express meaning" (Swidler, 1986).

These symbolic forms through which we communicate culture are not static; they change and adapt over time as the external environments in which particular cultures are enacted change. Thus culture itself is fluid and dynamic. One of the paradoxes of culture is that it is both enduring and changing. It gives its members a shared historical identity and a repertoire of symbolic forms that simultaneously recreate the historical identity and create a new identity as cultural forms are used "to meet the various contingencies of everyday living" (Carbaugh, 1990, p. 5).

The concept of repertoire is important in understanding how culture functions in people's lives. Culture is not deterministic. My membership in a particular culture not does determine my response to a given situation. My culture, instead, gives me a tool kit that I can use in constructing my response (Swidler, 1986). People choose, however, how they will use those tool kits; "any person can choose variously to reaffirm, to create with, to live by, or against such patterns" (Carbaugh, 1990, p. 153). Growing up as a young Jewish woman in suburban New Jersey in the 1950s and 1960s, I learned a repertoire of appropriate cultural behaviors that identified me as a woman. Choosing to pursue a serious career was not one of them.

Primary- or secondary-school teaching was the preferred career option for young women in my cultural cohort because it was the kind of career that ensured that women would have something to fall back on if they divorced or became widowed at an early age. I refused to major in education, and in doing so, I chose not to affirm my cultural background, but rather to act in opposition to it. My culture, however, shaped that choice: One cannot act in opposition to things unknown.

Membership in a Culture

Social scientists can define the elements of culture and we can all point to specific examples of the influence of culture in our own lives. For example, I value argument and I argue a lot, often in a loud voice. This behavior, which frequently irritates others, is a discourse mode characteristic of sociability in Jewish culture (Schiffrin, 1984). Despite our ability to identify the elements of culture, it is difficult to pin down the parameters of a particular culture. Who are the members of the culture? And what does it mean to be a member of a culture?

Although in the United States we tend to equate culture with nationality or ethnicity, membership in a culture is not defined by national, racial, or ethnic identity per se. Culture is the shared identity of a group. Although people may share a cultural identity with other citizens of the country in which they live, they also may not. My grandmother, although she lived in Poland until she was nearly 40 years old, never called herself Polish; she was Jewish. And even after she moved to the United States, she spoke Yiddish (even with her grandchildren, who didn't understand a word), read only Yiddish newspapers, and socialized with others who did the same. The same principle holds true for members of a particular race. An individual's national origin or skin color does not automatically place him or her within a particular cultural identity. To share an identity with others, you must share a symbolic community with them.

That point became clear to me several years ago when I taught a seminar at a university in northern California. I had only one black student in the class, and the other students felt compelled to turn to her when they had questions about how African Americans might respond to a particular issue we were discussing. Finally, she said that she had no idea because she never thought of herself as a black woman. Although her parents were black, they raised her in an all white suburb. They had no black friends and no other family members lived nearby. She attended white schools, worshipped at a white church, and socialized with whites; she even had a white boyfriend. Her cultural identity was as a white woman. Although many black Americans would argue that racism in the United States makes it impossible for blacks to identify culturally with whites (even if blacks forget their racial identity, whites won't let them), this young woman had not encountered sufficient resistance to her participation in white culture to believe that she was not a member of the culture, regardless of the image in her mirror.

Membership in a culture is also problematic because cultures are not monolithic. Diversity exists not only across cultures but also within cultures. Each of the groups that I will discuss in this chapter reflects broad diversity. For example, the term Hispanic comprises cultural groups that range from Mexican American to Puerto Rican to Cuban to Guatemalan to Haitian to Brazilian, and so on. Within that list we find a range of skin colors, religions, ethnicities, and languages. One reason, in fact, that many Hispanics do not like being labeled either Hispanic or Latino is that the label hides the uniqueness of their particular culture within the larger cultural rubric.

Whites in the United States are always surprised when they read about tensions among black communities in the United States. Those tensions are not surprising, however, when you recognize the diverse experiences of black Americans. Contrast, for example, the world views of African Americans who have lived in the United States for generations with those of black immigrants from Haiti. African Americans have lived in a culture in which they have always been an oppressed minority, in which their original African heritage was systematically suppressed, in which their first identity was as slaves. Haitian immigrants, on the other hand, grew up as members of a majority black culture. They have a rich cultural heritage from both Africa and France that has flourished for hundreds of years. They have a deep sense of personal pride in the fact that Haiti achieved its independence from France in 1804. Although white Americans rarely distinguish between the two groups (except to sometimes comment that black immigrants from the Caribbean work hard, implying that U.S. born African Americans do not), black Americans recognize clear differences among themselves. When they first come to the United States, my Haitian students are always surprised by the feelings of hopelessness and isolation that they encounter among many African Americans in the inner city.

I first became aware of the diversity within cultural diversity a number of years ago when I was discussing feminist theory in one of my classes. I was presenting some of the basic principles of feminism and talking about how they are grounded in women's experience. As I was describing Betty Friedan's (1963) concept of "the problem that has no name" (the nagging sense of something being wrong that Friedan said many bored, suburban housewives in the 1950s felt), one of my African American students jumped up and said, "That may be your experience, but it sure isn't my experience or the experience of my mother or my grandmother. Black women in the United States have always had to work to support their families." Although women share a community through their gender, that community is not homogenous, and women's experiences differ by race, class, ethnicity, sexual preference, age, and so forth.

Cultural membership is also confused by controversies over which culture is superordinate in an individual's life. For example, are black women in the United States a subculture of African American culture or a subculture of women? The controversy over the preeminence of race or gender in the lives of black women has, at various times, split apart the feminist community. It is a controversy, however, that serves no useful purpose.

Two other issues are far more critical than trying to determine whether race or gender is more important in black women's lives. First, black women, precisely because they are seen as either a subculture of women's culture or a subculture of black culture, are often ignored in discussions of either culture. To dramatize that point, Hull, Scott, and Smith (1982) titled their book on Black Women's Studies *All the Women Are White, All the Blacks Are Men, But Some of Us Are Brave*. Second, it is the intersection of race and gender and the tensions that are created by that intersection that provide the keenest insights into black women's lives. The intersection of race and gender provides a basis, for example, for understanding the occupational discrimination that consistently places black women at the bottom of salary surveys in the United States (behind white men, black men, and white women, in that order). The tensions inherent in the intersection of race and gender provide some understanding of why many black women were so supportive of Clarence Thomas after Anita Hill's allegations of sexual harassment became public. Black women often talk of the guilt they feel because historically black men have been denied access to meaningful work in the United States. Although they would agree that black women also have been discriminated against, having access to well-paying jobs allows men to support their families, a fundamental aspect of male identity in our culture. Many black women believe that because black men in the United States have been denied their male identity, black women must subordinate their own concerns to the concerns of black men. In this context, the strong support for Clarence Thomas rather than Anita Hill throughout much of the black community was not surprising.

PARTICULAR CULTURAL IDENTITIES

The remainder of this chapter focuses on the cultures of Asians, Hispanics, African Americans, and Women. It includes descriptions of the values, norms, beliefs, and behaviors that mark the cultural identities and performances of members of these cultural groups, and shows how those identities and performances differ from what are often referred to as "American" cultural identities and performances.

Characterizing American culture is a difficult, if not impossible, task. As a society created and recreated through waves of immigration, both voluntary and involuntary, the United States comprises diverse cultures. What we call American culture often has its roots in other cultures. Not infrequently, some artifact or behavior has, in fact, been coopted from another culture, although many, if not most, Americans would be hard pressed to identify the culture that supplied the artifact.

I was reminded of that fact recently as I was watching a children's television show with my sons. The show was introducing children to different national cultures, one of which was Mexico. After the children danced to the Mexican Hat Dance, one young boy said that he often heard the music played at sporting events but he hadn't known that it was Mexican; he just assumed it was American.

There are, however, certain modes of interpreting and acting that are peculiarly American; I refer to these modes as *mainstream* American culture. These cultural modes appear throughout the United States, but they are particularly embedded in our primary public institutions, such as education, politics, and business. Because these cultural norms, values, behaviors, and symbols tend to be reflections of the men who shaped these institutions, some feminist writers prefer the term *malestream* American culture. Whenever I refer to mainstream American culture, keep in mind that I am identifying cultural features that reflect the white, nonethnic, male experience.

Before I begin to describe the various cultures, three caveats are necessary. First, it is important to remember here that my purpose is primarily heuristic. The descriptions that follow are by no means complete and do little justice to the richness of the cultural lives of members of the cultures I am describing.

Second, my discussion of the historical determinants of the different cultures is necessarily simplistic. A complex web of factors establishes the conditions for the creation and recreation of culture. Hofstede (1984) posits a model of cultural stability and change in which he identifies seven ecological factors that contribute to the origins of cultures (geographic, economic, demographic, genetic/hygienic, historical, technological, and urbanization). Cultures are then passed on through the value systems of major groups in the population; these value systems are embedded in the structure and functioning of various institutions, such as families, religion, and politics. These institutions, through their form and function, reinforce the societal values. Cultures change primarily through outside sources, either the forces of nature or the forces of humans. My intent in discussing some of the historical antecedents of cultures is not to deny the complexity of cultural development and change, but only to illustrate the relationship between particular historical conditions and cultural consequences.

The third caveat is that the descriptions of particular cultural groups do not necessarily apply to specific individuals who are members of these cultures. This caveat is particularly important to keep in mind throughout this and subsequent chapters. Descriptions of cultural groups can easily lead to the error of "essentializing" people, or reducing each member of the group to particular essential characteristics (Wood, 1994). All members of a cultural group do not possess such characteristics. As I noted earlier in this chapter, culture is not monolithic; there is a wide range of differences among members of a cultural group. The descriptions that follow comprise generalizations about the beliefs and behaviors of cultural groups— not individuals; individual members of the group will vary in the degree to which they share those beliefs or exhibit those behaviors.

Numerous factors affect the extent to which any individual's beliefs and behaviors are isomorphic with the beliefs and behaviors of his or her cultural group. For example, the degree to which individuals have acculturated to the majority culture varies, as does the degree of cultural identity individuals have with their cultural reference group. Some Hispanics, for example, may be more Anglo in their identity and performance than some non-Hispanic whites. Because a person looks Hispanic or Asian or African American does not mean that he or she will conform fully or even partially with the cultural descriptions that follow.[2]

For several years, I worked on an affirmative action plan with a nonprofit organization in Boston. In one of the first conversations I had with some staff members about the affirmative action issues facing the organization, they told me that they had concerns about defining affirmative action goals simply in terms of whether a person was black or Hispanic or Asian because she or he might not be "black enough." They wanted to know how you could tell if someone was "really black." What they meant, of course, was whether that person self-identified as an African American and perceived the world and acted as one.

Another reason why individual cultural identities and performances may differ from the group identity and performance is that cultural identity is situational. We often shift our cultural identities based on our goals in a particular situation. Shifting cultural identities is a concept that is quite familiar to most minority group members in the United States. Because Anglo males are the normative group in defining American culture, especially in public contexts, their cultural identity is generally transparent. The transparent nature of their own cultural identity means that culture is an unseen and, therefore, unknown concept as applied to their own lives. Minority group members, on the other hand, see culture quite clearly, for they are constantly confronted by people—both real people and fictional representations in the media—who are different from themselves. In order to survive in the majority culture, minorities are forced to become bicultural. In other words, minorities are able to function in at least two different cultures. Being bicultural enables minorities to take on the cultural identity that is most appropriate or most functional in a particular situation.

African Americans in organizations often talk about the relief they feel when they go home at night and can take off their white organizational identities and return to their genuine cultural identity as African Americans. They understand that "gettin ovah" (achieving success in a white world) means "talkin like the Man," but the Man's identity is one they assume only for its instrumental value in helping them to achieve success in a particular context (work); the identity is quickly abandoned in another context. In fact, moving back into African American styles of acting is essential for acceptance in the black community. Blacks who cannot shift their cultural identities back to the African American community are ostracized.

Although the descriptions that follow may not fit any particular individual with precision, they do provide the conceptual base that underlies the theoretical perspective for this book. Keeping the limitations of the descriptions in mind, I turn now to examining the cultural identities of Asians, Hispanics, African Americans, and Women.

Asian Culture

As is true for each of the groups included in this chapter, it is misleading to identify a monolithic culture that encompasses all Asians. There are many Asian cultures. Asia crosses many national boundaries, from Japan across China and westward to India. Each nation comprises numerous cultures. The Philippines, for example, is a highly multicultural society that includes 87 languages and dialects. Even in China, where 90 percent of the population are Han, several dozen other ethnic and national minorities are represented in the population.

Although there is no one Asian culture, there are several important similarities among Asian cultures that differentiate them from mainstream American culture. My discussion of these similarities will focus primarily on the cultures of the three largest Asian groups represented in the United States: Chinese, Filipino, and Japanese.

One fundamental distinction between Asian and American cultures is the definition of self. The United States is an individualistic culture that stresses the importance of individual goals over group goals. The centrality of the "I" in the United States is embedded in our Constitution and the Bill of Rights, and permeates virtually every facet of our lives. I recall my father telling me during the energy crisis in the early 1970s that he would not buy a small car because it was his right as an American to drive a big car. A radio personality in Massachusetts led a successful citizens' drive to repeal the state seatbelt law based on his appeal to the individual's right to choose whether or not to wear a seat belt. The individualistic focus of American culture is not surprising given the history of the United States. The early settlers came here to escape the constrictions of group identity. The identity of the New World was forged in the exploits of individuals who sought to determine their own destinies by conquering and controlling other people and the environment.

Asian cultures, on the other hand, are "we oriented" (Servaes, 1988). Personal goals are subordinated to the goals of the group, and the identity of individuals is "defined by, and linked to, the identity of the groups of which they are members" (Gochenour, 1990). The individual's identity is submerged in the group; without connections to the group, the individual no longer exists.

Just as the individualism of the United States is rooted in its early history, the collectivism of Asian cultures is also. Historically, Asian economies were agrarian. Families depended on one another for survival; all of the children and adults were needed to work the land. The interdependence of people was critical in shaping the Asian cultural understanding of individual identity. Scholars consistently identify interdependence as the basis of individual identity in Japan (Gudykunst, Nishida, & Morisaki, May 1992). In a study of family-owned businesses in Japan, Kondo (1990) observed that "persons seemed to be constituted in and through social relations and obligations to others. Selves and society did not seem to be separate entities; rather the boundaries are blurred" (p. 22). For Filipinos, the family is the first and central group in creating the individual's identity. The family is the "ultimate place of security" (Gochenour, 1990, p. 17), and Filipinos have a deep sense of obligation to the needs of family members. In contemporary China, four groups (or collectives) are critical in the individual's identity: The family, the class collective to which a child is assigned (i.e., school), the work unit, and the local community (Wenzhong & Grove, 1991).

The interdependence of the individual and the group is a critical concept in understanding motivation and decision-making in Asian cultures. The individual is obliged to place the group's well-being ahead of her or his own. Thus, it is not unusual to see Asian family members all work in the family business, even if the children would prefer a different career. The extraordinary success of Asian-owned small businesses in the United States, especially among Korean Americans, is often attributed to the practice of having the entire family work in the business, thus ensuring a low-cost, reliable work force. Children's obligations to their parents continue throughout their lives. Elderly parents live with their children and continue to command respect from them.

But it is not only the children who are obligated. Familial responsibilities are reciprocal. Parents are obligated to care for their children—to feed, clothe, house, and educate them. Reciprocity, in fact, governs all individual/group relations. In China, for example, the work unit in which individuals are placed is responsible for not only assigning tasks and paying wages, but also for ensuring that workers have housing, medical care, and schools. The work unit will even negotiate family disputes (Wenzhong & Grove, 1991).

In addition to emphasizing the group as the source of individual identity, Asian cultures value group harmony. Wenzhong and Grove (1991) identify "intragroup harmony and avoidance of overt conflict in interpersonal relations" as a fundamental Chinese value. For Filipinos, maintaining group harmony is as important as getting things done. If conflict emerges in a work group, the conflict must be smoothed over—even if doing so means that the task cannot be completed. Among the Chinese, decision-making is a group process that is achieved by consensus building. Harmony is valued more than productivity, so organizational decisions often take much longer than they do in the United States (Wenzhong & Grove, 1991).

Asian social relationships are not only harmonious but also hierarchical. Asian cultures are characterized as *large power distance cultures*, what Hofstede (1984) calls cultures in which people believe and accept that power is distributed unequally. American culture is based on the premise of egalitarianism. Although most Americans agree that equality is a dream rather than a reality, it is a dream most of us believe we can achieve. Thus, most Americans are highly motivated to change the system, to work for egalitarian relationships. And we tend to be suspicious of inequalities, generally believing that power corrupts and that those who have power and wealth have achieved them only by abusing those who do not.

Asians, on the other hand, believe that hierarchy is a natural occurrence in nature and human relationships. Authority and power are natural to the human condition, and they "derive from the moral and ethical excellence of those who hold it" (Fieg, 1989). Those people who have power and authority tend to be older males with seniority who come from respected families. Power and authority carry with them, however, a complex set of obligations. Just as reciprocity governs individual/group relations, it also governs superior/subordinate relations—superiors and subordinates have mutual obligations. Managers are obliged to take care of workers. In times of need, influential people help others who are less fortunate.

The Chinese concept of *guanxi* provides an example of the centrality of reciprocity in governing social relationships. *Guanxi*, which means "relationship, connection, obligation, dependency" (Wenzhong & Grove, 1991, p. 61), governs friendships in China. Although relationships are more formal among the Chinese than among Americans, at least initially, once the bonds have been established, the relationship carries with it a set of mutual obligations. The Chinese have very elaborate gift-giving rituals and practices, which establish the extent of the reciprocal obligations. The giving and receiving of gifts creates a relationship between the giver and recipient in which the recipient is now obligated to the giver; "giving in the *guanxi* system is a kind of social investment upon which one may draw later" (Wenzhong & Grove, 1991, p. 61).

These social values in Asian cultures—submerging individual identity in the group, harmonious group relations, and hierarchical and reciprocal social relationships—underlie a communication style that differs markedly from mainstream American communication, especially in organizations. Servaes (1988) says the stylistic differences reflect different understandings of the function of discourse. He says that for westerners, "the end product, the message, is the most important part of the communication process," while "for Asians the emotional exchange, the being together, the pleasure of communicating are equally important" (Servaes, 1988, p. 68). Asians value the process rather than the product of communication.

The concern with the process of communication is consistent with the Asian emphasis on formal rules of communication. Uncertainty avoidance is another dimension of cultural variability that Hofstede (1984) uses to distinguish cultures from one another; it measures the degree to which members of the culture attempt to avoid uncertainty—a trait that manifests itself in communication. Asians are not comfortable with uncertainty and avoid it whenever possible (Gudykunst, Nishida, & Morisaki, May 1992). The United States, on the other hand, is a low uncertainty avoidance culture; Americans tend to accept ambiguity and uncertainty as normal features of everyday life. Low uncertainty cultures create elaborate rules for interaction as a means of reducing as much uncertainty as possible. Asian cultures have clear rules for communication in all situations, which serve to maintain hierarchical relationships and group harmony.

Several features of Asian communication provide an important contrast with the norms of organizational communication in the United States. First, Asians tend not to raise controversial issues or to disagree, especially with superiors; they also avoid saying "no." Second, anger is neither expressed nor tolerated. The person who shows anger undermines the dignity of the group and loses "face" for himself or herself. Maintaining face is extremely important in Asian cultures; individuals will repress their own feelings or even knowingly say something that is not true in order to maintain harmonious relationships and save face for themselves and others.

My choice of language here is very important. I do not mean that Asians will lie in the sense that Americans use the term. Since Asians value humility and modesty, the untruths told in order to maintain face are not bold self-assertions of their own accomplishments or lies told to cover up immoral or unethical behavior. In fact, being accused of telling a lie or being caught doing so would create a serious loss of face for an Asian. Wenzhong and Grove (1991) tell a story about a Chinese woman and an American acquaintance that exemplifies Asian face-saving behavior. The Chinese woman had a bad cold and her acquaintance suggested that a hot bath would make her feel better. When they met again, the Chinese woman's cold was gone and her acquaintance asked her if she had taken his advice. The Chinese woman said yes, that the soak in the hot tub had been beneficial. Another American who was present and knew that the Chinese woman did not have access to a bathtub and therefore could not have taken a hot bath asked her later why she had not told her acquaintance the truth. She replied, "I didn't want him to feel bad because I don't have a tub." Her untruth, what we often call "a little white lie," was intended to save face for both herself and her acquaintance.

Although face appears to be an important concept in all cultures, its social significance is much greater in Asian cultures than in mainstream American culture. For Asians, maintaining and saving face is a central value in interaction; it is a primary influence on behavior (Redding & Ng, 1982).

These attempts to maintain harmony by suppressing anger and avoiding conflict create an indirect style of communication. Asians usually will not state a problem or ask for help directly; instead, the other person in the interaction is expected to read between the lines, to recognize the nonverbal cues in the discourse, or to understand the meanings that underlie the precise form of the communication. To avoid direct communication, Filipinos even use go-betweens to act as intermediaries on their behalf when they are having problems or want to ask for something (Gochenour, 1990).

In addition, Asians are embarrassed by "immodest self-assertion" (Gochenour, 1990, p. 48). The Chinese believe that humility is a virtue, so they generally will not respond to a compliment (even though they do like to receive them), and sometimes they will even deliberately disparage themselves (Wenzhong & Grove, 1991). Asians, therefore, are not likely to offer their opinions in group discussions or to argue forcefully for their own ideas. Employees who are asked to make decisions are likely to enlist the opinions of their superiors rather than decide for themselves—not because they are not capable of deciding but because they would not presume to act independently. Filipinos believe that the written word has an inherent authority of its own. They are not likely, therefore, to write memoranda about organizational problems since doing so would be considered presumptuous (Gochenour, 1990, p. 20).

There is an additional point of contrast between western and eastern cultures that is important in understanding Asian modes of thinking. Philosophers and linguists have long debated the exact parameters of the relationship between language and thought. That there is a relationship, however, is not in question. Language provides a cultural form through which ideas can be expressed; the structure and content of a particular language shape and influence the structure and content of the thoughts of the people who use that language. The relationship here is not causal but constitutive. Language and thought are "two aspects of the same entity" (Tung-Sun, 1970, p. 123); they are "fundamentally indivisible" (p. 126).

Chinese and Japanese differ from English in two fundamental ways that affect thought.[3] First, Chinese and Japanese are ideographic or word-writing systems that use characters to represent the meaning of a word rather than its sounds. Ideographic languages focus on signs that represent meanings. In contrast, English and other western languages are alphabetic systems that use symbols (letters of the alphabet) to represent sounds. In alphabetic systems, language is an arbitrary symbol system that represents the underlying substance, for example, the word "chair" in English is an arbitrary representation of an object on which people sit. The ideographic nature of Chinese and Japanese affects the philosophical assumptions of the Chinese and Japanese people. While western philosophy has always been concerned with substance (materialism) and its attendant concept of causality, eastern philosophy puts much greater emphasis on signs (omens) rather than their underlying substance. Tung-Sun (1970) says that western thought is concerned with questions of "What is it?" In contrast, the Chinese are concerned with "How do we respond to it?" The distinction I cited earlier between the Asian and American concepts of the function of discourse provides a behavioral manifestation of the philosophical differences. Americans are concerned with the message of discourse (its substance); Asians are more concerned with the process and form of communicating (how it is done).

Second, English and other western languages have a grammatical structure that creates a logic of identity; Chinese grammar, on the other hand, emphasizes the relational qualities of things, creating a logic of correlation (Tung-Sun, 1970). The logic of identity is consistent with Aristotelian logic, which is the logic that dominates western thought, especially science, and provides the foundation of organizational decision-making in the United States. The logic of identity defines things in opposition to each other (i.e., A is not B). The logic of correlation "emphasizes the relational significance between something and nothing. . . . With the *yang* or the positive principle we presuppose the *yin* or the negative principle, and with the *yin* we presuppose the *yang*. Each is dependent upon the other for its completion" (Tung-Sun, 1970, p. 131). The principle of reciprocity in Asian social relationships is an example of the logic of correlation. Those with power and authority exist only *in relation to* those who do not have power and authority; each has responsibilities to the other.

Although my purpose in this section has been to examine similarities among Asian cultures, there is one difference across the cultures that is significant in understanding workplace interaction in the United States. Unlike China and Japan, which have remained independent countries for most of their history, other Asian nations have a legacy of colonialism that has shaped their national characters. The Philippines is such a nation. First controlled by Spain and then by the United States following the Spanish-American War, the Philippines has a strong western orientation. The colonial experience played a significant role in shaping Filipino culture. Filipinos are likely to believe that light skin equals higher status, that foreign equals authority, that indigenous equals inferior, and that officialdom serves its own ends (Gochenour, 1990). While Asians generally perceive authority in more personal terms than do Americans (recall that superior/subordinate relationships have reciprocal obligations in Asian cultures), Filipinos may try to subvert or defy authority; often they want to "placate authority, keep it at a distance, or use it to their advantage where possible" (Gochenour, 1990, p. 20). The colonial experience has created a set of assumptions, values, and behaviors that shares many similarities with other cultures that have had similar experiences, such as African American and Hispanic.

Hispanic Culture

Characterizing Hispanic culture is more difficult than characterizing Asian culture. First, the term Hispanic comprises numerous diverse cultures throughout the western hemisphere that are linked through their "roots in and connection with the peoples and cultures of Latin America as well as their blend of indigenous, African, and European influences" (Ferdman & Cortes, 1992, p. 273). Although Hispanic cultures "share important linguistic, cultural, religious, and other features common to most people of Spanish descent," they also have "rich differentiation" among them, ranging from accents and food preferences to sociopolitical and economic characteristics (DeFreitas, 1991, p. 7). With the current interest in the United States in identifying new markets, marketers have begun to court the Hispanic market, identifying 20 distinct markets with their "own cultural, racial, and linguistic differences" (Swenson, Feb. 1990, p. 40). The difficulty of characterizing these different cultures is reflected in the problems that the U.S. Census Bureau has had in collecting census data on Hispanics in the United States. The criteria used by the Census Bureau for categorizing Hispanics by ethnicity has changed with each census, making it impossible for researchers to use census data for longitudinal comparisons on the experiences of Hispanics in the United States (DeFreitas, 1991).

A second reason for the difficulty in characterizing Hispanic culture is the scarcity of literature on the subject, especially in organizational or work-related contexts.[4] There are several likely reasons why so little has been written about Hispanics, either in general or in the U.S. work force in particular. First, Hispanics are not represented in significant numbers in managerial positions in U.S. companies; in fact, they are half as likely as non-Hispanic whites to hold managerial or professional jobs (DeFreitas, 1991). As I noted in Chapter 2, most studies of organizational behavior focus on managers. Second, most of the work on cultural differences in the workplace has been done under the rubric of international business issues. The focus of these studies has been primarily on Asian business practices, especially Japanese management techniques. American business historically has been highly ethnocentric. As we have become enamored of international business issues in recent years, our interest has been in the success stories, which are mostly Asian. Despite the "Japan bashing" that often appears in newspapers, Americans tend to admire, or at least envy, the

Japanese, for in many ways Japan represents the modern version of the American success story. Their economic success and eminence in technology make the Japanese worthy of our attention. The nations represented in the Census Bureau's definition of Hispanic, on the other hand, tend to have weaker economies, and so we have been less interested in learning about their cultures.

The Census Bureau currently uses the following categories for Hispanics: Mexican, Puerto Rican, Cuban, Central and South American, and Other Hispanic (those from Spain or those identifying themselves as Hispanic, Spanish, Spanish-American, Hispano, Latino, and so forth). Mexicans are by far the largest Hispanic group in the United States, accounting for 64 percent of the total Hispanic population (Garcia & Montgomery, 1991a). Central and South Americans are the next largest group at 13.7 percent; followed by Puerto Ricans, at 10.5 percent. Although Cubans account for only 4.9 percent of the Hispanic population in the United States, they represent an economically and politically powerful group in southern Florida, and their experience in the United States is a study in contrasts with other Hispanic groups, especially Mexicans and Puerto Ricans.

Although Hispanic cultures vary widely, language and religion provide commonalities across cultures. The Spanish language is the most consistent marker of Hispanic identity; most Hispanics are bilingual in Spanish and English. For Hispanics, Spanish is not only a means of communication, it is also a symbol of Hispanic identity. Speaking Spanish differentiates Hispanics from members of the majority culture, not just from the perspective of Anglos, but as a matter of pride from the perspective of Latinos themselves (Ferdman, 1990). Catholicism is a second commonality. Seventy percent of Hispanics are Catholic, and "Catholicism is a strong bond . . . that crosses all lines of national origins and levels of assimilation" (Swenson, Feb. 1990, p. 40). For Hispanics in the United States, Catholicism is important not only in terms of prescribing their spiritual lives and their participation in religious rituals, but also in creating their social network. The local parish is the center of social activities.

U.S. Hispanics share more than language and religion; with the exception of the Cuban population in south Florida, Hispanics are among the most economically disadvantaged groups in the United States. They are the fastest growing "low-wage, high-unemployment group" in the United States (DeFreitas, 1991, p. 7). Also, despite the widespread belief that the majority of U.S. Hispanics are migrant farm workers who have illegally entered the United States from Mexico, the U.S. Hispanic population is primarily urban, the vast majority of which is legally entitled to be here. Hispanics are concentrated in urban centers; over 55 percent live in San Antonio and Miami. Further, the clear majority of Mexicans in the United States are either legal aliens, naturalized citizens, or U.S. born citizens (DeFreitas, 1991).

Mexicans and Puerto Ricans, who together represent nearly 75 percent of the U.S. Hispanic population, are the most economically disadvantaged Hispanics. The two groups share many cultural similarities. Both Mexico and Puerto Rico are former Spanish colonies that were later invaded by the United States. Their economic development was highly influenced by U.S. policies and practices, and both areas suffered economically. Most Mexicans and Puerto Ricans who emigrated to the United States did so because of the lack of jobs and low wages at home; they came here seeking work and economic security.

The experience of Cubans in the United States has been much different. In fact, from an economic perspective, the Cuban experience has been quite similar to the experience of whites. Cubans began to emigrate to the United States in large numbers after Fidel Castro came to power in Cuba; from 1959 to 1980, one in ten Cubans emigrated, and the Cuban population in the United States grew to over 600,000. Unlike immigrants from Mexico and Puerto Rico who came seeking better jobs, Cubans came seeking political asylum. The Cuban immigrants who came during this time period were more likely than the average Cuban to be well-educated, urban professionals (DeFreitas, 1991). Although many of them were forced to take nonprofessional jobs when they first arrived in the United States, as a whole, Cuban immigrants have been better employed and more continuously employed than other Hispanic immigrants. Further, over time their family income levels have approached white family income levels (DeFreitas, 1991). In 1980, the United States received a wave of Cuban immigrants from the port of Mariel. At the time, there was a flurry of negative publicity in the United States about the Mariel boat people, which said that most of them were from the Cuban underclass, including many prisoners released by Castro from Cuban jails. Survey data about these immigrants, however, show that they had similar characteristics to earlier groups. Thus, Cuban immigrants overall have been more educated, more urban, and less poor than Hispanic immigrants generally. In addition, they have stayed together, maintaining a strong sense of cultural integrity and group cohesion. Most of the Cuban population remained in southern Florida, especially Miami. Nearly half of all Cuban immigrants in the work force work for other Cubans. There is a high rate of self-employment in the Cuban population, and Cubans frequent Hispanic-owned businesses in far greater numbers than do other Hispanic groups (DeFreitas, 1991).

In describing Hispanics it is important to differentiate not only among the different national and ethnic cultures that comprise the Hispanic community, but also between Hispanic immigrants and Hispanics who have lived in the United States for one or more generations. Hispanics of Mexican descent who live in the United States are known as Chicanos; and although they share many cultural characteristics with the people of Mexico, they have also developed unique cultural characteristics through their experiences in the United States. Puerto Ricans who have remained on the island often call those who have emigrated to New York City "Newyorricans" (the city has the largest Puerto Rican population in the United States and is the second largest Puerto Rican city in the world) in order to point out that they have different ethnic identities now that they live among the Americanos. U.S. Puerto Ricans, however, continue to claim their Puerto Rican ethnic identity. I will briefly describe the national cultures of Mexico and Puerto Rico in order to describe the cultural roots of Hispanic peoples from these cultures. I do not mean to suggest, however, that there is a consistent and full correspondence between Mexican and Puerto Rican nationals and their counterparts in the United States.

Mexican Culture

Mexico's history and geography played a large role in shaping Mexican culture. Mexico was originally inhabited by numerous warring tribes that enforced rigid class lines. The land was inhospitable: Less than one-fifth of the land was arable and there were many volcanoes and earthquakes. The vagaries of nature and war created a sense of fatalism. Unlike the United States, where the first Europeans came seeking a better life for themselves and their children, Mexico was conquered by the Spanish conquistadors who came to plunder the land and, in the process, destroyed tribal life. Mexican identity developed through loss, creating a culture that looks to the past.

The contrast to U.S. culture is striking. U.S. identity developed through hope, creating a culture that is future-oriented. The rhetoric of the 1992 Democratic Convention provides a superb example of the contrast. The Democrats convened in New York City having lost five of the last six Presidential elections. Southerners, traditionally Democrats, had voted overwhelmingly for the Republican ticket since Jimmy Carter's election in 1976. Young people were joining the Republican Party, registering as Independents, or not voting at all. The political pundits argued that the Democrats needed to disavow the special interest groups of the left that they were now identified with (racial and ethnic minorities, labor, gays and lesbians, the poor), and to reclaim the political center by appealing to white, middle-class voters. What was most striking about the rhetoric of virtually all of the speakers at the convention, however, was not that it reflected a more moderate, centrist view. It would be hard to characterize the appeals of either Jesse Jackson or Mario Cuomo, for example, as moderate and centrist. Instead, what was most striking was that the rhetoric consistently looked to a better future and called on all Americans to have hope that together they could achieve that better future. This optimistic appeal to the future is peculiarly American.

In addition to creating a culture that looks to the past, the loss of tribal culture through conquest by outsiders also meant that the Mexican character was forged in humiliation, leading to a sense of national inferiority (Condon, 1985). The relationship between the United States and Mexico over the years has served to deepen that sense of national inferiority. Our frequent invasions and annexations of Mexican territory, coupled with abrupt shifts in immigration policy, created a relationship in which the United States was identified as the powerful neighbor to the north that used Mexican labor and resources for its own benefit. Our immigration policies provide a telling picture of our attitudes toward Mexicans. Throughout the nineteenth century, the United States had an open door policy, allowing unrestricted immigration. Movement across the Mexican-American border was essentially uncontrolled until 1924, when the U.S. Border Patrol was created. In fact, the labor shortages created by World War I prompted the United States to look elsewhere for labor and we began a policy of encouraging Mexicans to cross the border to work here. With the coming of the Great Depression, however, the United States closed its borders. Our policy shifted when we entered World War II and again faced labor shortages. Since 1965, more immigrants have come to the United States from Mexico than any other country in the world. The current economic problems in the United States, however, especially the high rate of unemployment throughout the country generally and in the Southwest in particular, have fostered strong feelings against Mexican immigrants (and immigrants in general). This push-pull dynamic in U.S. attitudes toward Mexican immigration feeds the Mexican sense of national inferiority.

Demoralization and humiliation co-exist in Mexican culture with a deep sense of idealism. Although the juxtaposition of beliefs at first glance seems contradictory, they grow out of the same roots. The fatalism of Mexican culture leads to a natural emphasis on spiritual and humanistic values. People may not be able to control nature and their destiny, but they can control their lives by nurturing their spirits and their souls. The Latino belief in *la raza* (the race) is a belief in the spiritual unity of Latin America, not a belief in the physical or material superiority of Latinos. In contrast to the spirituality of *la raza*, many Mexicans believe that Americans are materialistic, mechanistic, and irreligious (Condon, 1985).

Mexico is both a collectivist culture and a high power distance culture (Hofstede, 1984). Loyalty to the group, most especially the family, is supremely important. Mexicans also believe, however, that the dignity of the individual must always be protected. Unlike the American belief in the dignity of the individual, for Mexicans, the individual's dignity depends on internal spiritual qualities rather than external material accomplishments (Condon, 1985). Respect for others is also valued, but respect carries with it deep emotional overtones that convey the understanding of the power differentials inherent in the relationship between people. One's personal power is the result of fate or circumstance. Individuals, therefore, do not earn respect through hard work; rather, they command it through their position.

And they demonstrate their credibility through their personal connections rather than their achievements (Condon, 1985).

The collectivist culture of Mexico emphasizes interpersonal relationships. As in many Asian cultures, truth is grounded not in objective reality but in interpersonal reality. Mexicans are more concerned with saying something that will please another than something that will provide an objective description. Mexicans are also a passionate people. This passion, the emphasis on the interpersonal, and the idealism and spirituality of Mexican values all combine to create a communication style that is flowery, ornate, emotional, and dramatic (Condon, 1985). Mexicans enjoy creating artful word plays in much the same way that African Americans play with language.

Puerto Rican Culture

History and geography were as important in shaping Puerto Rican culture as they were in shaping Mexican culture. Columbus landed in Puerto Rico in 1493 and the island became a Spanish colony for over 400 years. Although Puerto Rico did not have Mexico's wealth, its strategic location and excellent natural harbor made it the front line of defense for the Spanish empire in the Americas (Ginorio, 1987). Throughout the eighteenth century, Spain had to fight to retain control over its possessions and had little interest in using its resources to develop Puerto Rico. The island remained undeveloped; by 1898, only 21 percent of its arable land was cultivated (Ginorio, 1987). In the nineteenth century, Puerto Rico sought its independence from Spain in a series of violent confrontations. The United States, however, invaded the island during the Spanish-American War in 1898. The U.S. soldiers encountered little resistance from the Puerto Ricans and easily gained control of the island. Puerto Rico was now free of Spanish domination but still had not achieved national autonomy. The long history of colonial rule and the continued lack of national autonomy played a critical role in shaping Puerto Rican culture.

Cultural integrity is an important issue for Puerto Ricans. Puerto Rican history is filled with ethnic and political conflict, beginning 500 years ago with the conflicts between the oppressors (the Spanish) and the oppressed (native peoples and slaves) and continuing today in the conflicts between those who support an independent Puerto Rico, those who support U.S. statehood, and those who support the status quo. Despite these conflicts, Puerto Ricans claim a shared cultural identity that first differentiated themselves from their Spanish oppressors and now differentiates them from Americanos in the United States.[5] Puerto Rican cultural characteristics include:

The Spanish language; the centrality of the family; a sense of *personalismo* (emphasis on the individual rather than systems or institutions), *respeto* (respect), and *dignidad* (dignity) in all interactions; the Catholic flavor if not practice of the culture. (Ginorio, 1987, p. 188)

Perhaps the most telling measure of the importance of cultural integrity is the fact that about 7500 more Puerto Ricans leave the United States to return to Puerto Rico each year than emigrate to the United States (Ginorio, 1987).

The islanders are a true multicolored society (Ginorio, 1987, p. 185), with a racial mix of native Indians, black Africans, and white Europeans. The original inhabitants of the island were the Tainos Indians, most of whom died from either disease or forced labor. In the early 1500s, the Spanish began bringing black slaves from Africa. Although the slaves were not emancipated until 1873, intermarriage among the Tainos, Africans, and resident Spaniards occurred frequently. The Spanish did not allow voluntary immigration to Puerto Rico until 1815, but when the doors opened, large numbers of immigrants arrived from both Europe and other countries in the Americas. These immigrants included French Catholics who feared the Protestant U.S. government after the Louisiana Purchase in 1803. The number of immigrants was so large that by 1830 the majority of residents on the island were white.

The definition of racial identity is another feature of Puerto Rican culture (and other Hispanic cultures) that distinguishes it from U.S. culture. Intermarriage among the Tainos, Africans, and European immigrants created a racial mix with many different shades of color. Racial differences in Puerto Rico appear on a continuum from white through shades of brown to black. In Puerto Rico, racial identity depends on not just physical characteristics, but also on nonracial factors such as socioeconomic status. In the United States racial identity is black or white, and is based solely on blood lines. Biracial children in the United States, regardless of how light their skin is, are considered black and face the same discrimination as African Americans with much darker skin. Southern Europeans in the United States, on the other hand, regardless of how dark their skin is, are considered white and enjoy the same privileges as lighter-skinned Anglos. The differences in racial identity between the two cultures is significant, for "in Latin America racial identity can be achieved, in the United States it is ascribed" (Ginorio, 1987, p. 197).

The fact that race and color are more subtly shaded in Hispanic cultures (although racism is no less pervasive) may explain why some Hispanic managers are less aware of race as a work force issue than members of other minority groups. Cianni and Romberger (1991) conducted extensive interviews with 16 managers from a Fortune 500 financial services company. Although black women and men and white women all reported feeling excluded in the organization, Hispanic managers were less certain about how their minority status affected them. One Latino said, "There's black

Hispanics and white Hispanics so I've never perceived myself as anything other than a white male. . . . But I think the company has" (Cianni & Romberger, 1991, pp. 359–360).

Ferdman and Cortes (1992), however, examined the management styles of Hispanic managers in a predominantly Anglo organization and found that they believed that their preferred managerial styles were directly connected to their experience of being different in the organization. The Hispanic managers were generally more collectivist than their Anglo counterparts: They valued the group over the individual, had greater need for consensus, and stressed interpersonal behavior over task achievement. They also favored a direct and immediate response to conflict and did not hesitate to disagree openly with their supervisors. And despite the fact that Hispanic cultures are generally large power distance cultures, these Hispanic managers had a flexible attitude toward hierarchy and preferred autonomy in their work. Ferdman and Cortes talked with these managers and found that the discussions about cultural identity led to an emergent view of group-level cultural features, including sensitivity to others and emotionality, that is consistent with cultural patterns found in Hispanic cultures outside of the United States. Ferdman and Cortes point out the danger, however, of applying group-level cultural features found abroad to the experiences of Hispanics in the United States. They believe that the cultural features reported by Hispanic managers that are consistent with cultural characteristics found abroad are just as likely the result of the managers' experience of being different as they are the result of cultural transmission.

I suspect that the answer lies in the intersection of historical cultural identity and current cultural experience. Most minority group members experience a sense of isolation in white male organizations. Different cultural groups manifest different behaviors in response to that sense of isolation, and those behaviors most likely reflect a particular group's cultural heritage.

African American Culture[6]

Recent scholarship in literary studies provides compelling evidence that the character of Huckleberry Finn was modeled after a black child that Mark Twain met in the 1870s (Fishkin, reported in Winkler, July 8, 1992). This discovery not only transforms how literary critics read American literature (*Huckleberry Finn* is a major work in the traditional literary canon in the United States), but also "suggests that traditional views of the dichotomy between majority and minority cultures may be flawed" (Winkler, July 8, 1992, p. A6). Shelley Fisher Fishkin, the American Studies scholar who uncovered the evidence, argues that full understanding of either culture demands an understanding of the other. She says:

I'm suggesting that African American voices have helped shape what we have thought of as mainstream American literature. The implication is that we need to pay more attention to African American culture, even when we study the canon. By the same token, we have to be aware of the influence of canonical works on African American writing. (quoted in Winkler, July 8, 1992, p. A6)

Fishkin's point is well taken and has implications that reach far beyond the study of American literature. African Americans have been part of American life since the first Europeans came to these shores. A human resources trainer for a Fortune 500 company told me a revealing story about a diversity workshop that she had facilitated. Participants were asked to divide up according to whether they were born in the United States or elsewhere. All first generation U.S. citizens were then asked to join those born outside of the United States. Second generation U.S. citizens then followed them. Finally, only a small group of people were left standing on the side of the room that represented those participants who could trace their ancestry back through several generations in the United States. All of them were African American.

It is impossible to deny the influence of African American culture on mainstream American culture. From music to fashion to hairstyles, black Americans have helped to shape the cultural lives of all Americans and the perception by other cultures of what is uniquely American. For example, many musicians throughout the world recognize jazz as the quintessential American musical form. The converse, of course, is also true. African Americans look not only to Africa for an understanding of their culture, but also to their experiences in the United States. It is the recreation of African ways of understanding and being for blacks in the United States that produces African American culture. African American culture is neither fully African nor fully American. For many years, scholars denied the existence of an African American culture (Foeman & Pressley, 1987), saying that black Americans had made no unique cultural contributions to American life. The scholarly argument was that slave owners had systematically stripped African slaves of their identity, taking away all markers of their ancestry, including their names and languages, and thus had destroyed their cultural heritage. The one marker they could not deny, of course, was their color.

Culture has a peculiar way of resisting destruction, however. In fact, the combination of the oppression of slavery and the continued transmission of African ways of knowing and behaving created a new culture. Scholars no longer debate whether there is an African American culture. A wealth of evidence now exists to document the existence of a persistent and unique set of cultural characteristics that have been passed down by generations of African Americans, including language, art, music, literature, and modes of being and behaving. Current controversies center more on issues related to the relative salience of particular attributes of African American culture (for example, the debates among black scholars about the importance of Afrocentrism) or the extent to which the culture is reflected in the lives of all African Americans rather than a particular group (for example, some scholars argue that the dense African American culture described by sociolinguists is really the culture of inner city male teenagers). Although Fishkin's work on *Huckleberry Finn* forces scholars to reassess how they define minority and majority cultures in the United States, it also reaffirms the fact that there is a unique African American culture. Weber (1991) concluded that 80 to 90 percent of black Americans use behavioral expressions of African American cultural identification at least some of the time.

Racism

Racism is the defining experience in the lives of most African Americans. It is a pervasive, historical fact of everyday life that has melded African and mainstream American beliefs, values, and behaviors into a unique set of cultural characteristics. Both the experience of racism itself and the internalization of the implicit and explicit attitudes in racist behavior and assumptions shapes the African American world view.

My analysis here is not intended to imply that racism is an issue only for black Americans. Members of all racial minority groups in the United States may encounter individual or institutional racism in their personal and professional lives; and for some it may be a fact of everyday life. Racism also knows no color lines; whites do not hold a monopoly on racist beliefs, attitudes, and behaviors. The ethnic and religious rivalries raging throughout the world provide vivid testimony to the pervasiveness of racism among all peoples. Racism is a cultural issue for African Americans, however, because the experience and effects of racism are central to the creation of African American culture. The majority of African Americans in the United States are descendants of African slaves who were brought here against their will and who lived their lives in a culture that denied them their basic human rights.

Understanding the effect of the denial of humanity is critical to understanding the experience of racism for African Americans. Asante (1987) argued that European protest movements are not comparable to the struggle of black Americans to achieve freedom. He said that European protest movements grew out of the repression of particular rights to which all parties presumed they were entitled. So, for example, the key rallying cry of the American Revolution, "no taxation without representation," presumed that the colonists had a right to be represented in the British government if that government was going to tax them. The American colonists were considered no less human than their English counterparts. The British government simply repressed their right to representation. In contrast, Asante stated that African peoples in the United States had been oppressed, meaning that their "rights and humanity" (1987, p. 159) were denied. African slaves were, in fact, considered less human than those people who claimed to own them. The history of the United States is filled with examples of verbal and visual depictions of blacks as subhuman, and, until only recently, our institutional policies and practices made concrete the beliefs and attitudes embodied in those depictions. Even now, more than a century after the abolition of slavery and a quarter century after the end of legal segregation, blacks in the United States still experience discrimination and de facto segregation.

Racism has affected all aspects of African American life, from family structure to employment opportunities to self-identity. In a powerful essay about the racism embedded in the English language, Ossie Davis (1976) identified 134 synonyms for whiteness, 44 of which were positive and only 10 of which had negative implications, and 120 synonyms for blackness, 60 of which were strongly negative. He concluded that English teaches "the Negro child 60 ways to despise himself, and the white child 60 ways to aid and abet him in the crime" (Davis, 1976, p. 313).

Some sociologists believe that the continuing economic, social, and political disadvantages of black Americans are the "legacy of the cumulative effect of historical discrimination" (Hatchett, 1991, p. 88). Slavery "constrained the formation and maintenance of stable families" (Hatchett, 1991, p. 85) and profoundly affected gender role identity. For example, surveys suggest that African Americans are more egalitarian about gender roles than white Americans. Researchers believe that this attitude is an adaptation to the constraints that precluded blacks from achieving the gender roles prescribed by the majority culture (Hatchett, 1991). Black men first born into slavery and later freed only to face chronic unemployment or underemployment because of racism never had the opportunity to enact the white male gender role of family breadwinner. Black women, whether slave or free, have always had to work to support their families, a reality at odds with the white female gender role of wife who needs to be taken care of by her husband.

Racism has had a profound effect on the work lives of African Americans, leading to persistent underemployment and poverty. Historically, blacks have lacked access to primary jobs (i.e., those jobs that have future job opportunities attached to them); both black men and women tend to get tracked into deadend secondary jobs, such as unskilled manufacturing and service jobs (Bowman, 1991). Overall, blacks are underrepresented in professional and technical jobs, and those who do hold higher-level positions face the added stress of racism along with the stress created by their job responsibilities. Dickens and Dickens (1982) observed that racism pervades the lives of black managers; "minority managers must acquire additional coping behaviors other than those acquired by managers in general" (p. x).

Foeman and Pressley (1987) concluded that "the sensitivity of blacks to the issue of race shapes their perceptions of the world" (p. 304). We see a striking example of the effect of racism in the differing attitudes that many black and white Americans have toward the police. Young black men and women often see the police not as protectors of the community but as fascist harassers. That perception is understandable if you consider the experiences that young blacks often have with the police. A young black male walking alone at night in a predominantly white neighborhood is likely to be stopped by the police and questioned as if he were a criminal, even if he is just returning to his home around the corner. The police presumption is, of course, that he doesn't live around the corner. A young black woman standing alone on a street corner at night is likely to be asked by the police to move along. The police presumption in this case is that she is a prostitute looking for customers. A young white woman in the same circumstances is likely to be offered a ride home.

Racism has had a profound effect on black aspirations. In African American culture, individuals are taught not to brag about their accomplishments, possessions, or social achievements. Bragging about these things offends the basic sense of egalitarianism in the culture. At another less-positive level, the prohibition about bragging is the result of the belief among African Americans that a black person's ability has little to do with his or her success in American society. Because African Americans see racism as pervasive in the society, they believe that those who make it in mainstream American society do so because they received special breaks and/or gave up their cultural identity. This belief is the basis for the African American admiration of entertainers, athletes, and hustlers—people whose success is based on their skill and retained "blackness" (Kochman, 1981).

Black perceptions of the workplace are also shaped by racism. Surveys reveal that black employees are more dissatisfied about workplace issues affecting the treatment of women and minorities than are other groups in the workplace, especially white men. Fernandez (1981) surveyed over 4000 managers about workplace issues and found that black managers were more critical than managers of other races about the treatment of women and minorities in the workplace. Black managers also strongly supported the need for affirmative action and Equal Employment Opportunity programs in the workplace. In fact, black men were the only male group who identified with women's issues in the workplace. A study of gender and race issues that I conducted at the Environmental Protection Agency (EPA) revealed a similar pattern of concern and dissatisfaction.[7] Although minority employees believed as strongly in the mission of the EPA and liked working for the organization as much as did white employees, they were much more critical of the EPA's efforts to address the needs of women and minorities, and they were more likely to believe that the Agency was not truly committed to doing something about gender and race issues. Further, although white men responded that they believed that racism was an issue of the past, minority employees strongly believed that women and minorities continued to face obstacles at work.

Although women and minorities agreed that both groups face obstacles to success in the workplace, they had very different understandings about how individuals achieve success. Consistent with Kochman's (1981) analysis about the black belief that black success in white society is not based on merit alone, minority employees said that "who you know" is an important factor in getting a promotion. White women, on the other hand, believed that the EPA is a meritocracy that rewards competence.

African Americans are often quite vocal about their dissatisfaction. Asante (1987) says that the discourse of resistance that marks the talk of African Americans is a healthy response to the "exploitation of the African through ideological impositions" (p. 87) of European culture. Studies of social identities of blacks in the United States support Asante, suggesting "that being socialized to challenge inequities somehow more fully integrates one into the system and results in closer intergroup relations" (Asante, 1987, p. 252). The discourse of resistance appears to enhance the self-esteem of African Americans. Ironically, although white Americans often seem to lose patience with black complaints about racism, the rhetoric of resistance is a quintessentially American discourse. It is based on the assumption that social inequities are wrong and that social relations can and should be changed.

Cultural Abstractions

The roots of African American beliefs and values are found in what Daniel and Smitherman (1976) call the "Traditional African World View." Although there are some variations in world view among African tribal cultures, four principles appear to be invariant across all tribes:

1. Unity exists between people's material and spiritual lives.
2. Religion is central in people's lives and permeates all aspects of their lives.
3. People should live in harmony with nature and the universe; all things are complementary rather than dichotomous, such as night and day, good and bad, and life and death.
4. Society is patterned after the natural rhythms of the universe.

These principles provide the foundation for understanding African American identity and performance.

In the Traditional African World View, the community and its coherence is central to the identity of the individual. The individual has no identity independent of the community; "neither 'I' nor 'We' have meaning apart from the other" (Daniel & Smitherman, 1976, p. 32). The individual's humanity exists only within the community; "the person is defined as human by his or her actions that lead to harmony" (Asante, 1987, p. 185). Maintaining the coherence of the community means that conflicts within the community cannot be allowed to continue; they must be worked out. In the African American community "public discourse . . . function[s] to restore the stability that conflict creates" (Asante, 1987, p. 67).

Working through conflict and restoring harmony are critical points of difference between African American culture and mainstream American culture. White Americans tend to suppress or smooth over conflict. In the workplace, for example, "white managers tend to value the appearance of tranquility" (Foeman & Pressley, 1987, p. 297). African Americans, on the other hand, want to achieve tranquility, which, at times, may mean bringing conflict out into the open and creating the appearance of disharmony.

The importance of community is reflected in a variety of ways in African American culture. African Americans generally have an "overwhelming perception of family solidarity" (Hatchett, Cochran, & Jackson, 1991, p. 67). The family is an extended network of kin, many of whom are not related through bloodline or marriage and, therefore, would not typically be defined as family members by mainstream Americans. The African American custom of informal adoption is well-documented among social workers; it is not unusual for a child to be raised by her or his grandmother, aunt, sister, or even a family friend. Informal adoption reflects both the importance of the African belief in community and the legacy of slavery, for it developed during slavery as a mechanism for family survival (Hatchett, Cochran, & Johnson, 1991). Although the fact that the number of black babies waiting for adoption is greater than the number of black families waiting to adopt children gives the impression that African Americans have abandoned the children of the community, the reality is that blacks adopt children in far greater numbers proportional to their total population than do whites. The combination of formal and informal adoption patterns paints a picture of a culture committed to the community.

The commitment to community is also evident in the high level of volunteerism among African Americans. Several years ago, I attended a Congressional hearing in Boston on the mandatory domestic service bill proposed by Senator Edward Kennedy. Johnetta Cole, the first black woman to serve as President of Spellman College, an historically black women's college in Georgia, testified at the hearing. She was fully in favor of the proposal that all college-age young people be asked to spend a year doing community service, but she insisted that those present understand that community service had always been a part of the experience of students at Spellman and other historically black colleges. Students were expected to work in their communities and they did so willingly without the force of law.

The sense of community and identification of the self within the group means that African Americans place a high priority on collective responsibility. Because things are complementary rather than dichotomous, collective responsibility does not absolve the individual; instead, it leads to a greater sense of personal responsibility and higher personal standards (Foeman & Pressley, 1987).

This heightened sense of personal responsibility as a function of group responsibility is consistent with the creation of individual identity within the collective identity. In some cultures the relationship between individual and group identity is such that individual identity is suppressed within the group (i.e., the individual is defined solely through the group). Several years ago a dance troupe from Bali appeared in Boston. In describing the art of Balinese dance, a local dance critic said that the highest compliment that one could give to a Balinese dancer is that she is indistinguishable from the other dancers. That is not how individual identity is created and performed within African American culture. Instead, individuals are encouraged to "do their own thing" within the group; through individual improvisational performances within the group performance, "the individual can actualize his or her sense of self within the confines of the group" (Smitherman, 1977, p. 104).

In addition to the family and community, the church is also a central social group in the lives of African Americans. Blacks in the United States are overwhelmingly Protestant: 52 percent identify themselves as Baptist, with Methodist as the second most common religious affiliation (Taylor & Chatters, 1991). Although African Americans brought the importance of religion with them from Africa, the black church in the United States developed as a response to the fact that blacks were denied access to institutions in American life. The church assumed the functions of a social organization in the black community, providing education, social activities, civic duties, community welfare, and business enterprises. The role of the church as the center of community life continues today. Organizations that are trying to reach African Americans (e.g., colleges seeking students, political organizations seeking members, or businesses seeking employees) usually start by contacting black churches and their affiliated organizations such as youth groups, choirs, and community service groups. Black church leaders usually serve as spokespersons for their communities, and many of the African Americans who have achieved national political prominence such as Martin Luther King, Jr. and Jesse Jackson began their careers in the black church. The black church has been critical in sustaining the culture and communication of African Americans.

The shaping of society to conform to natural rhythms rather than imposed ones and the belief in the complementarity of all things creates a sense of time in African American culture that differs substantially from white, western concepts of time. Time is seen as phases, "recurring, harmonic cycles" (Daniel & Smitherman, 1976, p. 32) in which people participate in events. Rather than identifying time as a fixed point, "being on time has to do with participating in the fulfillment of an activity that is vital to the sustenance of a basic rhythm. . . . The key is not to be 'on time' but 'in time'" (p. 32).

Several years ago I attended the wedding of a close friend; the events of the wedding and the responses to them by those who were present highlight the difference between being "on time" and "in time." The wedding invitation read 12 o'clock sharp; the invited guests began assembling at the church about 20 minutes before the ceremony was supposed to begin. At noon, nothing happened. Those of us who were friends of the bride began to joke a bit; she had a reputation for being late, although we didn't think she would miss her own wedding. At about 12:30 there were some signs that a wedding would, in fact, take place. A member of the wedding party appeared and began to practice the song she would be singing during the ceremony. The minister appeared in the front of the church, but without his robes. The whites in the church began to whisper that the bride and groom hadn't arrived yet. Had something happened? At about 1:30 the groom and various others took their places at the altar, the organist began the Wedding March, and the bride came down the aisle. The bride's only comment afterwards was that she and the groom had a few things to finish that morning before they could leave for the church. The confusion over the definition of time continued after we arrived at the reception. Many of us hurried over to the reception hall several miles away thinking that the caterers would be concerned that everyone was so late. No one was there. The food arrived long after the guests. The white friends of the bride and groom were alternately perplexed, embarrassed, and angry that nothing about the day had been "on time." Their black friends were enjoying themselves, talking and joking about the event and generally unconcerned about the absence of food. They were marking time by their participation in the event, the marriage of two close friends, an event that itself is a part of the natural rhythm of life; they were "in time."

Moving with the natural rhythms of the universe creates a spontaneity that is evident throughout African American culture, especially in the creative arts. The spontaneity and exuberance natural to African American culture is often at odds with the imposed structure and tempered style of white American culture. White culture values the ability of people to rein in their impulses; black culture, on the other hand, gives people greater freedom to express and assert themselves, and "views showing off—in black idiom *stylin' out, showboating, grandstanding*—positively" (Kochman, 1981, p. 30). The contrast between black self-assertion and white self-restraint and the stress it creates can often be seen in the organizational lives of African Americans. In a study of black women managers, Bell (1990) interviewed one woman who described herself as "magenta and teal blue functioning in a white world of grey and navy blue" (p. 472). Another woman said, "I show my white side here, which means I must be more strategic, not as spontaneous. My white side is precise and accurate" (Bell, 1990, p. 473).

Communication Style

Just as African American cultural abstractions grow out of the intersection of the Traditional African World View and the experience of life in the United States, so, also, do African American communication styles. The underlying structures or rules of black communication are grounded in the Traditional African World View (Daniel & Smitherman, 1976), while the cognitive content of black communication is situationally grounded in life in America.

The "word" is of central importance in African society; "without the word, nothing can be, for the word creates reality" (Asante, 1987, p. 70). Through words and their vocal expression, people create religion, music, medicine, and dance; "creativity is called into existence by man speaking" (Asante, 1987, p. 70). For Africans brought to the United States against their will and forced to live in an oppressive white society, the word became a vehicle for survival (Smitherman, 1977, p. 73). The oral tradition and verbal artistry flourished during slavery as blacks were denied access to the written form of language:

Unable to read or write English and forbidden by law (in most states) to learn, the African in America early cultivated the natural fascination with *nommo*, the word, and demonstrated a singular appreciation for the subtleties, pleasures, and potentials of the spoken word. . . . Vocal communication became, for a much greater proportion of blacks than whites, the fundamental medium of communication. (Asante, 1987, p. 83)

The emphasis on the spoken word continues in contemporary African American culture; "blacks tend to place only limited value on the written word, whereas verbal skills expressed orally rank in high esteem" (Smitherman, 1977, p. 76). The preacher, the politician, and the street rapper all share the same love of oral language and the same respect of the community for their linguistic skill. The current craze among young people in the United States for rap music represents the appropriation by the white majority of a cultural form that is part of the African American oral tradition. Rap, as a form of storytelling, has long played a central role in acculturating young blacks into the black value system.

Although the majority culture has appropriated the form of rap, it has not taken along an understanding of the meaning of rap. Rap represents the joining of African American communication rules with the words of white English. Although whites and blacks hear the same rap, they understand it differently. The recent controversy in 1992 over the rap song "Cop

Killer" by rap artist Ice T provides a case in point. Raps are a way that an individual both makes a point and establishes his or her reputation in the group (although rapping is primarily a male form); "black raps are stylized, dramatic, and spectacular" (Smitherman, 1977, p. 80). The black audience does not necessarily expect the speaker to act on his or her words; in fact, if the rap is forceful enough, action is unnecessary. African Americans refer to strong language that is only idle boasting as "woofin." As Smitherman (1977) says, however, white Americans don't understand the concept of woofin, "or at any rate, they wasn't buyin none" (p. 83). Instead, they take the meaning of the words literally. In the case of "Cop Killer," whites were convinced that Ice T's lyrics were intended to encourage black youths to kill police officers. Blacks were generally bemused by the fuss over the rap. In the wake of the not-guilty verdict in the trial of four Los Angeles police officers accused of beating Rodney King, a black man taken into custody by the police, and the subsequent riots in South Central Los Angeles, Ice T's lyrics made an important point about justice, or the lack thereof, for blacks in the United States. And the power of his words replaced the need for deeds to match them.

The African American oral tradition embodies the African belief in the complementarity of all things. Style and substance, thought and sound, art and activity are inseparable; one cannot exist without the other. For example, a poem exists when it is recited (Asante, 1987); "word *sound* and word *meaning* are combined in Afro-American communication dynamics" (Smitherman, 1977, p. 137). Discourse persuades, therefore, not only through its substance, but also through its style. The rhetorical qualities of African American discourse include exaggerated language, mimicry, proverbial statement and aphoristic phrasing, punning and word plays, spontaneity and improvisation, image-making and metaphor, braggadocio, circumlocution and suggestiveness, and the use of voice rhythm and vocal inflection to convey meaning (Smitherman, 1977).

Different forms of African American discourse also reflect African belief systems. For example, one of the most pervasive forms in African American discourse is the call-response. In the call-response, one member of the group calls to the other members, who, in turn, respond. Call-response is found in both sacred and secular settings. Contrast, for example, a church service in a white congregation and one in a black congregation. White worshippers are silent unless the minister asks them to read or sing collectively. Black worshippers, on the other hand, are constantly participating in the service, responding to the minister's calls with "amen" or "right on, brother" or even more extensive replies. The call-response form is rooted in the African belief in the harmony and balance of the universe and in the transactional relationship of the individual and group. It builds a bond between the speaker and the listener, making one inseparable from the other. It also creates a format in which the speaker can assert his or her own identity while still maintaining the cohesiveness of the group.

African American discourse also exhibits a creative tension between directness and indirectness. The African emphasis on harmony and the transactional nature of the individual-group relationship places great value on assertiveness and forthrightness. African Americans often engage in bravado, which is the bold and unselfconscious assertion of positive qualities of the self (Foeman & Pressley, 1987). They also confront conflict directly. However, racism and the experience of slavery have created a discourse style that exhibits indirectness. Through shucking or jiving, blacks accommodate to whites in authority, in order to appear acceptable to them. They also use signifying, which is language that indirectly implies, goads, brags, or boasts. The less direct style is most often used to get personal information, while the more direct style is to deal with conflict (Foeman & Pressley, 1987). For example, if a black woman wants to know if a black man is married, rather than ask him directly, she might say to him, "What does your wife think about that?"

Black English Vernacular

As a final comment about African American culture, let me say just a few words about Black English Vernacular (often called Black English or black dialect). Many Americans believe that the speech of some black Americans is a substandard form of English. Because African Americans who speak Black English Vernacular (BEV) do not follow the linguistic rules of standard English (the form of English we learn in school), speakers of standard English assume that they are uneducated or less intelligent. BEV, however, is not a substandard version of standard English; it is, instead, a different version of English. BEV is a complete linguistic system. It has its own syntax (grammar), semantics (meaning system), phonolology (sound system), and lexicon (vocabulary). Linguists recognize the integrity of BEV as a language system. BEV is not bad English; it is, rather, different English.

It is important to understand that the assumption that the dialect is substandard and that the related inference that speakers of the dialect are educationally and intellectually inferior is based on a form of cultural imperialism. The dialect is substandard only if standard English is defined as the norm against which all other forms of English are judged. The process is similar to the process of comparing other cultures to mainstream American culture and judging them deficient because they are different. The danger in the process is not the comparison per se; recognizing difference is critical to multicultural understanding. The danger is in the assumption that standard English (or mainstream American culture or the American way of doing things) is correct. Starting from that assumption forces the conclusion that anything that is different is deficient, and that people who speak a different language, use a different dialect, or hold a different set of values are also deficient.

My purpose is not to engage in the debate over the utility of BEV in particular contexts, especially organizational life. The issue is complex and volatile, and creates divisions both between and among whites and African Americans. My discussion is intended to acknowledge the integrity of BEV as a linguistic system and as an integral part of African American culture, and to dispel the idea that BEV is sloppy or incorrect language.

Women's Culture

The extraordinary success of Deborah Tannen's (1990) *You Just Don't Understand: Women and Men in Conversation* points to the strength of the belief, in the United States at least, that women and men are different. That belief is pervasive in American culture. We hear it repeated in nursery rhymes that ask what little girls and boys are made of, in advertisements for deodorants that tell you they're "strong enough for a man but made for a woman," and in the corporate talk of those who believe that women aren't suited to be executives because they cry too easily.

The belief that women and men are *culturally* different, however, is not generally acknowledged. More often, we confuse biology with culture, arguing that gender differences are sex differences, that women and men are biologically different. The difference between cultural symbols and biological determinants is significant. Culture is socially constructed; it is created, passed down, and recreated among people who share common experiences. Biology is given. Few would argue that there are not biological differences between women and men. Women bear children, men do not; on average, men are significantly larger than women physically. But biological differences alone cannot explain the belief that "little girls are made of sugar and spice and everything nice" or that "boys will be boys."

Some people recognize the limits of biological explanations but point to psychology rather than culture as a way to explain the differences between women and men. The *Harvard Business Review* readers who said that women were temperamentally unfit to be managers based their conclusion on the assumption that women lack certain psychological traits necessary for leadership roles, such as motivation, commitment, persistence, and strength of character. Psychological studies of women and men, however, belie that assumption. Jacklin and Maccoby (1975) surveyed the literature on psychological differences between women and men and found few differences, except in aggressive behavior, which they attributed to male hormones. They concluded that "leadership, task persistence, achievement motivation, intellectual abilities, and many other psychological abilities do not favor one sex over the other for job performance" (Jacklin & Maccoby, 1975, p. 37).

Biology and psychology provide inadequate explanations of gender differences precisely because their concern is with sex rather than gender. Gender is a social construct. Gender identities, or what we commonly refer to as masculinity and femininity, refer to modes of culturally sanctioned, appropriate behavior for men and women. They do not identify a particular man or woman, except to the extent that an individual may exhibit masculine or feminine behavior. So, all men are not powerful, rational, logical, and unemotional. And conversely, all women are not weak, irrational, illogical, and emotional. These characteristics represent cultural expectations, and the expectations of feminine and masculine vary among cultures. In her brilliant autobiography, Eva Hoffman (1989) described the difficulty she had relating her understanding of being a woman, which she had learned in Poland, to the American understanding of being a woman. She wrote:

I'm not sure how to transpose myself into a new erotic valence. The flattering sobriquets I heard as a young girl have no American equivalents: 'She's a maddening woman,' people would say about X, meaning that she had great quantities of classiness and brains and beauty. Or, 'she's a fabulous woman'—implying some favored combination of whimsicality and wit and a touch of ruthlessness. . . . The structure of personality is shaped at least as deeply by culture as it is by gender—or rather, each culture shapes both genders to be recognizable to each other in their difference. (Hoffman, 1989, p. 189)

In recent years, academics studying gender differences have extended the analysis of gender even further, arguing not only that gender is socially constructed within cultures, but also that each gender comprises its own culture (Johnson, 1989). This perspective provides a way of making sense out of the confusing and often conflicting array of research on the differences between women and men. Much of the research literature on the differences between women and men is inconclusive, with some studies suggesting differences and others finding none. In an exhaustive survey of studies on gender differences among managers, Powell (1990) concluded that there were no actual differences in behavior, only attributed differences. In other words, men and women acted similarly but those actions were interpreted and evaluated differently. Powell's findings support the position that gender is socially and culturally constructed. Our evaluations of the behavior of people depends to a large extent on our expectations of how they should behave. If we have different expectations for men and women, then women and men who "manage" similarly will be judged differently. And since our expectations include the assumption that men should be in organizational life and women should not, it is not surprising that many people conclude that men manage well and women do not, even when their managerial behaviors are the same.

There is, however, another explanation for the differences that can be found in some research studies. Although Powell (1990) generally did not find behavioral differences between male and female managers, he did find some evidence suggesting that women and men differ in their responses to poor performers in the workplace. Men based their response on whether they believed the performance was a result of lack of ability or lack of effort, while women treated everyone alike, regardless of what they believed caused the poor performance. The difference here is important because it suggests that women and men have a different set of assumptions about social structure and behavior. In fact, a growing body of research indicates that men and women characteristically have different assumptions and beliefs about the world, different communication styles, and a different set of shared experiences—in other words, they are culturally different.

Scholarly work in the area of gender as culture is relatively recent and scattered, so providing a coherent picture of women's culture is difficult. Revealing women's culture is also problematic because it is difficult, if not impossible, to distinguish women's genuine voices from male-imposed cultural norms of what women should be. Academics studying gender and culture have generally operated within a theoretical frame that posits genders as subcultures within a larger culture. Thus, discussions of male and female cultures usually presume that these cultures are subsets of some larger culture, for example, mainstream American culture. Johnson (1989) asserts that this theoretical frame is conceptually incorrect since mainstream American culture is actually male American culture. Johnson argues that a culture cannot be a subset of itself, and suggests that it is conceptually clearer to view male and female cultures as cocultures rather than as subcultures of some higher order cultural system.

Johnson's analysis is important for several reasons. First, removing women's culture from subculture status reveals and highlights the cultural contributions of women, which have been viewed as subordinate to culture itself (i.e., male culture), and, therefore, of lesser value than men's contributions. Second, the model provides a way of understanding the characteristics that are common among all women and those that are common among particular groups of women. A theory of women's culture asserts that common characteristics tie women together across cultures while also acknowledging that subcultures of women exist. Third, Johnson's analysis highlights the power differential between men's and women's culture. By refuting the myth that the larger culture is gender-neutral, Johnson shows that "what we know as culture . . . is the product of men and is maintained through the domination by men over the channels and institutions for the public expression of culture" (1989, p. 311).

Male domination of the "public expression of culture" makes it difficult to sort out women's culture and men's ideas about women's culture. For example, are the qualities that are typically associated with feminine behavior (e.g., soft, emotional, sweet, caring) characteristics of women's culture or fantasies that men in the dominant culture have about women? Public forms of culture (e.g., books, magazines, television shows, movies) are filled with feminine images, but since these public expressions are most often created and marketed by men, it is hard to know where woman begins and woman-created-by-man ends. Just as African American culture is a product of the intersection of African culture and the American experience, including racism, women's culture is created through the unique experiences of women, including the experience of male domination, especially in the public domain.

Although the efforts to uncover women's culture are less systematic than cultural studies of various racial, national, and ethnic groups, there is sufficient evidence to describe several central features of women's world view and communication style. Keep in mind that these features represent generalizations about women as a cultural group; individual women will vary in the degree to which they match the descriptions of these features.

Women's World View

The juxtaposition of intimacy and independence best captures the contrasting world views of women and men. Men see the world as a hierarchical social order in which people are either one-up or one-down. Women, on the other hand, see the world as a community in which people are placed within a network of connections (Tannen, 1990). For men, "life . . . is a contest, a struggle to preserve independence and avoid failure" (Tannen, 1990, p. 25). For women, life is "a struggle to preserve intimacy and avoid isolation" (Tannen, 1990, p. 25).

Carol Gilligan's (1982) work on moral development in women is among the best known research on gender differences. Gilligan, a psychologist specializing in moral development in adolescents, questioned the prevailing assumption among developmental psychologists that human development progresses in similar stages for boys and girls, men and women. Prompted by concern that women and girls often seemed to fall short or to be judged deviant according to the generally accepted theories of healthy adult development, Gilligan looked more closely at the genesis of those theories. Not surprisingly, she discovered that the male researchers who conducted the original research studies used male subjects. The resulting developmental theories, therefore, reflected the experiences of male development and did not necessarily provide an understanding of female development. To test the generalizability of one such theory—Kohlberg's model of moral development—Gilligan replicated Kohlberg's original research using women instead of men.

Although psychologists had long argued that "masculinity is defined through separation while femininity is defined through attachment" (Gilligan, 1982, p. 8), healthy adult development was equated with separation. Because women tend to fuse intimacy and separation, theories of human development in general and Kohlberg's theory of moral development in particular defined womanhood and adulthood as mutually exclusive. By including the stories of girls and women in the data set from which Kohlberg developed his theory of moral development, Gilligan demonstrated that women and men differ in their fundamental orientation to relationships, self-identity, and morality. These differences form the basis of different systems for making ethical judgments. Rather than having a deficient or inferior ethical system, women simply have a different system from men.

The imagery of a web is the recurring theme of women's understanding of relationships. The web shows the interconnection of people's lives within a nonhierarchical structure where everyone is equally worthy and deserves care. Individual identity is inseparable from the relationships in one's life; intimacy creates identity. The individual seeks to be at the center of the web, connected to everyone. Gilligan identifies women's morality as an ethic of caring. In articulating moral dilemmas, women see conflicting responsibilities to others and the need to find solutions that ensure that no one is hurt.

The contrast with men's imagery is stark. In a hierarchical world each person seeks to be alone at the top. Relationships are one-up or one-down, moral decisions are right or wrong. The male morality of rights assumes that rational people can agree on objectively fair solutions. Women's moral decisions are contextualized; men's are absolute.

Several factors are responsible for these differences. Historically, women and men have occupied different positions in social life, with men primarily in public roles and women in private ones. The public world of organizational life is hierarchical. People are identified in terms of their professional and educational accomplishments. Men are named through their titles—Dr. Jones, Professor Jones, Mr. Jones—and these titles reflect their positions relative to each other. Dr. Jones is in a superior position to Mr. Jones. Women, on the other hand, reside in an interpersonal world of nonhierarchical connections. They are identified interpersonally as Mary or Joan or Sue; both men and women tend to call women by their first names more frequently than they call men by their first names. Until relatively recently, women's titles, when women were given them, reflected not their personal accomplishments but their marital status and their husbands' or fathers' names—Mrs. Jones or Miss Smith. The creation of "Ms." as the female equivalent of "Mr." was intended to eliminate the practice of identifying women in terms of their marital status. The practice is so ingrained in our culture's way of identifying women, however, that "Ms." has come to mean unmarried professional woman to many people. Thus, women remain relatively equal to each other, connected primarily through their interpersonal relationships.

Enacting roles in each of these domains requires a different set of assumptions and skills. Women necessarily become adept at managing interpersonal relationships; they are attuned to the nuances of voice, gesture, and language. Women spend much of their lives engaged in talk, especially with other women. Talk serves to create and sustain their relationships with each other. Men reside in a world of action, where their relationships with each other are created and sustained through shared activities.

These relationships carry over into other contexts in women's and men's lives. For example, Johnson and Aries (1983) studied same-sex friendships and found that female friendships "encompass personal identities, intimacy, and the immediacy of daily life" while male friendships "involve more communication about matters peripheral to the self" (p. 356), such as work and sports. In a study of conflict resolution in the workplace, Johnson and Arneson (1991) found that women defined the workplace as "group-centered, interpersonally oriented, and a place of cooperation" (p. 31). Women said that conflict and anger were counterproductive in such an environment. Johnson and Arneson also said that women in the workplace faced "cooperation stress," which they defined as anxiety experienced when organizational hierarchies prevented "egalitarian approaches to task accomplishment" (1991, p. 32). Several years ago, a women friend of mine resigned her position after she received a promotion and new title. She had no objection to the promotion and its attendant salary increase. Her concern was that she now had a title that formally identified her as in a one-up position from other workers in the office. No one in the office had previously held formal titles and she had asked that she not be given one when she received her promotion. A male colleague who was also promoted at the same time, however, insisted that he receive a title, and therefore both new positions were given titles. She said she could no longer work cooperatively with the other staff and so she resigned. Her male coworkers were bewildered by her decision. Although I wasn't sure that I would have done the same, I fully understood why she chose to resign.

Women's world view is also reflected in the ways women come to know and understand the world. Women's epistemology, or ways of knowing, differs markedly from men's epistemology and from the ways of knowing that are embedded in institutional life in the United States, especially in education and business. Women tend to know things through subjectivity, experience, and passion (Belenky et al., 1986). Rather than looking to authority or theory for understanding, women learn through direct experience and personal relationships. And rather than valuing dispassionate objectivity as a necessary precursor to decision-making, women give credence to passionate subjectivity.

The concept of women's intuition has its basis in reality, for women do appear to know things by instinct rather than by conscious reasoning. Their instincts, however, are firmly grounded in real life experiences. The absence of the appearance of conscious reasoning may be an artifact of women's emphasis on holistic rather than reductionistic modes of thinking.

Women's ways of knowing are often at odds with the rationalistic approach to understanding and decision-making that forms the foundation of management theory and practice in the United States. I am deliberately using the term "rationalistic" rather than "rational" to describe managerial decision-making. Management theory and practice is rationalistic; it assumes that the exercise of reason provides the only valid basis for action or belief. That assumption, however, is not always realized. Many managerial beliefs and actions have a nonrational, or even irrational, basis. We tend to attribute rationality to bureaucratic decision-making because the decisions are enacted in a rational style (impersonal, distant, dispassionate) and they are conveyed in rational form (argumentative discourse that provides a rationale for the decision). We assume that the manager who calmly and quietly tells you that your job is being eliminated because the company is downsizing its operations has made a rational decision, when, in fact, we know only that it is rationalistic. The decision to downsize may or may not be based on the exercise of reason.

Women are told they are unfit to be managers because they are too emotional and lack objectivity, and their decisions are devalued or trivialized because they cannot always be explained in ways that are organizationally recognized and sanctioned. These evaluations are rooted, however, both in the denial of women's culture and the assumption of the superiority of male modes of thinking and being.

Women's Communication

Research in both linguistics and communication documents distinct differences between women's and men's communication. Early writings on women's speech equated different with deficient, and concluded that women's talk was less effective and decisive than men's talk, presumably because women were less effective and decisive than men. More recent research attempts to contextualize women's communication and understand it on its own terms. That research reveals a range of communication features that are culturally distinct, including vocabulary, semantics, grammar, and conversational style.

It is important to note here that these communication features characterize the speech of middle-class white women in the United States. Although women constitute a cultural group, all women do not share the same cultural characteristics. The linguistic and communication features of women's speech vary across race, class, ethnicity, and a variety of other factors. My primary purpose in this chapter is to describe the cultures of different groups in order to provide a frame for the reader's understanding of the organizational problems and conflicts created by a diverse work force in the United States. I have chosen to describe the communication of middle-class white women both because they represent the large majority of women presently in the U.S. work force and they have been the subjects in most research studies of gender and communication.

In *Games Mother Never Taught You*, Betty Harragan (1977) said that the language of business was the language of war, sports, and the locker room— a male linguistic repertoire that was either unknown or inaccessible to women. Although many women would laugh at the notion that they do not understand and cannot talk about the complex world of professional football strategy, most women in the United States have not participated in military life, competitive team sports, or locker room banter. People (and cultures) develop vocabularies that represent their experience. Women's words weave a tapestry of subtle colors and textures, reflecting their experiences as mothers, wives, and friends. Women don't see red or green; they see shades of burgundy, wine, magenta, lime, forest, or teal. Women don't "make end runs around the boss," "hit the ground running," or begin a project "full steam ahead."

Perhaps even more significantly, some words that are known to women are not allowed to them. Locker room talk, what we generally refer to as obscenity, has long been considered taboo for women. Most women have experienced being in a conversation with one or several men and having a man turn to them and say either "excuse my language, but . . . " or "I would tell you what I think except a woman is present." That taboo is not simply an artifact of age. Several years ago, I studied the use of obscenity among female and male college students (Fine & Johnson, 1984; Johnson & Fine, 1985) and found that although women and men identified the same obscenities as part of their linguistic environment, men were more likely to use obscene language. More importantly, both men and women agreed it was less appropriate for women to use particularly strong obscenities (although a few women said that these words were not appropriate for men or women).

Not only do women and men use different words, they also sometimes assign different meanings to the words they share. Studies of gender differences suggest that women and men define power differently (Belenky et al., 1986; Gilligan, 1982; Wyatt, 1984). In my own research (Fine, Johnson, & Foss, 1991), I found that men equate power with a personal style characterized by aggressiveness toward others, and women see power as a cognitive attribute that accompanies intellect. For years, feminists in organizations have used the term empowerment rather than power to describe managerial work, saying that managers empower others by nurturing them and sharing resources with them.

Success is another organizational term that carries different meanings for women and men. A number of years ago I was developing an outline for a workshop on success for managerial women and was startled when a member of the planning group said that the definition of success that I was using was too restrictive. She reminded me quite eloquently that women usually see their lives in larger patterns of interconnections and that success was not limited to movement up the organizational ladder. Such movement, in fact, often mitigates against women's opportunities for achieving success in other parts of their lives.

Researchers have also identified grammatical differences between men's and women's speech. Women are often referred to as the "keepers of the language" because of their use of proper grammar. Little girls are taught at a very young age to use language correctly. Grammatical errors, casually dropping consonant endings such as the "g" in "doing" and using "ain't," are unacceptable in the talk of little girls and generally ignored in the talk of little boys. In some cases, the emphasis on correct grammar becomes excessive and results in hypercorrect speech, grammatical forms that are incorrectly modeled after correct forms (e.g., "between you and I").

In addition to correct grammar, some researchers (Lakoff, 1975) have noted that women tend to use tag questions ("you know what I mean, don't you?"); superpolite speech forms ("please" and "thank you"); and hedges ("kinda," "well," "I wonder," or "I guess"). This constellation of grammatical forms has been used to justify the evaluation of women's speech (and, sometimes by extension, women) as tentative and unassertive. In the early research on gender and language, researchers concluded that women used hedges because they were uncertain about their conclusions and that they used tag questions because they were afraid to express a point of view without support from others. More recently, feminist scholars have questioned those conclusions, arguing instead that women define and use these forms in ways that differ from men's understandings of them. Tag questions, for example, are a way to encourage others to participate in the conversation; they invite a response and create dialogue rather than monologue in conversation. Hedges may well reflect the reality of uncertainty, as contrasted with the male tendency to make direct assertions regarding things about which they are uncertain.

These different understandings of the meaning and function of linguistic forms reflect fundamental differences between how men and women define the function of "talk." Men see talk as a means to preserve their independence and maintain their status. They engage in what Tannen (1990) calls "report talk," in which they exhibit knowledge and skill, tell people what to do, and hold center stage. Women, on the other hand, view conversation as a cooperative enterprise (McConnell-Ginet, cited in Case, Summer 1993), and engage in "rapport talk" (Tannen, 1990). Women use talk to establish connections and share experiences; talk allows women to create symmetry in their relationships. This understanding of talk is consistent with studies that indicate that women's friendships are developed and maintained through conversation, while men's friendships are based on shared activities (Johnson & Aries, 1983).

Defining conversation as a cooperative enterprise that establishes relationships leads women to a conversational style that is distinct from men's conversational style. In a study of workplace discourse, Case (Summer, 1993) identified three communication styles: (1) A facilitative/personal style, used mostly by women, which is relational, self-disclosing, and integrative; (2) an assertive/authoritative style, used mostly by men, which is directive, depersonalized, and commanding; and (3) a wide-verbal-repertoire style, used by a few women and men, which contains mixed elements of the other two styles.

CONCLUSION

In this chapter I have identified some unique cultural characteristics of the cultures of Asians, Hispanics, African Americans, and Women. For each culture I have included a description of the major values and beliefs in the culture, and the ways in which members of the culture enact those values and beliefs through their behavior and communication. As I stated at the beginning of the chapter, my goal is neither to describe these cultures fully nor to give readers the impression that any single member of these cultures would carry all of the characteristics I described. Instead I have provided an array of descriptors that shows the ways in which assumptions and behaviors vary culturally, in order to provide a foundation for understanding what happens when members of different cultures interact in the workplace. In the next chapter I will show how different cultural identities and performances, when they are unacknowledged or misunderstood, can lead to dysfunctional and nonproductive interaction in the workplace.

NOTES

1. Because different cultures have different patterns of thinking, acting, feeling, and interpreting, we would expect members of those cultures to interpret and evaluate their experiences through their own cultural lenses. Ethnocentrism, which is "the tendency to interpret and evaluate others' behavior using our own standards" (Gudykunst, 1991) is a natural human behavior rather than a horrible sin committed only by "ugly Americans." Ethnocentrism becomes dangerous when people are unwilling to acknowledge their cultural biases. That trait is generally strongest among members of homogeneous cultures and members of privileged cultures. Members of cultural groups that function on the margins of other powerful, privileged cultures are forced to understand the cultural assumptions of the more pow-

erful group in order to survive. Most members of marginalized culture groups, therefore, are bicultural. In later chapters I argue that because the United States is now a nation of diverse cultures, each of us must develop multicultural literacy to negotiate the public world.

2. The reverse logic is also true. We cannot assume that a person is not a member of a particular cultural group because she or he doesn't *look* like other members of the group. I have twice had the disconcerting and potentially embarrassing experience of assuming that blonde, blue-eyed, white women were Anglo. The first woman was an American Indian; the second was Puerto Rican. In both cases the women strongly identified with their cultural reference groups and both had encountered prejudice in the workplace once their cultural identities had become known.

A PBS television special on racism highlighted how easily people classify others based on physical characteristics. The program focused on a very successful antiracism training module used by the U.S. military. The trainer for the program was a tall, handsome man with white skin and classic Anglo physical characteristics. Throughout the seminar he provoked the participants, white and black, to share their feelings about members of the other race. As he won the trust of the participants, particularly the white members of the group, people began to express more honest feelings and to vent their frustrations about racial issues. The white participants began to look to the trainer for support for their statements, seeing in him a compatriot. When the training sessions were done and the group was debriefing about the experience, someone made a statement that presumed that the trainer, as a white man, would agree with a particular sentiment. At that point, the trainer moved to the front of the group and announced that he was African American. The group stared disbelievingly. No one believed him until he produced pictures of himself with his parents and siblings.

3. Despite some important similarities among Asian languages, they also differ in significant ways. For example, although written Japanese uses Chinese characters and over half of contemporary Japanese vocabulary is Sino-Japanese, the two languages are fundamentally different. Chinese is a branch of the Sino-Tibetan language family and Japanese is distantly related to Korean and the Altaic language family, which includes Turkish, Finnish, and Hungarian (Inoue, 1979).

4. A new collection of articles about Hispanics in the workplace (Knouse, Rosenfeld, & Culbertson, 1992) provides some information on managerial issues. Most of what has been published about the experience of Hispanics in the United States, however, focuses on the low economic and educational achievement in the Hispanic community in general. Hispanics have come to be identified by the majority culture as a disadvantaged group.

5. All of the peoples of North and South America are Americans. Many Latin Americans resent the appropriation of the term by the United States to refer only to the people of the United States. The use of American to refer exclusively to U.S. peoples and culture is seen as the epitome of U.S. ethnocentrism and imperialism. Puerto Ricans, however, commonly use Americanos to refer to Anglo Americans.

6. My choice of terms here is purposeful. The discussion of African American culture is not intended to include cultural characteristics of all black Americans. Blacks born and raised in the United States who trace their ancestry back at least several generations and whose forebears came to the United States from Africa

differ in significant ways from blacks who have recently emigrated to the United States from Caribbean, Latin American, or African countries. One of the more critical cultural differences is that recent emigres, in most cases, have grown up in majority-black cultures. The minority status of African Americans has had a profound impact on their cultural identity and performance. Much of the current racial tension within and among the various black communities in the United States is caused by a lack of understanding of the different modes of cultural knowing and being engendered by growing up as either a majority or a minority person. Many of my Caribbean students comment to me when they are new to the United States that they have a hard time understanding why the African Americans they meet are so sensitive about racial issues and so quick to cry racism when something bad happens to them. Sadly, those who remain here for an extended period of time begin to take on many of these same attitudes as they, too, encounter the racism so prevalent in our society.

7. Because the number of minority employees by racial categories was so small, we could not divide the category of "minority" into different racial groups without jeopardizing the anonymity of the employees. Although the data in the study are presented in terms of minority employees versus white employees, the large majority of minority employees were African American. The results, therefore, can be compared to the results of Fernandez's work. For a more detailed description of the study, see Fine, Johnson, & Ryan (1990).

4

DYSFUNCTIONAL
DIVERSITY:
THE WORKPLACE AS
A TOWER OF BABEL

The previous chapter provided an overview of cultural differences among particular cultural groups and a context for understanding the dynamics of diversity in the workplace. The different ways of thinking, feeling, acting, and interpreting that white Anglo men, African Americans, Hispanics, Asians, and Women bring to the workplace hold the potential for generating new insights into solving workplace problems and increasing productivity among all workers. Realizing that potential, however, requires both personal and organizational adaptations to cultural differences. Without those adaptations, cultural diversity in the workplace tends to recreate the biblical Tower of Babel, with workers of different cultural backgrounds speaking in mutually unintelligible forms and engaging in continual conflict.

In Chapter 3, I described some of the key cultural characteristics of Asians, Hispanics, African Americans, and Women, and juxtaposed them against the cultural characteristics of white Anglo men. This chapter explores the implications of those differences by looking at the interaction among culturally diverse people in the workplace.

Although cultural diversity holds the promise of numerous positive outcomes, it often creates negative outcomes, such as misperceptions, misunderstandings, and stereotyping. In his analysis of cultural differences in communication, Carbaugh (1990) uses the term "asynchrony" to describe "the interactional dynamics" that produce a "wide range of detrimental outcomes that, in turn, stem—in part—from cultural variations in communication" (p. 157). In this chapter, I examine the asynchrony that can occur when culturally diverse people work together.

In the scenarios that follow, it is important to recognize the limits of a cultural description and analysis of workplace behavior. First, cultural identity should not be confused with biological identity. An individual may be a member of a particular race or gender by virtue of his or her genetic background, but not identify culturally with other members of that culture group. Biological identity does not equal cultural identity. In fact, in some instances, an individual's cultural identity may be at odds with his or her biological identity. Transsexuals are an extreme example of this phenomenon. Transsexual men, or "she-males" as Raymond (1979) calls them, were born with male bodies but developed a female cultural identity, albeit a cultural identity based on gender role stereotypes rather than lived experience.

Second, individuals vary along a continuum in the degree to which they fit a particular cultural description. Culture is not the only factor that shapes individual behavior: Social class, age, individual idiosyncrasies, family dynamics, personal history, and a variety of other factors influence how individuals understand the world and behave in it. Also, individuals are often situated within more than one culture, and their behavior at any given point in time may reflect a particular culture or some hybrid of two or more cultures.[1]

It is important to remember that culture does not *determine* behavior; rather, it provides a guide to behavior. People are free to choose ways of thinking, feeling, interpreting, and being that differ from those of their native culture.[2] In fact, in some instances, people very deliberately choose to pass as a member of another culture. Members of an excluded or marginalized cultural group will try to pass as members of more "prestigious" cultural groups in order to have access to greater professional and personal opportunities. For example, in the 1940s and 1950s, some Jewish professionals Anglicized their names in an attempt to pass as Christians, and light-skinned blacks sometimes tried to pass as white.

The third limitation of the analysis reflects the scarcity of research on the experience of second and third generation Asians and Hispanics. Where an individual sits on a cultural continuum is directly affected by one's status as an immigrant in a new culture. Recent immigrants are likely to adhere more strictly to the cultural assumptions of their native culture than are subsequent generations born in the United States, although even that generalization varies by particular culture and individual family. The cultural characteristics of Asians and Hispanics described in Chapter 3 are based on studies of some of the particular national cultures represented within the more general cultural names. Very little research has focused on identifying the cultural characteristics of Hispanics and Asians born in the United States.

Although there are a few studies of the experiences and behaviors of women and African Americans in the workplace, there is little research on the relationship between cultural identity and workplace behavior in general. The limited research that does exist is based on a workplace in which conformity is both expected and the norm by which people are judged, so researchers are unlikely to find significant behavioral differences. Furthermore, most women and people of color who have made it in the workplace have assimilated into white male organizational culture, making their observable behavior nearly identical with that of their white male counterparts. A few articles have been written in which the authors infer from the existing research on African American or women's culture how African Americans and women behave when they are allowed, or would behave if they were allowed, to express their own cultures (see, for example, Asante & Davis, 1989; Foeman & Presley, 1987; Loden, 1985; Rosener, Nov./Dec. 1990).

Although there is little systematic empirical evidence on workplace behavior, we do have anecdotal evidence about what happens when culturally diverse people interact. Such anecdotal evidence has the power to suggest larger scenarios about interaction in culturally diverse organizations. The remainder of this chapter explores such actual or imagined scenarios. To keep the analysis both brief and relatively simple, I focus primarily on interaction between African Americans and whites and between men and women, with only a brief discussion about what happens when members of other cultural groups are added to the cultural mix.

BLACK AND WHITE ASYNCHRONY

Interaction between African Americans and whites has always been problematic. Most white Americans identify racism as the primary issue that divides blacks and whites. Whether because they feel liberal white guilt or fear being branded a racist for something they might say, whites often avoid extended conversations with blacks, especially on topics that might involve conflict. Blacks generally interpret white reluctance to talk with them as racist, especially when the interaction suggests that whites are not being honest and genuine about their feelings.[3]

Although racism, both institutional and individual, obviously shapes relationships between black and white Americans and continuously serves to undermine attempts to bring blacks and whites together, cultural differences also create asynchrony between them. These cultural differences not only create misunderstandings and misperceptions between African Americans and whites, they also place the two communication styles fundamentally at odds with each other, making successful communication between the races virtually impossible. Kochman (1981) says that black communication styles are disabling to whites. In other words, when African Americans communicate within their own cultural style, they create patterns of interaction in which whites, because of their cultural style, are unable to participate.[4] The styles of blacks and whites are not simply unknown to each other; they are in conflict with each other.

The conflict between African American and white communication styles is evident in a variety of attitudinal and behavioral differences. I will describe four communication features in which those differences are manifested in order to show the difficulties blacks and whites face communicating with each other in the workplace: Persuasive discourse, expression of individual feelings, eye contact, and conversational interaction.

Persuasive Discourse

Calm, rational discussion is a fundamental principle of persuasive discourse in white male organizations. Professionals are expected to use language that is careful, calculated, and unemotional; to keep their voices low and well-modulated; and to maintain polite decorum at all times. Intense emotional expressions and argumentative challenges have no place in the white male organization.[5] According to white norms of discourse, people who challenge and confront others are expressing anger and hostility, emotions that are inappropriate in the workplace. Further, intense emotional debate does not allow for the exercise of reason, since emotion and reason are considered mutually exclusive within white male culture.

In African American culture, however, self-control is defined as the ability to show anger fully while controlling the escalation of anger into violence. As I said in Chapter 3, the violent lyrics of some rap music function to express the anger of many young African Americans in order to prevent their emotions from erupting into physical violence. Young African American men pride themselves on their ability to engage in verbal duels without resorting to acts of physical violence.[6]

This heightened emotionalism carries over into other interactions, and can become a source of misunderstanding and conflict between blacks and whites. For example, I recall sitting at a staff meeting on affirmative action policy with five white men, one African American man, and one white woman, who represented the senior executives of a large organization. The African American male, who served as the organization's affirmative action officer, accused the organization of not being committed to affirmative action. He used very forceful and emotionally charged language to make his point, and became very angry when no one would respond or defend the organization's actions. The white staff at the meeting became more and more uncomfortable, and the angrier the African American male became, the quieter and more uncomfortable the others became.

In separate conversations with me afterwards, each gave me a different interpretation of what happened. The African American male was furious that no one in the organization cared enough about affirmative action to engage in dialogue with him about the issue. The white staff members were furious that their African American colleague refused to talk calmly and rationally about the issue; they concluded that he had a chip on his shoulder about racial issues and, therefore, his comments could not be taken seriously. They were also angry because they believed that their personal integrity and commitment to racial equality had been questioned by a peer.

In this particular situation (and many similar interactions between blacks and whites), the misunderstanding was magnified by the different meanings members of each group ascribed to the arguments that were presented. When the African American male accused the organization of not supporting affirmative action, he was making a general accusation that was not directed at any person in particular. In black culture, individuals are not expected to defend themselves against general accusations. When a black speaker accuses whites of racism, the speaker is indicting a system of institutional racism in which whites participate; the speaker is not accusing any particular white person, including the person or persons with whom she or he is speaking, of being racist. Denying one's guilt, therefore, is unnecessary. Individuals only need to deny specific accusations that are directed at them, and the denial should be firm but not overly vehement. In black culture, a vehement denial is taken as a sign of guilt.

In the staff meeting I described, the interaction between the African American and the white executives intensified as the whites began denying the accusation that the organization was not committed to affirmative action. A statement that the African American executive had hoped would provide an opening to an organizational discussion of affirmative action issues became, instead, a point of conflict, which both defined the differences between blacks and whites and further heightened them. The white executives first denied that they were not committed to affirmative action, pointing to various policies and programs they had endorsed. Their quick and forceful denials, which they believed were necessary to prove they were not racist, impressed the black executive that they felt guilty about something. As the discussion continued and the black executive became more emotional, the white executives' retreat into uneasy silence only reinforced that initial impression of guilt.

The addition of Asians into the mix creates even more asynchrony in persuasive discourse. Asians tend to be reticent in public situations, and often remain silent in group discussions. In conversations fraught with conflict, Asian silence is sometimes transformed into acquiescence, with Asians seeming to agree to most anything that is stated or asked by others in order to end the conflict. Asians generally avoid conflict at any cost, even if doing so means denying their own beliefs or feelings. The danger here is that the non-Asian participants usually read acquiescence as either passivity or a definitive yes rather than as a strategy to smooth over interpersonal conflict. Asian colleagues who today support a black peer's as-sertion that people of color are discriminated against may not sign tomorrow's petition on behalf of all people of color in the organization. They may even deny the assertion in subsequent conversations with white colleagues. Blacks and whites alike in this situation may interpret this be-havior as waffling (or even lying), and may begin to mistrust Asian col-leagues.

Expressing Individual Feelings

Another aspect of communication that differs in black and white cul-ture is how individuals express their feelings. In white culture, individuals often suppress the full force of their feelings in order to conform to accept-able behavior. Children are taught to control their anger, learning to "count to ten" before responding to someone or something that has made them angry. Whites are taught that it is natural and appropriate to suppress their feelings in particular situations or contexts, such as the workplace.

The workplace is a prime example of a context in which people are ex-pected to suppress their emotions. The ambiance of corporate offices re-flects the pervasiveness and power of organizational strictures against ex-pressing emotional extremes. The silence is often overwhelming as you enter the executive suite. Thick carpets mute most sounds; in the absence of carpets, the clicking of heels against stone floors is deafening, and high-lights the absence of other noises. The neatness and cleanliness of the of-fices suggests a compulsive desire for order. Managerial "how-to" books suggest ways that managers can keep their desks uncluttered; some orga-nizations even have policies forbidding employees to eat food at their desks or requiring them to clear their desks before they leave each day. Voices are hushed, and everyone is unfailingly polite.

The different perspectives that blacks and whites have about expressing the full force of individual feelings have their roots in the distinction that each culture makes between individual sensibilities and individual feel-ings. Sensibilities have to do with matters of taste, decorum, and refine-ment; feelings have to do with emotions. Individual sensibilities are pro-tected in white culture, while individual feelings are protected in black culture. Thus, African Americans believe that they have a right to express their feelings even if that expression offends the sensibilities of another person. Whites, on the other hand, will suppress their feelings in order not to offend the sensibilities of others, or even of themselves.

When African Americans negotiate situations or contexts that are de-fined by white cultural expectations, they are compelled to subordinate their feelings to the sensibilities of others. This behavior is called "fronting," or not being free to act in accordance with the force of personal feelings (Kochman, 1981). Because fronting is normalized in white culture, whites rarely even notice it as a distinct behavior. Fronting is a way of being that is expected; it is neither applauded nor derided. To African Americans, however, fronting represents unacceptable behavior; they must consciously suppress their own feelings and cultural norms in order to conform to white behavioral norms. That conformity takes an enormous psychic toll on African Americans, especially in the workplace, where any deviations from fronting may have serious professional and economic consequences. Because whites rarely notice fronting, they are generally unaware of the toll it takes on African Americans.

The different attitudes toward expressing personal feelings in African American culture and white culture also create misunderstandings between blacks and whites. Whites sometimes misread cues from blacks. For example, in a mixed group setting, if blacks do not voice dissatisfaction about a policy or procedure, whites tend to assume that the black group members are satisfied. Their silence, however, is just as likely to be a sign that the black group members feel uncomfortable speaking up in this situation because they do not believe that they are free to express their real feelings. Numerous organizational studies show that African Americans often have strong negative feelings about their working environments (see, for example, Fernandez, 1981; Fine, Johnson, & Ryan, 1990). Whites are often surprised by these findings, not only because those feelings are at odds with their own, but also because they rarely hear blacks in the workplace voice their true feelings.

Eye Contact

Eye contact is an important nonverbal component of conversational interaction that varies widely among different cultures. The cultural patterns regarding eye contact differ substantially in African American and white culture. African Americans generally have greater eye contact when they are speaking than when they are listening. Whites reverse the pattern, showing greater eye contact when they are listening than when they are speaking (Hecht, Ribeau, & Alberts, 1989).

The different patterns create interactional problems between blacks and whites that can become the basis for inaccurate judgments, especially by whites about blacks. For example, because blacks tend to maintain eye contact when they are speaking and whites tend to maintain eye contact when they listening, blacks and whites often stare at each other when blacks are speaking. This mutual staring can heighten the sense of confrontation between blacks and whites. Whites interpret direct and sustained eye contact by speakers as a sign of intensity and passion. It often also signals anger; for example, parents will demand that a child look at them when they are rebuking the child for misbehaving. What blacks consider normal conversational interaction, therefore, is interpreted by whites as not only unusual but also angry and confrontational, which further strengthens the belief held by many whites that African Americans have "a chip on their shoulder" and are difficult to work with.

When the conversational interaction is reversed and whites are speaking, the different eye contact patterns create a situation in which both whites and blacks appear to be inattentive (Hecht, Collier, & Ribeau, 1993). White speakers break eye contact frequently and black listeners look away from the speaker. Although the black listeners are not gazing directly at the speaker, they are well aware that the speaker is not looking at them. Black listeners interpret this behavior by white speakers in a variety of ways depending on the context of the conversation or their relationship with the speaker. The speaker doesn't care about them; the speaker is disrespectful toward them; the speaker is nervous about talking with them; the speaker is not telling the truth. Each of these interpretations, however, holds negative consequences for the immediate interaction between speaker and listener and the longer-term relationship between them.

The interpretation of the conversational interaction by whites is equally incorrect and potentially damaging. African Americans believe it is disrespectful to maintain eye contact with a speaker, especially if the listener is in a subordinate position to the speaker. Children are taught not to look directly at teachers, parents, and other adults. Whites, on the other hand, believe that looking away from a speaker is a sign of disrespect, or at best, proof that the listener is inattentive. When blacks and whites converse, white speakers assume that black listeners are not paying attention to them.

White teachers, for example, often complain that African American children do not pay attention in the classroom. The assumption that lack of eye contact equals lack of attention frequently leads white teachers to conclude that black children have poor attitudes in school. That conclusion has serious and detrimental consequences for African American children. Educational research shows a strong link between student performance and teacher expectations. If teachers believe that African American children have poor attitudes in school, they are likely to pay less attention to them and to lower their expectations of them, leading to a self-fulfilling prophecy, with African American students performing less well academically than white students.[7]

The same principle holds true in the workplace; there is a relationship between managerial expectations and worker performance. The perception, therefore, that African American workers do not listen attentively can have powerful negative consequences for African American employees, even though that perception is based on a misinterpretation of their nonverbal behavior. In the more immediate context, the misperception that an African American worker or coworker is not paying attention to a white speaker may lead to personal conflicts between them, making their future working relationship more difficult.

Conversational Interaction

Misperceptions between blacks and whites about listening behavior also occur because of fundamental differences in the structure of conversational interaction between African American culture and white culture. In Chapter 3, I described the African American discourse form named "call-response." In the call-response, one member of the group calls to the others, who, in turn, respond. The call-response is rooted in the African-American belief in the harmony and balance of the universe; it is a discourse form that is most evident in religious settings, but is also found in interpersonal discourse in secular contexts.

The secular use of call-response in conversations between blacks and whites creates communication problems for both groups (Daniel & Smitherman, 1976). White conversational discourse is governed by strict turn-taking rules; when the speaker speaks, the listener's role is to listen silently. The listener might provide some nonverbal feedback to the speaker, but for the most part, the listener is mute. In fact, listening textbooks instruct listeners to refrain from responding and to suspend their judgment of the speaker's ideas until the speaker has concluded. African American conversational discourse is much more fluid, with speakers and listeners essentially inseparable from one another. When one person speaks, he or she is issuing a call for the other members to respond; they, in turn, do so, both verbally and nonverbally, by interjecting comments and nodding their agreement or disagreement.

In conversations between blacks and whites, each group brings its own cultural understanding of how conversations are organized. Because whites adhere to the turn-taking rules that govern white conversational discourse and remain silent when blacks are speaking, blacks think that whites are not really listening to them. Conversely, when whites take over as speakers and call to others in the conversation, they think that blacks are not listening to them because the black listeners are talking back, dancing around, and otherwise interrupting them. Each group holds the other to its own cultural expectations, and the resulting deviations are negatively interpreted and evaluated, leading to further conflicts between them.

FEMALE AND MALE ASYNCHRONY

Cultural differences based on gender create numerous misunderstandings and conflicts between women and men. As I said in Chapter 3, the success of Deborah Tannen's (1990) popular press version of her sociolinguistic research on gender differences in communication, *You Just Don't Understand: Women and Men in Conversation*, suggests the extent to which women and men in the United States believe that they are unable to understand each other.

My purpose in this chapter is to look at some ways in which cultural differences between women and men lead to conflict between them in the workplace, both in their personal relationships and professional conduct and in their positions on organizational policies and practices. In doing this, I do not mean to minimize the effects of sexism in organizations, or to deny the power differentials that keep women in positions that are subordinate to men, but only to demonstrate how an understanding of cultural differences based on gender helps to deconstruct some of the misunderstandings and conflicts between women and men.

Intersection of Personal and Professional Lives

The contrasting world views of women and men lead them to very different understandings about the intersection of the personal and the professional, both in their own lives and the lives of others. Women see the world as a network of connections; each part of that network is intricately and intimately connected to the other parts, creating both continuity and community. Men, on the other hand, see the world as a hierarchical social order, with clear divisions and unequal status among its parts.

Women rarely compartmentalize their personal and professional lives. The personal and professional represent different contexts, with different relationships, but they are not compartmentalized and ordered in relation to each other. Instead, they form a whole that represents equal facets of a woman's life, with each facet adding depth and dimension to the whole. This sense of continuity and connection between the personal and the professional means that women don't leave their personal concerns at home. They continue to worry about a sick child even after they arrive at the office; their talk at the coffee machine revolves around children, spouses, and other home issues; they are likely to reschedule a meeting in order to take a child to a swimming lesson or to get home in time to see a class play.

Men are often frustrated by what they define as women's lack of commitment to organizational success. They see women torn between work and home, and, more often than not, choosing home over work. Women, however, do not account for their behavior in terms of choosing one over the other. Their lives are defined through their private interpersonal commitments rather than their public institutional commitments; those interpersonal commitments serve to set their priorities. Women take care of their children, spouses, parents, and friends not because society tells them that it is their job to do so, but because they value and respect the interpersonal ties that are represented by those relationships. Of course, the fact that men generally do not take responsibility for the care of family and friends provides an added incentive for women to do so.

This commitment to interpersonal relationships leads women to demand that organizations become more accommodating to families. The demands for on-site daycare or more community daycare, flexible work schedules, job sharing, and family leave policies represent the expectations of women, not their dreams. Work and family are not competing interests, but complementary ones.

Men, on the other hand, are often baffled by these demands. For men, these options are nice extras *if* the organization can afford them financially, but they are not necessary. Further, men tend to believe that workers who choose to exercise these options are not serious about their work and careers. For example, women who have chosen to work parttime while their children are young are generally not considered for promotions. When Felice Schwartz (Jan./Feb. 1989) made her controversial proposal in the *Harvard Business Review* that organizations establish "Mommy tracks" for women who want to raise a family and work, she explicitly stated that such a track was not for women who wanted to move ahead in the organization. Those women should, instead, remain on the traditional fast track, a career option that leaves no time for family and friends.

These different positions on the relationship between family and work lead to conflicts between women and men in the workplace. For example, women and men often disagree about whether an organization should adopt policies and job procedures that accommodate the family needs of employees. Men argue that these policies and procedures are too expensive. Women do not define the issue in financial terms. They believe that organizations have a responsibility to ensure that employees can adequately meet their family needs. The debates over making organizations more "family friendly," both within particular organizations and in the national public policy arena, often get stalled because on a fundamental level each side is incapable of understanding the other's arguments. Men demand quantitative proof that these policies increase organizational productivity; women conclude that organizations are hostile environments for them.

Ways of Knowing

Women's ways of knowing, or what philosophers call "epistemology," are very different from men's ways of knowing. People's epistemological stances shape their persuasive discourses, guiding their decisions about the validity of the evidence, the reasoning, and the conclusions in a discourse.

Men tend to be deductive thinkers; their discursive arguments rely heavily on general assertions that are supported by concrete data. The scientific method, with its emphasis on objectivity and testing hypotheses, is one of the best exemplars of male epistemology. Practicing the scientific method demands that researchers remain distanced from and objective about their subjects (or at least maintain the pretense of objectivity through an objectivist position). The data that they subsequently collect are used to verify or refute their hypotheses. The logic of scientific proof is rational, economical, and clean; once you accept its premises, it moves inexorably toward its conclusion. In addition to relying heavily on deductive reasoning, men also tend to develop arguments based on authority, using expert opinion to support their conclusions. Men also tend to identify themselves with authorities (Belenky et al., 1986), thus the expert opinion they use is often their own.

Women generally approach the world much more inductively than men do; women learn through subjectivity, passion, and personal experience. Consciousness-raising groups, a phenomenon born in the late 1960s as part of the Women's Movement, best characterize women's epistemology. Consciousness-raising is a learning technique that is based on sharing common experiences. In the early years of the Women's Movement, small groups of women would meet on a regular basis to talk about their experiences as women; the topics ranged from women's health issues to juggling work and domestic responsibilities to sexual practices to interpersonal problems with men. By sharing their personal experiences, the women in these groups discovered common patterns of discrimination against women in numerous public institutional practices—marriage, medicine, and work, for example—and simultaneously gained a sense of solidarity with each other. Consciousness-raising groups allowed women to see the political dimensions of their personal experiences and empowered them to work to change the institutional practices that discriminated against them. Conversational discourse among women today is often very like the discourse of consciousness-raising groups.

The rationalistic, scientific approach to management that has been the dominant perspective in both theory and practice throughout the twentieth century often makes little sense to women in the workplace. I recall my frustration with economic and finance theories when I was a graduate student because the theories did not reflect my experience. For example, I chafed at the concept of "rational man," which underlies economic theory. My professors would insist that economics is a rational, predictive science because "rational man" would always choose the basket of goods that contained the largest number of goods; more, of course, being better than less. I would sit in class and present counter-examples, such as selecting the basket with less goods in order to ensure that someone else might have some goods. I would obsess about the contextual issues that, in a particular instance, would undercut the generalizability of the theory. Those contextual issues would always be based on my experience or that of people I know or my understanding of how I would respond to a choice in a particular situation; the generic concept of "rational man" made no sense to me. At first, my professors were annoyed by my examples; later, they were annoyed by my persistence in refusing to accept their premises (and, implicitly, their authority). Although some radical economists have now embraced alternative explanations of economic decision-making, economics is still dominated by "rational man."

Many women in the workplace experience the same reluctance to accept established theories of how to do business. In making decisions in the workplace, they agonize over the particularities and peculiarities of the situation and the people involved. Rather than offering an unqualified judgment about a proposal, they point out the various circumstances that might undercut either its success or failure. Or they rely on intuition, and say that the idea does or doesn't feel right. Men listen to these comments and conclude that women are indecisive and illogical. Conversely, women say men are dogmatic, narrow-minded, and authoritarian.

Understanding Organizational Experiences

Women and men in organizations often find themselves at odds with each other because of their different understandings of personal experiences. As I said in Chapter 3, women and men have traditionally conducted their lives in different spheres, with men occupying positions in public life and women occupying positions in private life. Further, the unequal distribution of power between women and men gives each gender a different vantage point for making sense out of the world around them.

The continued pervasiveness of sexual harassment of women in organizations provides evidence that women and men understand their workplace experiences differently. The confirmation hearings for Clarence Thomas when he was nominated to the Supreme Court gave both genders a public forum in which to reveal their understandings of sexual harassment in the workplace.

When Anita Hill, the young female law professor who had accused Thomas of sexually harassing her when she worked for him at the Equal Employment Opportunity Commission, was questioned by an all-male Senate panel, the Senators' questions and comments clearly displayed not only their disbelief of her account but also their lack of understanding of the experience of sexual harassment. Why hadn't she reported his behavior to others? (Since Thomas was the country's top enforcer of the laws against sexual harassment, she had no one to report his behavior to. Furthermore, the experience of sexual harassment is painful and humiliating; most women are too embarrassed, and sometimes too frightened, to talk about it.) Why did she continue to have a professional relationship with him even after they had both left the EEOC? (Thomas was the most senior and powerful supervisor in Hill's legal career; she would continue to need his professional support and recommendation throughout her career.)

This male lack of understanding of women's experience with sexual harassment was poignantly demonstrated to me on two occasions when I was doing a research project on gender and race for a large federal agency.

As part of the research project, we asked employees if they had experienced sexual harassment during their employment with the agency. Although only three percent of the men reported being sexually harassed, nearly one-quarter of the women said that they had been sexually harassed at least once while working at the agency (the numbers are consistent with data from other federal agencies and large organizations generally). When I reported the findings at a senior staff meeting, the senior administrator present, who was male, said the numbers couldn't possibly be true because *he* was unaware of any incidents of sexual harassment. After a very long silence, the sole woman at the meeting spoke up and said that he wouldn't know because the women who had been harassed were unwilling to talk to men about it. He appeared stunned. On a second occasion, I presented the research results to a large group of agency employees. When I said that three percent of the men reported being sexually harassed, a man in the audience said, in a loud stage whisper, "Who's the lucky guy?" While many of the men tittered at the comment, the women looked horrified. Sexual harassment simply isn't funny to people who live with either the experience of it or the fear that it might happen to them.

Although most organizations now have explicit policies prohibiting sexual harassment and women can claim legal protection, sexual harassment in the workplace continues. Some sociologists say that it is because men and women are confused about the new rules of appropriate behavior in the workplace and confuse romantic overtures with sexual harassment. Others say that men are intimidated by women's new power and are fighting back. I think it is more likely that the organizational strictures against sexual harassment lack meaningful enforcement because many men in positions of authority do not believe that sexual harassment is a serious issue.

It has been interesting to watch men in the military respond to the pressure to allow openly gay men and lesbians to serve in the armed forces. Although the military establishment was slow to respond to the sexual harassment charges in the Navy Tailhook scandal, in which dozens of women accused male officers of blatant harassment, they were quick to mobilize their opposition to gays in the military on the grounds that straight men would feel uncomfortable showering with gay men who might be "checking them out" sexually. Although reports of gay men sexually harassing straight men in the workplace are rare or nonexistent, the fear that gay men might harass straight men is sufficient to justify denying an entire group of people access to military life. Yet, the numerous proven cases of men sexually harassing women in the workplace are not sufficient to convince men that the workplace is a hostile environment for women.

Two major new literary works, a play by David Mamet (1993), *Oleanna*, and a novel by Michael Crichton (1993), *Disclosure*, highlight the disparity between men's and women's understanding of sexual harassment. In both works, the typical sexual harassment scenario is reversed, with a woman harassing a man. Crichton simply reverses the scenario: In his novel, a female boss demands sexual favors from a male subordinate. Mamet's work is more complex. In *Oleanna*, a young woman student files false harassment charges against a male professor and proceeds to destroy his life. Although each of these works makes a dramatically different statement about sexual harassment in the workplace, in each one, a male author reshapes the experience of sexual harassment by describing and defining it from a male perspective.

By turning the tables and reversing the roles, Crichton gives the audience a woman who is far more powerful than most women in the United States today, both in terms of her organizational status and her gender role. Although the scenario can, and probably has, happened, it is enacted only rarely in real life. Women, in fact, have very little organizational power in the United States: And thus, a fictional story about a woman executive who sexually harasses a male subordinate reduces the woman's organizational power to sexual power. The scenario speaks to male fears of female sexuality, and redefines sexual harassment as a male sexual fantasy.[8]

Mamet also gives the audience a male definition of sexual harassment. Mamet defines the horror of sexual harassment in terms of the false accusation and its power to destroy lives. That definition fits with male fears about the new organizational rules and what might happen to them if they break them. Although most men who sexually harass women remain protected, either by women's silence or men's inaction, many men who don't sexually harass women fear that their comments or actions may be misunderstood by women in the workplace. What men see as a seemingly innocent joke or a comradely arm around the shoulder becomes potential grounds for a nasty lawsuit.

Women have a difficult time understanding either Crichton's or Mamet's conceptions of sexual harassment. Women generally do not experience sexual harassment as a sexual act per se; for women, sexual harassment, like rape, is a form of violence against women. Their harassers are men who use their power over them to gain sexual favors or to create a hostile working environment. Most women are far more familiar with the untold stories about sexual harassment than with the few charges that are publicly levied. Male fears about unfounded charges ring hollow to women who have remained silent about their own experiences because they fear reprisals or believe nothing will be done.

Sexual harassment becomes an even more complex issue when other cultural differences are added to the gender differences. African American men, for example, have very direct and sexually explicit courtship styles. Courtship styles in white culture are more restrained and indirect. Men are taught not to offend the sensibilities of women; the language of courtship, especially among well-educated Anglo men, is the language of Victorian romance: Delicate, refined, and highly euphemistic. White women are often startled, affronted, and sometimes even frightened by the way in which African American men approach them; more significantly, in the workplace that behavior can easily be perceived as sexual harassment. Although the office should not be a venue for courtship, it often is, and it would be impossible to prohibit women and men from courting, or attempting to court, each other there.

CONCLUSION

When people from different cultural backgrounds come together, misperceptions, misinterpretations, and conflict are the natural outcomes. The natural dysfunctionality of diversity may lead some people to call for a return to cultural homogeneity in the United States, especially in the workplace, where clear communication and cooperative relationships are viewed as essential to organizational productivity.

A return to cultural homogeneity in the workplace, however, is neither feasible nor practical. The demographic profile of the United States has changed too dramatically for organizations to rely on a pool of white male workers to fill the needed positions in the next century. More importantly, returning to cultural homogeneity in the workplace would come at a tremendous cost to organizations and individuals, and to the country as a whole. Forcing individuals to assimilate and give up their own cultural identity creates numerous psychological and physiological problems that decrease worker productivity. Organizations instead need to look for ways to make diversity functional. We need to create multicultural organizations in which all workers can be productive, rather than return to monocultural organizations that stifle individual creativity or endure cultural battlegrounds that resemble the proverbial Tower of Babel.

In the remaining chapters, I look first at the ways some organizations are responding to diversity in the workplace, and then offer both interpersonal and organizational strategies for creating multicultural organizations.

NOTES

1. African American women provide a case in point. Culturally situated at the intersection of African American culture and women's culture, African American women experience each culture differently. As African American women, they face a different set of cultural norms and expectations than African American men. As women of color, they create a women's culture that differs significantly from the culture of white women. In particular situations, however, they share fully the African American's experience (e.g., racism) and women's experience (e.g., sexism). For a more detailed description of the intersection of gender and race in the lives of African American women, see Chapter 3.

2. The struggle to move out of one's native culture and into a new culture has been movingly documented in numerous autobiographies. These descriptions testify to both the power of humans to embrace or reject particular cultural assumptions and behaviors, and the enormous psychological toll that such choices exact. Richard Rodriguez, in his brilliant autobiography *Hunger of Memory* (1982), provides a chilling portrait of a young man pulled between the world of his Hispanic parents who had emigrated to the United States and the world of scholarship that had become accessible to him through education and the English language.

3. That is, of course, when African Americans have some reason to care about whether whites are talking with them. Hecht, Collier, and Ribeau (1993) report that African Americans generally appear to be less interested in their interactions with whites than in their interactions with each other. African Americans will, however, choose to talk with whites in order "to negotiate status or get position, to obtain favorable future evaluations, to be seen as capable of getting along, and for mutual interest" (p. 90). In these conversations, African Americans are likely to shift their communication style to accommodate whites, a practice known as code switching.

4. Although Kochman's point is well taken, it is important to recognize that whites are not the victims here. White communication styles are equally disabling to blacks. Since whites are the numerical majority and control virtually all institutional power in the United States, blacks are negatively affected in more substantial and serious material ways by the disabling effects of white communication styles than are whites by the disabling effects of black communication styles.

5. The irony of this description, of course, is that most of us are familiar with the highly successful executive (usually, but not always, male) who manages through shouting. Although the behavior is sometimes nothing more than a quick way to let off steam that is just as quickly forgotten by both parties, more often it is an effective method of managing through intimidation. White fear of conflict and anger in organizations is sufficiently strong to make shouting a tool of intimidation. The use of anger, however, is tolerated only in one direction in the organization—downward. Subordinates rarely shout back, and when they do, they often pay dearly for the breach of organizational norms. That anger is not directed at either one's peers or superiors is further evidence of the strength of the prohibition against anger in the workplace.

6. The dramatic increase in violence among young black males in our inner cities makes it difficult for many whites to understand and acknowledge this feature of African American discourse. Although African American culture values the ability to express anger and hostility verbally without letting the emotions escalate into physical violence, a complex interplay of social, political, and economic forces have created a cultural nihilism among young black men in the inner city. The hopelessness that permeates their lives, along with the reality that many of them will not live beyond young adulthood, creates psychological and social conditions in which life and death are equivalent states of being. These conditions are even more devastating because they are coupled with the denial of responsibility and accountability that permeates personal, social, and institutional relationships in the United States. The violence that has become endemic among urban black teenagers underscores the ways in which white culture in the United States continues to tear at the fabric of African American culture. While the interactional patterns of

black and white discourse are linguistically disabling to whites, life in white America is downright dangerous to blacks.

7. This situation is the result of many more factors than simple misperceptions based on eye contact in conversational interaction. White teachers frequently enter the classroom with a set of preconceived assumptions about black students—that they have impoverished family situations, that they use substandard speech, that they are athletically inclined—many of which are incorrect when applied to a particular child, some of which are incorrect when applied to any child, and all of which add to a constellation of negative assumptions about African American children as learners. This constellation of negative assumptions exerts a powerful force in shaping white teachers' expectations of the academic achievements of African American students, and, ultimately, of the academic achievements themselves.

8. Although a story about a woman who sexually harasses a male subordinate reduces female power to her sexuality, the converse is not true. A fictional narrative about a man who sexually harasses a female subordinate does not automatically reduce male power in the same way. The difference lies in the relationship between the fiction and reality. Men hold power in this culture, and their power is manifested in a variety of contexts and forms. The magnitude and sweep of male power is far too great to be reduced through a single textual reading. Women, on the other hand, do not have power, especially in public and institutional settings. A fictional narrative that accords power to a woman stands alone in defining women's power; the images in such a narrative, therefore, carry much greater significance in shaping our understanding of women's power.

5

ORGANIZATIONAL RESPONSES TO CULTURAL DIVERSITY: CASE STUDIES IN CHANGE

This chapter is a significant point of departure from my previous work. The first four chapters detailed the increasingly diverse nature of the U.S. work force, showed how current organizational theory is inadequate for understanding and working with that diversity, summarized key cultural differences among the major new groups represented in the work force, and provided examples of how those differences can create problems for workers and their organizations. Those chapters provided a context for understanding cultural diversity and its impact in the workplace. This chapter begins our discussion of the ways that organizations can respond to a culturally diverse work force by reviewing the strategies and programs already undertaken by some organizations. My purpose is to show the wide range of options that are available, and to suggest what we can learn from the experiences of those who have already begun this work.

ORGANIZATIONAL INTEREST IN CULTURAL DIVERSITY

From the mid-1960s through the 1970s, public and private organizations put into place a variety of policies and programs intended to increase the representation of women and people of color. These initiatives were developed under the rubric of affirmative action or Equal Employment Opportunity (EEO), and, as such, they were attempts to comply with legal and legislative directives regarding the equal treatment of all employees. Affirmative action and EEO programs were created to redress past wrongs and to share organizational resources and rewards with those who had been excluded in the past: Women and people of color, particularly African Americans.

Twelve years of government inattention and judicial dismantling throughout the 1980s weakened the legal and legislative mandates undergirding affirmative action programs. Perhaps more significantly, poorly conceived and administered programs, whether through benign neglect, overly zealous efforts, or deliberate sabotage, created numerous doubts about the efficacy of these programs and spawned charges of reverse discrimination among white males and charges of ineffectiveness among minorities.

But as affirmative action programs lost their luster, several forces in the business environment converged to create an interest in, and, some observers would argue, an imperative for, cultural diversity initiatives. Although the term "cultural diversity" began to appear in the organizational behavior literature and in some corporate programs prior to 1987, most observers mark the publication of the Hudson Institute's *Workforce 2000* (Johnston & Packer, 1987) as the beginning of the cultural diversity efforts in U.S. corporations.

Workforce 2000 identified five demographic trends in the United States that will dramatically affect organizational life in the twenty-first century:

1. Both the population and the work force will grow more slowly.
2. The average age of the work force will increase and the pool of young workers will decrease.
3. More women will enter the work force.
4. Minorities will increase their share of new entrants into the work force.
5. Immigrants will make up the largest share of the increase in the work force since World War I.

Although the authors of *Workforce 2000* never used the term cultural diversity, the demographic trends they so compellingly documented established cultural diversity as the central work force issue for the next century. These five demographic trends suggest two significant conclusions about the work force of the future. First, the work force will be much more diverse than it is now. Although white males will continue to maintain a numerical edge into the next decade, they will constitute a shrinking percentage of the new entrants into the labor pool. The new work force will comprise greater diversity of gender, race, age, culture, and language. Second, apart from the cyclical demand changes created during downturns in the economy or the structural demand changes created as old industries decline and new ones emerge, demand for workers will exceed the supply of those previously defined as "qualified," thus creating intense competition among organizations for workers. The competition for trained professional and technical personnel and supervisory/managerial personnel will be especially intense. This second conclusion was important because it provided corporations, for the first time, with a bottom-line motivation for dealing in a serious and substantial way with the first conclusion—that the new work force will be culturally diverse.

Prior to the publication of *Workforce 2000*, most companies were either unaware of or chose to ignore the business and managerial implications of the demographic changes in the United States. Most U.S. companies opened their doors to women and people of color only to comply with federal affirmative action laws (for either moral or legal reasons), not because they believed that doing so was in their best strategic business interests. The projected shortage of white male workers documented in *Workforce 2000*, however, placed a premium on workers of color and women, and created a strategic incentive for organizations to develop ways to recruit, hire, develop, promote, and retain them.

Work force changes were not the only considerations that encouraged companies to recognize the importance of cultural diversity. Increasing competition for new consumer markets here and abroad; the growing importance of specialized market niches that are often within ethnic communities; the development of foreign outsourcing to cut costs; the increasing number of mergers across national boundaries; and a variety of other new global business strategies all demonstrated the necessity of having an understanding of other cultures and their ways of doing business. Companies, however, were still slow to respond.

In 1990, the Hudson Institute and Towers Perrin, an international management consulting firm, decided to find out how organizations were responding to *Workforce 2000*. They asked senior human resource executives at 645 U.S. organizations about their level of concern about the human resource issues in the report, and about the ways that their organizations were dealing with or planning to deal with these issues. The survey, which was published in 1990 as a report titled *Workforce 2000: Competing in a Seller's Market: Is Corporate America Prepared?*, suggested that organizations generally were aware of the issues but were unprepared to deal with them. The managers' responses revealed the following conclusions:

1. The work force was already diverse. Of the organizations in the sample, 60 percent reported that workers of color represent up to 20 percent of their work force, and close to 25 percent said that they represent over 26 percent of their work force.

2. Cultural diversity was a paramount concern to these organizations. Their diversity concerns focused on the hiring and promotion of people of color and what the human resource executives defined as the special needs of women (e.g., child care, family leave, and flexible work schedules).

3. Although some companies were responding to the particular issues raised in the *Workforce 2000* report, they were implementing very traditional solutions.

> For example, to deal with the lack of basic skills of many new entrants into the labor force, many companies offered tuition reimbursement to employees, but few companies offered in-house training programs.

Interestingly, although most companies in the survey had not responded to the demographic projections in *Workforce 2000* with new programmatic initiatives, the managers in these companies were able to articulate a clear set of concerns that they had about managing cultural diversity. They said they were most concerned about three managerial issues: (1) The ability to motivate diverse groups of employees; (2) the differences in values and cultural norms among employees; and (3) the challenge of communicating when employees speak different languages and have different cultural assumptions. Despite defining their concerns in terms of cultural differences among employees (i.e., differences in ways of thinking, acting, feeling, and interpreting), the managers indicated that their organizations were doing little, if anything, to address those concerns. The divergence between understanding the problem and knowing what to do about it were obviously enormous.

CASE STUDIES OF ORGANIZATIONAL INTERVENTIONS

Some companies, however, have grappled with the issues inherent in having a culturally diverse work force and have developed different approaches to the issues. Their approaches range from focusing on human relations within the organization, to creating organizational policies that are inclusive of other cultural perspectives, to making diversity part of the strategic business plan. In this section, nine brief case studies of organizations are presented to demonstrate different approaches to cultural diversity in the workplace.[1]

Digital Equipment Corporation (DEC)

DEC's "Valuing Differences Program" is probably the best known U.S. corporate effort to deal with diversity in the workplace. The workshops that are part of the Valuing Differences Program are widely emulated in business and government, and closely studied by academics.

DEC's efforts began in response to affirmative action policies. Although DEC's work force was primarily white, by the mid-1970s, DEC had opened two manufacturing plants in Puerto Rico and one in inner-city Springfield, Massachusetts, which employed primarily black workers. The company was planning to open another plant in Roxbury, Massachusetts, an inner-city, black section of Boston.

Some managers in these plants and at headquarters viewed the plants "as no more than experiments in corporate social responsibility" (Walker & Hanson, 1992, p. 122). The perception that these plants were inferior to

DEC's other manufacturing operations led to lowered expectations and fewer opportunities for the plants to succeed. Senior management decided to examine closely its own attitudes toward workers of color and women, and began a series of awareness sessions on gender and race. These sessions, with the help of outside consultants, eventually developed into what came to be known as "Core Groups," an informal network of small, ongoing discussion groups. Each group included six to eight people, mixed by gender and race, who met with a facilitator each month and worked on building relationships with people who were different from themselves. The discussions focused on testing their stereotypes and assumptions about others.

The goal of the original Core Groups was empowerment and awareness. The consultant who first developed the groups, Barbara Walker, believed that "dialogue is the key to personal growth and change" (Walker & Hanson, 1992, p. 129). DEC's strategy in developing and maintaining the Core Groups was to identify and educate leaders so that they could seed the organization with new ideas. The fundamental premise of the Core Group strategy was that organizational change and growth would happen as a result of individual change and growth.

The genesis of DEC's diversity efforts necessarily placed the focus of the activities at the interpersonal level. The initial concerns were about individual perceptions and stereotypes and how they affected people's relationships at work. The original Core Groups developed in response to those concerns. Subsequent diversity efforts spun off of the premises embedded in the Core Groups and in DEC's own corporate culture, which saw "employees as the company's most valuable asset" and believed in respecting individuals (Walker and Hanson, 1992, p. 122).

DEC now has a variety of ongoing educational and awareness interventions related to diversity. The company sponsors monthly celebrations that honor different cultures or races. Employees can participate in different support groups, some informal and some more structured, but all legitimized in the system. Some groups focus on networking, others on learning about others, and some of the original Core Groups are still meeting. The company also offers a two-day course titled "Understanding the Dynamics of Difference," which is available to workers throughout the organization. In addition, DEC maintains resource libraries that include films, articles, and books that can be used to start conversations with employees about diversity issues, as well as a U.S. on-line calendar that publishes all diversity events in a given month.

The definition of diversity has also been expanded. Diversity at DEC used to refer to race and gender, but the range of differences included in the diversity activities has grown to include age, culture, ethnicity, disability, religion, sexual orientation, personal style, and function within the organization.

In 1991, Sue Aaronson became Manager of the Valuing Differences Program, with responsibility for implementing diversity programs through-out the United States. DEC had recently opened a Worldwide Diversity Office and a Worldwide Office for Upward Mobility. At that time, Aaronson had three overarching objectives for all of DEC's U.S. operations: (1) To increase the representation of different groups at all levels throughout the company; (2) to allow all employees to be fully productive by creating a climate at DEC where people can feel that they are heard, trusted, and valued; and (3) to ensure that management practices and processes are bias-free.

To achieve these objectives, Aaronson planned to shift DEC's diversity focus to the group and organizational level while continuing the learning and skill building at the interpersonal level. When she discussed her plans with me, she articulated two important differences between her approach to diversity at DEC and the previous diversity initiatives. First, Aaronson saw diversity work as critical to DEC's business success. Second, she be-lieved that managers should be held accountable for their diversity efforts. Aaronson also hoped to integrate diversity issues into all of DEC's training and all aspects of its business.

ABC Corporation[2]

ABC Corporation provides another example of a company whose ef-forts are primarily (although not entirely) focused on interpersonal rela-tionships. The company has several different corporate initiatives related to diversity, including a formal alliance of various ad hoc groups that rep-resent different interests, such as women and African Americans, and a corporate committee comprising the head of minority programs, an em-ployee of color, a woman, the chair of the company's employees commit-tee, and five corporate officers. Corporate officers have participated in workshops on gender and race, and internal communications have been used to educate employees about diversity.

ABC Corporation, however, is highly decentralized, and most of the company's diversity work is decentralized by division, as is training in the company. One manufacturing division, the XYZ Division, has been work-ing on diversity issues since 1989. The initial motivation for dealing with diversity in the division came from racial tensions in the plant. At that time, there were few managers of color. Also, women in the division tended to be excluded from technical positions, and older workers perceived some discrimination. An education and training specialist in the division had a background in racial issues, having been a civil rights activist in the 1960s and later having held an elected position with a local NAACP chapter. His background and personal commitments provided a perfect match for the problems surfacing in the plant.

As did DEC, the XYZ Division initially brought in an outside consultant, who first interviewed people in the division and then developed a proposal based on the interviews. The proposal included general plant training (beginning with a four-hour awareness-training workshop to which people were assigned) and senior-staff training to be done three to four times each year. Senior staff also participated in the general plant training. The awareness training started with a discussion of why the company had developed the program. The philosophy that underlay the training was that people need to start by valuing themselves first. The training approach was based on an "assumption" model; in other words, what assumptions do employees have about other groups and their members? After the awareness training, employees could choose to go to a three-day leadership workshop.

The approach in this division was interpersonal and focused on human relationships. The approach was built on a therapeutic model for understanding diversity, which held that organizations that have diversity problems are like dysfunctional families. In this model, diversity training was an intervention strategy that helped organizations to regain their health.

The workshops appear to have had an impact in the division. The language and behavior of employees have changed. Senior staff, in particular, have changed their behavior. For example, to break down the social divisions among employees, they have made a commitment to sit in the cafeteria with employees who differ from them by gender and/or race.

In addition to the training program, the division has several other diversity projects. One is the Valuing Differences Employee Advisory Board. The employees on the Board are trained to be cofacilitators and discussion group leaders. Membership on the Board is an extension of the leadership training, and is designed to keep people involved with diversity issues. Another project has been a learning-disabilities support group, which was started by an employee. The division won an Exemplary Voluntary Efforts (EVE) Award from the federal government. The plant also has a Valuing Differences visual display in the entrance to the manufacturing facility. The exhibit changes periodically; one Christmas, for example, employees displayed holiday cards in many different languages.

Environmental Protection Agency, Region I

As a federal agency, the Environmental Protection Agency has long been required to have several formal programs inside the organization that focus on the concerns of women and people of color. One of these is the Federal Women's Program (FWP). In most federal agencies, managing the FWP is considered a half-time job. In the mid-1980s, a group of women in EPA Region I, which is located in Boston, Massachusetts, convinced the Regional administrator to hire a fulltime Federal Women's Program Manager. The manager who was hired, Connie Griffin, was new to the EPA and to the federal government, and she decided that she needed to gather more information about the needs of women and people of color in the agency before she developed any new programs for them. In 1985, two colleagues and I were hired to do a needs assessment for the agency and then develop training modules based on the assessment.

Our efforts were supported by both the senior staff of the regional office and the senior staff in the EPA central administration in Washington, DC. Our study was exploratory. We began with no hypotheses about what we would find; our purpose was to explore and document the experiences of employees in the agency and to identify the issues that concerned them.[3]

At that time, the agency employed approximately 500 people, so we used a questionnaire to do the assessment. To develop the survey questions, we first interviewed 51 employees (11 percent of the work force), who represented a variety of constituencies within the agency: Secretaries, senior management, administrative and technical employees, white male managers, white women, and male and female minority employees. After completing the focused interviews, we developed a questionnaire based on the issues employees raised in the interviews. Those issues included barriers that created an underrepresentation of women and minorities in supervisory and management positions; sexual harassment; training programs for all employees; the impact of equal opportunity and affirmative action on white males; the career paths of women and minorities; and perceptions of the organizational culture.

The final questionnaire comprised two parts. Part I had 102 closed-ended questions (i.e., questions that require a choice among two or more answers). Part II contained 10 open-ended questions, which are more difficult to analyze but provide more in-depth data. All employees received Part I; a random sample of white employees and all employees of color received Part II. To ensure anonymity, the questionnaires were returned directly to the researchers. In addition, because the agency employed so few people of color, their responses were analyzed as a group rather than by race or ethnicity.

After the questionnaire data were analyzed, we prepared both a written report, which all employees received, and several oral presentations. Some presentations were open to all employees. Senior staff and participants in the FWP each had their own briefings, although many of them also attended the briefings for all employees. The written report and oral briefings simply reported back what employees said about gender and race issues. Our goal was neither to blame any person or group for gender or race problems nor to tell the agency what to do about its problems. Rather, we wanted employees to understand the context in which they worked, to know how others in the agency experienced the workplace.

Connie Griffin then asked for employees interested in these issues to volunteer to serve on a Needs Assessment Steering Committee, which was charged with developing the Agency's responses to the needs assessment. The Steering Committee included both white employees and employees of color, and had representatives from all levels in the Agency, but because it was formed under the auspices of the FWP, white women in professional and managerial positions predominated. One of the steps the Steering Committee took was to work with me over the next two years to develop a series of training modules on gender and race issues. The content during the first year focused on interpersonal interaction; the topics included perception, stereotyping, and communication styles. The training format relied heavily on personal exploration.

The training modules in the second year focused on workplace interaction. The topics were similar, but the format required participants to look at the topics in the context of the workplace. For example, a member of the Steering Committee (a white male manager) developed a case study based on the procedures the EPA uses to identify and recommend employees for promotion. I then used the case study in a training module on hiring and promotion assessment for managers. The case study allowed participants to see how their judgments about people were shaped by their perceptions and stereotypes of people who were different from themselves. After the participants understood why they recommended particular candidates for promotion, they could then develop and discuss strategies for changing their behavior to ensure that they were making fair judgments about others.

Morgan Memorial Goodwill Industries, Inc.

Morgan Memorial Goodwill Industries, Inc. is the Boston branch of Goodwill Industries, an international nonprofit organization that provides vocational and rehabilitative services to people with developmental, physical, mental, emotional, social, or economic needs. Although Morgan Memorial Goodwill operates under the aegis of Goodwill Industries of America, it is administratively and financially autonomous, and has its own president and board of directors.

Historically, Morgan Memorial Goodwill was a very conservative and male-dominated organization. In 1987, however, the Board of Directors voted to move the organization's headquarters from its location in downtown Boston to a site in Roxbury, a primarily black and economically disadvantaged section of Boston. The move symbolized Morgan Memorial Goodwill's commitment to serve disadvantaged communities, and marked a shift in the organizational culture. The Board also appointed Deborah Jackson, an African American woman, President of Morgan Memorial Goodwill in 1989. Jackson not only was the first person of color to head the organization, she was also the first woman to do so.

The geographical move and change in leadership were public manifestations of changes that were occurring throughout the organization. Morgan Memorial Goodwill's work force was becoming increasingly diverse, both racially and ethnically. The organization always had numerous female employees, although generally not at senior levels. Women now account for half of all employees at all levels of the organization. Although nearly half of the nonmanagerial positions in the organization are staffed by people of color, minority representation is significantly less among department heads (14%) and managers and supervisors (24%). As the work force diversified, the staff became concerned about how to manage that diversity. Staff members went to senior management and said, "We need help." Senior management and the Board were both supportive and open to the idea of developing a diversity initiative.

Morgan Memorial Goodwill's diversity work began as a training program. The organization first identified a consultant that could work with its diverse constituencies. Finding a consultant proved difficult. The organization is not only racially and ethnically diverse, but also occupationally diverse. The work force comprises teachers, psychologists, rehabilitation specialists, retail salespeople, donation center collectors, administrators, and numerous others, each with vastly different educational backgrounds and work experiences. A diversity training program would need to speak to the needs and concerns of everyone in the organization.

In 1990, Morgan Memorial Goodwill hired Gwen Cochran Hadden of Cochran Hadden Royston Associates to design its diversity initiative. Hadden began by conducting a needs assessment. Based on the assessment, she developed a three-phase training model that emphasized interpersonal relations. Phase I focused on the needs of managers. All senior and middle managers, department heads, and supervisors attended four full-day training seminars, which focused on identifying personal biases, cultural differences, and techniques for managing a diverse work force. Because the organization had not done any training for a number of years, the managerial staff simultaneously participated in training seminars in good management practice. Although the management-practice training and diversity training were separate programs, the content frequently overlapped, and participants were able to discuss the relationships between them.

Phase II of the diversity initiative comprised two half-day sessions in which managers developed their own agenda of issues and concerns about diversity in each of their departments. Those discussions often focused on defining acceptable behavior in the workplace, and they led to two important projects. First, the managers developed two equal opportunity codes of conduct, one for managers and supervisors, and one for all employees. Second, they developed a new management handbook with revised management policies. Also during this phase of the initiative, Hadden ran a "Train the Trainer" workshop for employee facilitators who would assist in the employee training sessions in Phase III. The purpose of identifying and training employee facilitators was to allow the organization to become self-sufficient in providing diversity training in the future.

Phases I and II represented the management model of the diversity initiative. Using focus groups, senior management evaluated the model when those phases were completed. The evaluation was generally positive; managers said that the training had been both supportive and empowering. Senior management also believed that they could see behavioral changes among managers and supervisors, especially in the area of employee relations. Disciplinary actions appeared to be more objective, and managers spent more time coaching their employees.

The experience with and evaluation of the management model formed the basis for the design of the employee training that was presented in Phase III of the diversity initiative. As did the management training, the employee training sessions emphasized interpersonal relations and focused on identifying personal biases and cultural differences. Because participation in the workshops was mandatory for all employees, the organization offered numerous sessions and scheduled them at a variety of times that were convenient for employees, including Saturdays, so that everyone would be able to attend. They also ran three bilingual sessions (Spanish and English) and two sessions with an interpreter for hearing-impaired employees.

In addition to the training initiative, Morgan Memorial Goodwill has other projects related to diversity. The cafeteria in the Roxbury headquarters building plays the music of different cultures, and the chef often experiments with foods from different cultures. The organization is also planning a Diversity Celebration for all employees. Morgan Memorial Goodwill's diversity work has received recognition outside of the organization. Its diversity training programs were supported by a grant from Boston's Human Services Personnel Collaborative, and the Association of Affirmative Action Professionals awarded Morgan Memorial its 1992 Ray Frost Award, which "salutes organizations for exemplary leadership in pursuit of affirmative action, equal opportunity, and social justice."

Polaroid Corporation

The diversity initiatives at Polaroid, although prompted by vocal women and people of color in leadership positions, are the result of the commitment and actions of Polaroid's CEO. At the end of the 1980s, a number of women and people of color who had been identified as potential leaders within Polaroid left the company, saying that they felt they had better professional opportunities elsewhere. Polaroid had just been through a takeover and was in the middle of a major corporate restructuring, which was taking place without the involvement of women or people of color. Several advocacy groups on diversity issues, such as the Women's Action Team and Senior Black Managers, were already in existence at Polaroid, and these groups provided natural forums in which women and people of color could voice their concerns about being excluded from decision-making and leadership positions in the company. The CEO participated in one forum with several particularly vocal members of these advocacy groups. The forum sparked the CEO's interest in and concern about diversity issues at Polaroid, and through continued discussions with the Women's Action Team and the Senior Black Managers, the CEO became convinced that Polaroid needed to do something about the situation.

His first step was to bring together approximately 30 people in leadership positions in the company for nine days of workshops over the next 12 months. The group of managers included approximately equal numbers of women, black men, and white men, with approximately equal numbers of people the CEO believed he could learn from and people he believed were also open to learning from others. The group members focused their discussions on identifying who they were, how they were, and who they wanted to be.

The sessions were developed and led by external consultants who told the participants that working on diversity issues required substantial effort, and that, as organizational leaders, they must change their behavior. The sessions focused on stereotypes and the discussions were very intense. Participants worked initially in homogeneous groups (women, black men, and white men) to identify what they thought about other groups, what others thought about them and why, and what they had done to create those stereotypes about themselves. Having participants identify ways that their own behavior may have created or reinforced stereotypes other people have about them made everyone accountable for their own behavior and created a shared sense of responsibility for changing behavior in the organization. The workshop discussions then focused on the participants' vision of who they wanted to be and ways that they could achieve that vision.

This first diversity initiative prompted a corporate decision that the company needed for leadership to continue its diversity work. A new position was created, Assistant to the President, to provide formal leadership for Polaroid's diversity efforts. In addition, the corporate officers were organized into a task force called the "I Team" (short for Improvement Team), that was charged with developing and implementing a new organizational environment. The I Team comprised the key corporate officers, all of whom were white men; several senior women and black male managers; and a representative from a company employees' group.

The I Team established a two-part agenda for the corporation's diversity work: (1) Educational initiatives and (2) changes in corporate policies and practices. The educational component was based on a learning model, and began with a two-day internal Diversity Leadership Conference (DLC). The DLC was designed like a trade conference and utilized experiential learning in a variety of large and small workshops. The workshops covered a broad range of diversity issues, including, for example, "Young, Black, and New to Boston," "White Men Have Issues Too," "Work and Family Issues," "Gays, Lesbians, and Bisexuals in the Workplace," and "Physical Challenges." The workshops featured representatives of advocacy groups and employees who had been identified as model leaders, who discussed their best practices. The workshops emphasized inclusivity, respect, and learning in a nonthreatening environment. Participants told their stories, sharing their experiences of being different and/or excluded. The learning assumption was that individuals are better able to recognize the pain that others feel if they remember their own pain. The DLC has been repeated, with 120 to 150 employees participating each time.

In addition to developing the DLC, Polaroid decided to build diversity training into its regular training programs. Polaroid's own training personnel worked with an external diversity group to develop and implement a Train the Trainers program. Polaroid now has an internal group of trainers who are capable of offering training in diversity issues.

The second part of the I Team's agenda, changing corporate policies and practices, began with the creation of a work and family platform. Polaroid now has a Work and Family Manager, who provides leadership for the company on issues related to work and family. In 1993, Polaroid was named one of the 100 best companies for working women.

Pay equity was another concern for many women and people of color, so the company did a statistical comparison of salaries across the corporation and corrected any inequities. The pay analysis was initiated by a committee led by corporate officers, which developed the statistical model used in the analysis. That first study uncovered salary inequities for about 10 percent of the population at Polaroid. The inequities, however, were not limited to women and people of color; some white men also received salary adjustments. Salary data are now analyzed each year, and the company does yearly salary adjustments.

Polaroid also has started some internal conversations about how to measure its diversity work to determine if the company is meeting the needs of its employees. Five percent of the employees recently participated in an internal survey about work life. The survey revealed that work and family issues are important to employees, especially women, and that there is a growing interest in parental care policies. Employees who participated in the survey also said that they believed that diversity is an issue that is here to stay and that the diversity initiatives help build a better environment for all employees. In addition to discussions about how to measure the impact of diversity and diversity initiatives, Polaroid is also talking about ways to incorporate diversity into interview designs, the selection process for committees and task forces, and succession planning.

Polaroid is a highly interactive organization that encourages discussion among and between employees and management. The company now has three kinds of advocacy groups that initiate discussions on diversity issues. The first type of group is a traditional advocacy group that represents a homogeneous group of people with a common cause, for example, Hispanics in Polaroid, the Asian Society, Senior Black Managers, and various women's groups and African American groups. These are grassroots organizations that usually include employees throughout the corporation. The second type of advocacy group is a management-aligned diversity group that serves as a sounding board for management on diversity issues. These advocacy groups typically include members of local business groups. The Diversity Alliance, which Polaroid is now building, represents the third type of advocacy group. The Diversity Alliance serves as an umbrella organization for the other advocacy groups in the company; it is the place where the other advocacy groups can share their concerns about diversity issues and where they can highlight and share examples of good diversity policies and practices. The Assistant to the President, who provides leadership on diversity issues, serves as the head of the Diversity Alliance, and also sits on the I Team. In addition, Polaroid now has a Corporate Office of Work Force Diversity, which serves as a corporate overseer of diversity initiatives at Polaroid.

Grand Metropolitan, Food Sector

Grand Metropolitan, Food Sector is better known in the United States by its pre-takeover name, Pillsbury. The company is located in Minneapolis, Minnesota, an area of the country characterized by racial and ethnic homogeneity. Yet GrandMet is a company on the cutting edge of diversity efforts in the United States. GrandMet's approach to diversity was put into place by the company's Chief Executive Officer; diversity has been added to the corporate mission statement, complete with a long-range plan that includes strategy and tactics. The impetus for the diversity efforts at GrandMet is not to meet affirmative action requirements, but to enhance the company's bottom line. Diversity is in the best interest of the corporation: GrandMet needs "internal informants" for marketing purposes.

The company takes a broad perspective in defining diversity. It acknowledges differences based on such characteristics as geographical region, occupation, race, age, and gender. The company believes that this approach is one to which every employee can relate because each person is different in a particular way. The company is trying to find a way for people in the work force to be at ease with each other. The purpose is to have greater sensitivity to the marketplace, and therefore, to improve results in the corporation.

GrandMet has a three-pronged approach to diversity: (1) Education in cultural diversity issues, (2) redesign of human resource systems, and (3) support group networks. The goal of each of these efforts is to change corporate culture by widening the "band of acceptance" of difference in the organization.

The education component begins with senior management, including the heads of each of the brand groups and the different businesses in the Food Sector. The training programs include a broad range of material related to diversity issues, generally including how they relate to the business mission, and then more specifically including the various "isms" (racism, sexism, and so forth) and communication patterns of different cultural groups. The programs also emphasize the skills executives need to manage diversity, including self-learning, identifying their own leadership styles, learning about others, and team-building. The groups are well mixed by gender and race. The company has senior women but few senior people of color, so people of color at other ranks in the organization are invited to join the senior workshops. Rebecca Chou, Director of Cultural Diversity, believes that rank has not affected the discourse in the workshops; she says that people of color have been willing to share their experiences and that white executives have been willing to listen. After completing the workshops for senior management, GrandMet planned to start a round of workshops for managers and supervisors in headquarters.

The education strategy also includes a less formal component. The corporate headquarters in downtown Minneapolis hosts numerous cultural events intended to introduce employees to different cultures, such as Hispanic, Native American (named Original American at GrandMet), African American, and Women's culture. The events include visual exhibits, lectures, and performances.

The second component of the strategy is to redesign the human resource systems. For example, GrandMet is developing a work/family project that addresses ways the company can support a better balance between work and family life. When GrandMet acquired Pillsbury in a hostile takeover, there was a culture clash between the two corporations. GrandMet culture was entrepreneurial and maverick, committed to working long hours and putting the company first. Pillsbury, on the other hand, was a very midwestern culture; the work ethic meant putting in an honest day's work and then going home to family and community, which are both considered more important than work. GrandMet believes that it must find ways to balance work and family in order to keep its Minneapolis work force productive.

The third component of the strategy is developing support groups. These groups are places where people can take a break from the corporate culture and return to their own culture, where they can talk with others who share their language and other concerns, where they can "let their hair down." Most of the support groups are informally organized, although the Black Network has officers and a more formal structure. Many of the informal networks are structured around community issues. Most employees are active in the community and seek identity with others who are similar to themselves through community projects.

GrandMet faces a particular set of diversity problems because of its location in a racially and ethnically homogeneous geographical area. Although the Minneapolis area provides an ample, well-trained work force, GrandMet recruits nationally for key jobs in order to bring in people of color.

Lotus Development Corporation

Lotus Development Corporation is nearly as well known as Digital Equipment Corporation for its diversity efforts, but for very different reasons. Unlike DEC, Lotus emphasized diversity from its inception; diversity was included as one of seven values in the company's statement of values when it was formed in 1982. Russell Campanello, Vice President for Human Resources, says that "diversity is the language" at Lotus. For example, the culture at Lotus does not tolerate offensive jokes; each employee receives an electronic mail message about their unacceptability. Although there is no enforcement of the cultural norm, it does give employees license to have conversations about the issue and to say "no."

Lotus has a Diversity Advisory Group, which comprises a cross section of employees and reports directly to the CEO. Campanello calls the group an "internal Amnesty International." Every year, the Diversity Advisory Group issues a report card on the company's diversity efforts. The first report, issued in 1990, called attention to the fact that although diversity is a central value at Lotus, the company had not been attentive to diversity issues. Lotus began to recast its diversity work in response to the report.

The diversity efforts at Lotus are similar to those at GrandMet, and include education, the redesign of human resources policies, and internal support networks. Lotus believes that it is important for senior management to understand diversity. To ensure that senior management does understand, the company developed three days of training off-site with an outside consultant, during which participants discuss issues of difference to raise participants' awareness of difference. Eighty percent of Lotus's managers have participated in diversity training. In addition, the company has developed employee facilitators who function as inside ambassadors. The company also sponsors monthly cultural awareness programs, where they display art, provide different foods, and share information about different cultures.

Lotus has numerous internal networks that provide support for members of different cultural groups. For example, the company has a multicultural network, a gay and lesbian network, and a women's network. Lotus also has a Women at Lotus electronic bulletin board that has an ongoing dialogue on women's issues. The internal conversation about naming the multicultural network indicates the degree of sophistication and openness that Lotus employees have about diversity issues. The multicultural network was originally called a people of color network, but the group wanted to include Asians, who often do not like to be identified as people of color, and white ethnic men. To accommodate both groups, the group renamed itself the multicultural network.

Lotus is best known for its human resource policies that attempt to be inclusive of all employees, especially its "spousal equivalent" policy for gays and lesbians. The spousal equivalent policy creates a vehicle for committed gay and lesbian couples to receive the same benefits as married couples. The policy intentionally reads "spousal equivalent" rather than "domestic partner" so that unmarried heterosexual couples or family members who live together are not eligible.

Lotus has also looked at performance appraisals and promotion rates in order to see if the procedures are biased in favor of or against particular groups. The company offers a multicultural interviewing course in which participants discuss their cultural filters.

Medtronic

The diversity initiative is relatively new at Medtronic, a large manufacturer of medical products and instrumentation. Located in Minneapolis, the company has always had a relatively homogeneous work force and affirmative action was not a strong function in the organization. The company is highly decentralized and each business unit had its own affirmative action function, although not its own affirmative action officer. In the early 1990s, Medtronic hired a new CEO, who came from a company with a strong affirmative action record. He was concerned about the lack of diversity in Medtronic's work force, and began to push for increased affirmative action efforts, primarily to prepare the company to meet the challenge of the shrinking labor pool.

One of those efforts included creating the position of Work Force Diversity Manager, a position that is not part of the affirmative action function. Prior to creating this position, the only intervention in diversity was a one-day training course in diversity awareness that focused on the changing demographics in the United States. But management and employees increasingly need to understand diversity issues. Medtronic is a global company; it distributes its products in 80 countries worldwide. It also has acquired companies in other regions of the United States, including California, New York, and New England. The company is faced with the challenge of gaining a better understanding of difference in order to work with its acquisitions here at home, to market its products globally, and to deal with the shrinking labor pool.

Medtronic's first step toward creating a diversity initiative was to begin training managers. The company has developed a training program based on the Meyers-Griggs assessment of individual differences in work groups. Trainers also use films from the Valuing Diversity series produced by Copeland Griggs.

The second step was to develop a two-part plan for increasing the representation of women and minorities throughout the work force. The first part of the plan involved creating an Advisory Council that had representatives from almost every business unit, who ranged across different levels in the organization, from senior management to clerical workers, and who were mixed by gender and race. The role of the Advisory Council is to create a vision of the kind of organization Medtronic needs for continued success. The Council will decide what is needed to achieve the vision, set objectives and priorities, and then develop strategies and tactics for achieving that vision.

The second part of the plan involves developing policies and programs that provide opportunities for women and people of color to advance in their careers. For example, the company conducted a work and home life study to identify the factors that keep employees from being fully productive. Based on the results, Medtronic plans to develop a sick child care support program, flexible workplace policies, on-site education and awareness sessions, and perhaps even on-site daycare with an infant room, where parents can visit infants and mothers can breastfeed them. The company has also started an internship program to address the shortage of technical people in the field. The program is offered to local students and focuses primarily on people of color, since a commonly given reason for not hiring people of color is that they do not have a medical products background.

In addition to the specific internal programs aimed at increasing the representation of women and minorities in the work force, Medtronic is working with the community, both to train young people generally and to enhance Medtronic's reputation in the minority communities in Minneapolis. Carolyn Miller, the Work Force Diversity Manager, works internally with the Medtronic Foundation on projects that encourage and support math and science programs for children, especially disadvantaged students and people of color. Externally, she makes Medtronic visible in the minority communities by attending dinners and award ceremonies, and developing partnerships in the community.

Although Medtronic tends not to have formal support groups, several informal groups have emerged. African American employees meet socially; Asian Americans have an informal group; and, at the suggestion of the

CEO, women have formed a Women's Council. Clerical women have had a separate formal organization for many years.

New England Electric Company

The diversity initiatives at New England Electric, which supplies electric power to Massachusetts, New Hampshire, and Rhode Island, were not developed in response to diversity issues per se. Instead, several forces in the external environment combined to create a unique impact on the company and set the foundation for the company's diversity efforts. The context for understanding New England Electric's approach to diversity starts with the Civil Rights Acts in the 1960s, which served to motivate companies, including New England Electric, to begin recruiting women and African Americans. The oil embargo in the early 1970s, however, counter-acted the efforts of New England Electric. In order to keep overall costs down while oil was scarce and expensive, the company decided to reduce its work force from 8000 employees to 5600. That reduction in the work force precluded the company from meeting its affirmative action obligations during the 1970s.

In the early 1980s, the CEO noticed some significant facts about both the company's work force and its customer base. Utility companies are known generally for their low employee turnover, and New England Electric was no exception. The average age of its employees was increasing; in the mid-1980s the average age was 48. That meant that the company would have to replace about one-third of its work force in the coming years as its older workers reached retirement age. The CEO also realized that the demographics of the major population pockets in New England had changed, particularly in those areas serviced by New England Electric. For example, Lawrence, Massachusetts was 47 percent Hispanic; Lowell, Massachusetts had become heavily Southeast Asian and Hispanic; and 51 percent of the population of Providence, Rhode Island was minority. The CEO realized that New England Electric was now serving a diverse population, and would also be drawing on that diverse population as it needed to replace workers.

At the same time that the CEO recognized the demographic changes in the company's service territories, quality improvement programs were becoming popular in the United States. These programs focus on meeting customer needs, and implementing them requires that companies have a keen understanding of their customers. Understanding cultural diversity, therefore, became important to New England Electric from a strategic business standpoint.

The company developed a strategic plan to deal with increased competition in the industry and the anticipated work force turnover. To implement the plan, the company needed to change the corporate culture, which it decided to do by educating the existing work force in the principles of quality improvement. The company developed a three-year training program. The company also assumed that the turnover in the work force would complement the training efforts by allowing cultural change in the organization to happen naturally.

During the first year of the training program, diversity was not an issue. The top 800 employees received training in small groups on topics including change in the competitive environment, motivation of employees, and managerial strategies. The program was built on the assumption that the company needed to have evaluation processes in place before it dealt with diversity issues. The first year of training, therefore, emphasized managerial processes and strategies.

The second year focused on customer orientation and taught the participants the importance of being customer driven. The topics that year also included leadership and performance appraisal. One result of the training was that the company changed its performance appraisal system. Exempt personnel now work with managers to identify mutually agreed on expectations for their performance that year. Built into the new system is a structured approach to dialogue between the manager and the employee on the individual's performance throughout the year.

In the third year, the training focused on managing the organizational climate and performance. Topics included the financial implications of organizational climate and the changing customer environment. Employees closely examined affirmative action, looking at both the legal standards and the relationship between affirmative action and the company's financial health. Diversity became the central topic in the training and employees were told why the company was diversifying its work force and how they could help it to do so. That year, hiring targets were set that were tied to affirmative action plans for each business unit in the company, and meeting the hiring targets was tied to incentive compensation plans for managers. The initial effects of the work force turnover were also felt during the year, and significant numbers of women and minorities were hired.

The company now has a "quality team," which is mixed by gender and race and represents people at all levels of the organization. The team is charged with figuring out how to achieve the company's new vision and with taking diversity issues to the next level through diversity training that educates all employees about the reasons for and benefits of a diverse work force.

In addition to emphasizing training, New England Electric has an active program for recruiting women and people of color. They set specific targets based on their affirmative action plans. To identify potential employees, they use state job fairs in Massachusetts. They also have a rolling allocation of five slots in upper- and middle-management that are reserved for women and minorities. The company has developed several employee programs that it identifies as woman-based, such as dependent care assistance, flextime, and job sharing. These are offered to both men and women, but were designed to help working couples in order to retain women employees.

GENERAL FEATURES OF ORGANIZATIONAL INTERVENTIONS

These nine case studies provide a sampling of the cultural diversity efforts already underway in U.S. organizations. They characterize the types of interventions that are commonly undertaken by organizations, and, as such, they offer some lessons for others who are planning diversity initiatives. In the final section of this chapter, I summarize three key issues in these case studies and assess how well our current responses to diversity in the workplace meet the goals of the multicultural organization described in Chapter 2.

Legal/Moral Imperative or Strategic Business Decision?

For most U.S. organizations, the primary impetus for developing any diversity initiatives has been compliance with affirmative action and equal employment opportunity laws and regulations. Initially, companies were interested in developing programs for recruiting women and people of color so that the firms could meet the goals established in their affirmative action plans. For some companies, the sole concern was meeting the letter of the law. For others, the concern went beyond the law to a moral imperative to do the right thing. Whether the concern was legal or moral, however, the emphasis was on bringing new people into the organization.

Some public and private organizations that were successful in diversifying their work forces expanded their diversity initiatives beyond recruiting as they realized the need to ensure both that employees could work together productively and that white women as well as women and men of color would have ample opportunities for advancement. These expanded initiatives were primarily educational, and involved various forms of human relations training. The needs assessment project and subsequent training program at EPA Region I is a typical example. The initial concern about the needs of women and people of color grew out of affirmative action policies that established the Federal Women's Program. DEC's Valuing Differences Program evolved out of earlier training programs that were developed in response to problems the company encountered when it opened manufacturing plants in minority communities. Those plants were part of DEC's affirmative action plan.

When diversity initiatives grew out of either a legal or moral commitment to affirmative action, they focused on education. As I noted in Chapter 2, in the early years of affirmative action, education most often was in the form of skill building for women and people of color. The "different equals deficient" assumption led employers to assume that these new employees lacked the skills necessary for organizational success. As women and people of color gained visibility and credibility in the work force, employers also realized that they needed to provide training to help employees understand and get along with one another.

When diversity was approached as a strategic business issue, however, the focus moved beyond training to encompass human resource policies that made the workplace more accessible, more accommodating, and more attractive to workers who are different. Firms like Lotus, GrandMet, and Medtronic have recognized that having a diverse work force is in their best strategic interest, either because they need to understand global markets, establish ethnic market niches here in the United States, ensure diverse perspectives in decision-making, or attract the most talented workers. That recognition has led them to adopt policies and practices that range from making health care and other benefits available to the domestic partners of gay and lesbian employees, to developing flextime and job sharing options for women or men who are juggling family and job responsibilities, to reassessing their performance evaluation and promotion systems.

Top Down or Bottom Up?

The prevailing wisdom about doing diversity work says that diversity initiatives cannot be successful unless they have the support and involvement of senior managers (Loden & Rosener, 1991). Obviously, identifying diversity as a strategic business issue happens at the top of the organization. Others in the organization may see the strategic importance of diversity before senior management does, but in order for diversity to shape organizational strategy, senior management must be convinced of its importance. New England Electric's diversity efforts permeated the entire company because the CEO recognized the changing demographics of the company's customers and future workers, and, together with his senior managers, developed a company-wide plan for changing the organizational culture.

However, although the need for change and the process for initiating it were identified at the top of the organization, the work of creating the new organization happened at the bottom. As every New England Electric employee went through quality training, he or she participated in defining quality for the company. The company's quality team, which comprised employees at all levels of the company, developed the process for achieving this definition of quality. According to William Watkins, Jr., Vice President for Human Resources, the vision of the company is being created bottom up rather than being imposed top down. The quality team is also charged with developing the diversity training program for the company, and Watkins says that they are changing the top down approach to training also.

In contrast to diversity initiatives that are part of a strategic business plan, diversity initiatives that are motivated by affirmative action concerns can be created at different levels of the organization, and do not necessarily require the participation or even the support of senior management. In the ABC Corporation, for example, training is decentralized. Although there are some corporate diversity initiatives, each division can develop its own diversity training, and those efforts vary widely by division. EPA Region I's decision to hire a fulltime Federal Women's Program Manager (most federal agencies have only a halftime manager) was heavily influenced by lobbying from women employees. One middle-level manager in particular became known as the "Tiger" for her persistence and tenacity in arguing for greater support for women in the organization. At one point she organized the women to picket the JFK Federal Building in downtown Boston. Shortly thereafter, senior management agreed to hire a fulltime FWP Manager and provide money for the needs assessment. Even special hiring and recruiting activities can be developed and implemented within an organization rather than be imposed from the top down.

Management support is helpful, however, in gaining widespread employee participation. Although the idea of doing a needs assessment to identify the concerns of women and people of color in the EPA Region I came from middle management (the Federal Women's Program Manager) and women who were active in the FWP, our success in getting employees to voluntarily participate in both the survey and the subsequent training program was aided by the endorsement of senior management. The Regional Administrator and Deputy Regional Administrator signed the cover letter that accompanied the questionnaire, and the Deputy Regional Administrator attended the briefings and participated in some workshops, as did all of the other senior managers in the Agency.

Change that is initiated at lower levels, particularly when it is initiated by employees rather than management, can be very powerful. When employees can claim ownership of organizational change, they are more likely to participate fully in the new policies and practices and to ensure that they will be successful. Change that is imposed from the top down is often sabotaged by employees in the middle or at the bottom. Affirmative action efforts, for example, have sometimes been undermined by less than enthusiastic managers who make half-hearted attempts to recruit people of color, or who deliberately hire unqualified women or minorities, hoping that they will fail at their jobs and prove that affirmative action policies don't work.

On the other hand, when diversity initiatives are decentralized, they often fail to transform the organizational culture. Transformation requires consensus about the importance of diversity. Unless all, or most, employees within the organization believe that working on diversity issues is in their strategic interest, there will not be sufficient pressure to shift the vision of senior management. That convergence of employee interests is not likely to happen, especially in organizations that are primarily white and male. Without the cooperation and endorsement of senior management, diversity initiatives cannot permeate the entire organization and they lose their transformative power. Diversity initiatives require time and money, both important and usually scarce organizational resources that are controlled by senior management.

Components of Diversity Initiatives

The nine case studies in this chapter suggest that current diversity initiatives comprise three components: Education, support groups, and human resource policies.

Education

Education is the most frequent response to diversity concerns, and even large-scale diversity initiatives tend to focus on education as the central component. Typically, diversity training begins with a brief session that serves to justify having the training. In companies that initiate training programs as part of a strategic business plan, the justification session focuses on why diversity is important to the company's bottom line. All too often, however, the company's financial resources are exhausted after introducing employees to the importance of diversity work. The majority of employees in the organization, therefore, never have the opportunity to learn about other cultures and/or to develop any personal skills for working in diverse organizations.

Most organizational training programs in diversity emphasize interpersonal relationships. The goal of such training is to help people who are different from each other understand each other and get along together. Interpersonal or human relations training typically identifies the roots of prejudice in the individual's personal history. Trainers ask participants to share their experiences learning about others. By examining their own prejudices, participants begin to understand how their assumptions and stereotypes about people who are different were formed and to realize that those assumptions and stereotypes don't necessarily fit the people with whom they are working. Human relations training assumes that as the participants begin to see each other as unique individuals rather than as representatives of stereotyped groups, they will discover commonalities among themselves, learn to tolerate and even appreciate their differences, and henceforth, will work together productively.

Diversity training that is primarily focused on interpersonal relationships rarely includes an analysis of the cultural and sociopolitical roots of prejudice and the oppression of others. Racism and sexism are reduced to personal misunderstandings between individuals, much in the vein of Deborah Tannen's (1990) *You Just Don't Understand: Men and Women in Conversation.* Tannen demonstrates, quite convincingly, that women and men define the function of talk differently and use different conversational styles. These differences lead to misperceptions of the other sex and misunderstandings between women and men. Tannen's analysis is helpful—as far as it goes. What Tannen leaves out is an explanation of how the conversational differences between women and men reflect and reinforce the social, political, and economic power differentials between women and men. Not surprisingly, Tannen's book remained on the *New York Times* bestseller list for over a year. Reducing sexism in discourse to a series of personal misunderstandings allows women and men to say, "I always knew he/she didn't understand me," without fear of conflict or the possibility of changing the social arrangements. Personalizing racism by reducing prejudice and oppression to personal misunderstandings between people of different races or cultures also ignores power differences in organizations, and precludes re-visioning organizations in ways that are inclusive of all workers.

There are several reasons why diversity training tends to avoid analyzing the sociopolitical and cultural roots of oppression. First, discussions of causes inevitably lead to blame, defensiveness, and eventually conflict. It is less painful and far more harmonious to see diversity issues as personal and interpersonal misperceptions rather than as micro-examples of cultural power struggles that are reproduced within the organization.

The desire to avoid discussing the roots of oppression is intensified by the frequently heard charge that diversity efforts are a form of reverse discrimination. Organizations often worry that diversity training will turn into a "white male bashing" session. Many employees, especially but not exclusively white males, believe that discussions about diversity are nothing more than opportunities to dump all of the world's ills on white men. White employees in general are more receptive to discussions of racism and other forms of oppression that don't identify the oppressors. Like most things in bureaucratic organizations, oppression is a passive state of being.

An even more palatable analysis identifies white men as victims of oppression too. Some white men have been persecuted for their ethnicity or religious beliefs; many are victims of classism; all have been oppressed by cultural norms that force them to repress their emotions and to conform to strict codes of organizational behavior. The success of Robert Bly's (1990) *Iron John,* sometimes called the male *Feminist Mystique,* is based on the appeal of male victimization. Because "real men don't cry," we are all—male or female, black or white—victims under the skin.

A second reason why diversity training avoids analyzing the causes of oppression is that the root causes of racism, sexism, and other "isms" are multiple, complex, and not always agreed on by experts. Most organizational consultants are not knowledgeable about those issues, and are not trained to teach others about them. Organizational consultants are trained to teach people about individual differences, such as differences in management styles. Management training has long focused on helping people to identify and assess their own leadership and management styles. It is much easier to develop a training program that builds on the knowledge and skills of trainers and the curricular design of existing training than it is to develop new content and modes of learning. Diversity training tends to be a mirror image of human relations training in general; the only difference is that the categories of difference are culturally rather than individually based.

A third reason why diversity training tends to focus on interpersonal relationships among workers is that a sociopolitical analysis of oppression requires a larger view of the organization and its place in the social, political, and economic systems in the United States. Management theory, especially organizational theory, tends to view organizations as independent cultural entities. Although environmental scanning is an accepted part of any long-range planning schemas, organizations tend to be viewed as unique cultures that are independent of the larger culture in which they are situated. To look at the suppression and devaluation of difference in the organization within the larger context of American cultural life implies that there are social, political, and economic causes and consequences of that suppression that are reproduced within the organization. Such analysis cuts at the core of capitalism and bureaucracy, making it dangerous to discuss these issues inside of organizations. Few, if any, organizational consultants who propose analyzing the roots of oppression find work in U.S. organizations, private or public.

In addition to avoiding an analysis of the roots of oppression, another shortcoming of current training efforts is that they rarely include specific content or skills development related to the workplace. Workers need to see how diversity issues affect their daily interactions in the workplace; managers need to understand how their cultural assumptions shape their decisions about whom to hire or promote. We all need to learn strategies for remaining open to differences.

Support Groups

A second component of diversity initiatives is support groups. Although these groups may be mixed by gender, race, or sexual orientation, as they are in the ongoing Core Groups at DEC, they more often comprise people who are alike in some fundamental way. Many organizations have support groups for women and African Americans; more recently, some organizations are developing Asian American and Latino support groups. A few organizations, such as Lotus and DEC, have support groups for gay and lesbian employees. The groups range from highly structured and institutionalized organizations, such as the Federal Women's Program, which exists in all federal agencies, to informal networks that meet periodically over lunch.

The purpose of support groups is evident in the name: They provide support and sustenance for their members. The concept was popularized in the Women's Movement in the 1960s and 1970s. As individual women joined the Women's Movement and began to realize that they were not alone in their experiences (workplace discrimination, sexual harassment, husbands who refused to do housework and childcare), they sought solace and support from each other. At the same time, a few women and African Americans were beginning to make inroads into American corporations. As tokens in their individual departments or offices, they often felt isolated from others like themselves and with whom they could be themselves. Organizational support groups, especially for women,[4] appeared, sometimes with the support of management and sometimes without it.

Support groups play an important role in diversity initiatives. They give employees an opportunity to test reality with others who are like themselves and who may be experiencing the same problems that they are experiencing. Organizational life for those who are different is often crazy-making. The isolation, the inability to be accepted as part of the group, the sense that others are keeping information from them, can be overwhelming. A common response is to internalize those feelings and identify the self as crazy. Talking with others who share those experiences and feelings can help employees see that they are not crazy and that they are not alone. Support groups also give employees a place where they can let down their defenses, speak their own language, and just be themselves. Women and people of color in organizations often talk about how exhausted they become from controlling and monitoring their behavior so that it meets the expectations of the organization. This function of support groups may be increasingly important as all of us in the United States begin to renegotiate our cultural assumptions and recreate our communities, including our organizational communities.

Another function of support groups is mentoring. Studies have consistently shown that mentors are important in achieving organizational success. Mentors teach their protégés the organizational rules, give them access to important people, counsel them through difficult decisions, and give them challenging assignments. Successful men and women usually can point to several significant people in their organizational careers who served as their mentors.

Although effective mentoring can and does occur with dissimilar people, mentors tend to choose people like themselves to mentor. Because there are fewer women and people of color in senior positions in organizations, women and people of color generally have fewer opportunities to be mentored. Support groups often serve to bring together mentors and protégés. Because they draw their members from across organizational functions and departments, support groups increase the number of available mentors.

Human Resource Policies

Creating new human resource policies or making existing policies more flexible is the least developed and implemented component of diversity initiatives. The Towers Perrin and Hudson Institute study (1990) of the responses to the demographic issues in *Workforce 2000* included a listing of the specific programs that the 645 organizations surveyed had undertaken. Few organizations in the sample were redesigning their human resource policies. The human resource policies that were reported primarily involved assistance to parents (most often defined as mothers), including daycare assistance, sick child care, maternity or paternity leave, or opportunities to have more flexible work time, including job sharing, flextime, and compressed work weeks. By far the most prevalent human resource policy was a sexual harassment policy; approximately 85 percent of all organizations surveyed reported having a formal sexual harassment policy, and nearly 70 percent said that they provided supervisory training in harassment issues.

The nine case studies presented in this chapter reveal a similar response. I described the human resource policy component of five of these organizations. GrandMet has its work/family project; Polaroid's work and family platform represents a similar effort; Lotus extends benefits to the partners of gay and lesbian employees and is committed to maintaining a system of unbiased performance appraisals and promotions; Medtronic hopes to provide sick child care support and is considering on-site daycare; and New England Electric offers several woman-based programs, such as dependent care assistance, flextime, and job sharing. These policies and programs reflect efforts to make the workplace more accommodating to particular workers, especially women, and to ensure that human resource practices related to hiring, evaluating, and promoting employees are perceived as free of bias in their application.

Current efforts by U.S. organizations are commendable, and many of the policies do serve to make the workplace more hospitable to workers who are different. But these policies are not enough. We must do more, and we must do some of it differently. As U.S. society becomes more diverse, our goal should not be to create a raceless, genderless society. Instead, we need to create a society that recognizes, understands, and celebrates diverse interests. Most importantly, we need to foster those diverse interests rather than sublimating and submerging them. We need human resource policies and practices that offer people flexible responses to different needs. New England Electric's new performance appraisal system, which requires managers and employees to set mutually agreed on expectations each year and then to talk about those expectations and the employee's performance throughout the year, offers a potential model for such policies and practices. The success of the system in actually accommodating the differing needs of employees of different cultural backgrounds depends on the knowledge and attitudes of the managers and employees using the system.

The remaining chapters of this book are devoted to exploring ways that organizations can develop and implement diversity initiatives that will help to create genuine multicultural organizations that are prepared for the challenges of the twenty-first century.

NOTES

1. The case studies presented here are based primarily on interviews with the individuals who are or were responsible for managing all or part of these efforts within their organizations at the time when the interviews were conducted. The exception is the Environmental Protection Agency, Region I, where I was part of an external consulting team (with Dr. Fern L. Johnson and Dr. M. Sallyanne Ryan) that worked with employees, first, to identify gender and race issues in the organization and second, to develop and implement training programs around those issues. Some of the individuals I interviewed now hold different positions within their organizations or have left entirely. Only one company did not want to be identified by name. I would like to thank the following individuals for talking with me about their organizations and projects (their titles reflect their positions at the time they were interviewed): Sue Aaronson, Manager, Valuing Differences Program, Digital Equipment Corporation; Russell J. Campanello, Vice President, Human Resources, Lotus Development Corporation; Rebecca Chou, Director, Cultural Diversity, Grand Metropolitan, Food Sector; Joyce Cofield, Assistant to the President, Polaroid Corporation; Susan Forth, Human Resources Training Specialist, Morgan Memorial Goodwill Industries, Inc.; Carolyn Miller, Work Force Diversity Manager, Medtronic; Larry Walrod, Training and Development Manager, Polaroid; Barbara Waterman, Affirmative Action Manager, Polaroid; and William Watkins, Jr., Vice President for Human Resources, New England Electric. The case studies presented are necessarily brief since they are not the focus of this volume and my goal is only to suggest the range of initiatives that have been implemented. Nor do the programs that I describe represent the full extent of the diversity work at any of these organizations. For a more complete treatment of current organizational strategies, see Jackson and Associates (1992).

2. ABC Corporation is a fictitious name, as is the XYZ Division within the company. The names were created to maintain the anonymity of the actual company used in this case study. The description of the diversity efforts is essentially accurate; minor details have been changed to ensure anonymity throughout the description.

3. For a full description of the study and an analysis of the data, see Fine, Johnson, and Ryan (1990).

4. It is not surprising that women's support groups were more likely to develop and find acceptance in organizations than support groups for African Americans. Whites in the United States have always feared blacks in groups. That fear intensified after several summers of race riots in major U.S. cities, beginning in Los Angeles in 1965. Women in groups (at least in the 1970s) were much less likely to evoke fear in men. In fact, a women's support group conjured up images of housewives gathering over their morning coffee to discuss their husbands and children and other domestic concerns. Women's support groups were acceptable precisely because women and their concerns were not taken seriously by men. Conceptually, women's support groups also were consistent with cultural stereotypes about women. Men believed that women did need additional support to succeed in organizational life.

6

IMPROVING INTERPERSONAL RELATIONSHIPS: MULTICULTURAL LITERACY FOR EMPLOYEES

As the case studies in Chapter 5 demonstrate, most diversity initiatives focus on improving interpersonal relationships among culturally diverse individuals. These efforts generally comprise training workshops, most often for senior executives and managers, and sometimes include ongoing personal support groups, such as DEC's Core Groups.

Diversity initiatives that focus on interpersonal issues are intended to improve working relationships among employees; to ensure equity in hiring, evaluation, and promotion decisions; and to enhance individual and organizational productivity. The interpersonal focus assumes that greater knowledge and understanding of other people and their cultural backgrounds leads to greater tolerance among employees and respect for each other as individuals. Individual tolerance and respect are assumed to be transformative, ultimately creating more inclusive organizations that respect and nurture all employees, regardless of cultural orientation. *The locus for organizational change in these efforts is within individual employees and their relationships with one another.* The responsibility for providing the organizational tools to accomplish the transformation lies with the training and development function in the organization.

In this chapter I describe the content and pedagogy of typical diversity training programs, suggest a content and pedagogy that are consonant with this book's perspective on cultural diversity in the workplace, and offer specific suggestions for developing diversity training programs. Although interpersonal support groups are often part of diversity initiatives that focus on changing interpersonal relationships, they will be discussed in Chapter 7 as part of organizational policies and practices.

DIVERSITY TRAINING

Numerous training materials on diversity are available to organizations, including film and videotape series, books, games and simulations, and newsletters. Despite the abundance of materials, most organizations choose to hire external consultants to develop and implement diversity training for their employees. Diversity training, a relatively new field, has become increasingly popular among consultants. Until recently, organizations could find few trainers with backgrounds in diversity work. The increasing real demand and the presumed potential demand have combined to create a new market niche for organizational consultants.

Diversity consultants come from a broad range of backgrounds and offer many different theoretical and pedagogical approaches to understanding diversity. This book provides one perspective for understanding cultural diversity and thinking about its implications in the workplace. There are, of course, other perspectives. Regardless of theoretical perspective and pedagogy, however, consultants generally offer organizations one of two kinds of training—"canned" or individualized.

Canned training programs are very much what their name suggests: Predeveloped, generic training modules that are formulaic and can be used in any organization. Individualized training is developed for a specific organization. The training program is based on the particular training needs of the organization and is usually developed after the consultant has done an assessment of the organization's needs.

Canned training programs on any organizational topic generally have limited viability. At the very least, a training presentation on any topic needs to include examples, data, and situations that are relevant to the organization and its employees. However, the impetus and needs for diversity training vary greatly among organizations, depending on the demographics of the local population, the current and projected demographics in the workplace, and the degree of structural integration of women and people of color throughout the organization. In addition, the breadth and depth of training vary according to whether the organization has had previous diversity initiatives, whether the organization's strategy is to begin its training program with senior personnel, whether all employees will participate in the diversity training, and numerous other factors.

Individualized diversity training, therefore, is preferable to canned diversity training. That is not to say, however, that canned programs serve no value. Any exposure that employees have to the value of diverse points of view, to differences among cultural groups, or to information about the changing demographics of the workplace lays the foundation for personal growth and change. Education and training have intrinsic value in that they expand people's knowledge and experience, and, in so doing, hold the potential to change attitudes and behaviors. Employees may have a more difficult time generalizing from the information or experiential exercises in canned training programs than in training programs that are more tailored to the needs of their own workplace, but they can potentially benefit from having gone through the training program.

Types of Workshops

Although consultants vary widely in their approaches to diversity training, they tend to use three types of workshops, either singly or in different combinations, depending on their personal pedagogical assumptions about training and a particular organization's needs: (1) Informative presentations, (2) consciousness-raising, and (3) experiential skills building.

Informative Presentations

Informative presentations most often provide an introduction to diversity efforts in an organization. For example, a diversity initiative might begin with a short (three to six hour) workshop on demographic trends in the United States and how they will affect (or already have affected) the organization. The demographic information becomes a backdrop for presenting an overview of the diversity efforts that the company plans to take. This kind of presentation is an efficient, relatively inexpensive, and effective way of presenting a lot of information to a large number of employees. It does, however, have serious limitations.

First, the informative presentation allows little or no time for questions and audience interaction. It is an efficient mode of presenting information for precisely that reason. The presenter decides what information is relevant, develops and organizes the information in a manner that should be understandable and interesting to the audience (or audiences if the presentation is to be repeated), and then presents it. A good presenter leaves some time for questions, and an experienced presenter with some depth of knowledge on the subject will be able to add new material if the audience questions suggest it is necessary. Generally, however, presenters are constrained by the information that must be included in the presentation and the time that has been allotted for the workshop.

Material that is factual and noncontroversial is well-suited to this mode of presentation. Thus, demographic information generally can be presented this way. The audience can listen, take notes, and be better informed at the end of the presentation. Diversity issues, however, are emotionally charged and highly controversial. An informative presentation on the company's planned diversity initiatives is likely not only to raise lots of factual questions (e.g., who will participate? what will I have to do? when will these activities occur?), but also to heighten emotions and expectations among different employees. Diversity training, regardless of whether the trainer's theoretical perspective is based on acculturation to the majority culture, or a "melting pot" in which all cultures are joined into one, or a "tossed salad" in which each culture retains its uniqueness but also forms part of a new culture, presumes that the participants will develop greater open-mindedness about others.

Learning that is intended to change attitudes and behaviors is best done in experiential formats, in which participants can explore the issues more personally and directly. Although informative presentations are efficient, in terms of both time and money, they are generally not as effective as other formats for diversity training. They should not, therefore, be the only type of format that is used to deliver diversity training.

Consciousness-raising

Consciousness-raising is a technique for bringing new ways of under-standing and interpreting experience into one's conscious awareness. The term was popularized in the early 1970s by feminists. Small groups of women would meet regularly in informal discussion groups and share their experiences of being female in this culture. The shared recollections gave credence to each woman's experience by making her realize that she was not alone, and also helped women see the larger social and political con-text of each woman's personal experience. These consciousness-raising groups became both an educational and political tool for feminists. The group discussions educated women about the ways in which women are oppressed and silenced in this culture, and the shared support of other members empowered the women to act, both individually and as part of a larger political group, to change their lives.

Consciousness-raising can be used in similar ways to teach people about culture and cultural differences, making them aware of how culture has shaped their own perceptions and behaviors and the perceptions and be-haviors of others. Diversity workshops often begin by having participants tell their stories; participants describe key experiences in their lives that they believe shaped who they are now. These stories can bring coworkers closer together by giving people a better understanding of each other. The white woman who had been dismissed by coworkers of color as having led a privileged, upper middle-class life is now recognized as someone who worked her way through college and graduate school, often working several jobs, while raising two children as a single parent. The African American male, who coworkers presumed attended Harvard as an affir-mative action scholarship student, turns out to be the son of wealthy, Harvard-educated parents. Sharing stories clarifies our misperceptions about other people and breaks down stereotypes. It also makes people feel closer to each other because they have shared important, and sometimes intimate, details about their lives.

Several years ago I worked on a diversity initiative with a small, non-profit agency that had deep racial divisions among its employees. People generally refused to talk openly about the problems in the organization, especially when members of another racial group were present. After enduring two years of either near silence or extremely guarded comments during sessions with the group, my colleagues and I decided to begin a session with the group by having everyone share their personal stories. Our agenda for the workshop that day was to identify and discuss how our cultural background shapes our attitudes about work and how we do our work. We asked each person to answer the following five questions: What are the cultural roots you were raised in? What did the people who raised you do for a living? What other experience stands out as fundamental in how you understand your own work? What about these things helps you do your work in a way that you value? What about these things interferes with doing your work?

The stories that people told were powerful and insightful. One woman talked about growing up as a black person in a white community and not being included in other children's activities. She believed that the experience had made her reluctant to speak up at work because she continued to fear being rejected by others. A black man from a wealthy Haitian family said that he had grown up having little interaction with working class people, and really didn't understand their issues. His Haitian roots and French accent, which were a source of tremendous pride for him, were also a problem for him here in the United States because he believed that his accent got in the way of people trusting him. An African American woman, who spoke after him, said that she had grown up poor and had great disdain for privileged people, those she described as not having suffered. People from privileged backgrounds made her angry. An Asian American man whose parents were from Korea said that he grew up hearing many graphic stories about the atrocities committed by the Japanese when they annexed Korea. His parents escaped from Korea and came to the United States. He said that his parents' lives had taught him that people in the most inauspicious conditions can survive and can rebuild their lives.

Stories such as these gave people new insights into their own behaviors and feelings, and helped them understand the behaviors and feelings of their coworkers. They also brought forth powerful emotions. People felt each other's pain, cried tears for each other, and gave each other physical and emotional support. It was the first time in two years of working with the group that I had sensed that the staff members genuinely cared about the entire group rather than just select friends.

The intensity created by these questions with this particular group of participants is not always necessary or appropriate in diversity training. Less encompassing personal explorations are also valuable and productive ways to initiate diversity discussions. For example, I have put participants in small groups that were mixed by gender or race, and asked the group members to share with each other what they were taught about the other gender or race as children. After the group members explored how their stereotypes of others were created, they discussed when they began to question their stereotypes and what events prompted them to do so. These discussions can prompt some powerful memories and connections between people. I recall one white male coming to talk with me after a group discussion in which a black male had talked about being refused service at a lunch counter in the South when he was growing up in the 1950s. The black man's story had prompted the white man to remember something that had happened to him when he was stationed in St. Louis during World War II. He told me that he had gone to look at an apartment in the home of a widow. He decided to rent the apartment, and while he was discussing the details with the owner, he asked her where the nearest Catholic church was located. The next morning she called him and said that she was very sorry but the apartment had been taken by someone who had seen it before he had. His first reaction was surprise, since she had said the night before that the apartment was available and that he could have it. His next reaction was anger when he realized what must have happened. The apartment was located in a Jewish section of town. He was Italian, with dark hair and eyes and a swarthy complexion. The widow most likely assumed that he was also Jewish, until he asked the question about the Catholic church. Remembering that experience and the anger he felt when he realized that he could not live where he wanted to live simply because someone else didn't like his religion helped him to identify with his African American coworker. It also helped him to understand the attitude of some African Americans that he usually identified as having chips on their shoulders. He could now imagine how he would present himself to others if he faced discrimination every day in everything he did.

Consciousness-raising begins with the kind of deep personal exploration and sharing of experiences that these exercises provoke. Consciousness-raising continues, however, with further exploration of the connections between these individual experiences. Just as women's consciousness-raising groups in the 1970s helped individual women understand that their personal oppression was part of a larger social, cultural, and political pattern of oppressing women and suppressing their experience and voices, consciousness-raising in diversity training draws connections among the experiences of individuals in order to reveal cultural patterns of behavior and to provide a social and political context for the experience of being different in U.S. culture.

Without further exploration, consciousness-raising risks being nothing more than a feel-good strategy. Everyone has the opportunity to reveal a hidden dimension of himself or herself and be better known to others. We can all feel somewhat self-righteous about allowing others to speak, and now that we've told our stories and better know each other, we can return to business as usual. If conscious-raising is used only to give people an opportunity to vent their frustrations and anger, or to show their compassion, it may prove helpful to working relationships in the short-run, but over the long-term, it may do more harm than good. Women and people of color who have been historically excluded from organizational life may have heightened expectations about the outcome of the diversity training once they have been given the opportunity to speak. Those expectations include more than having people feel good about themselves for having allowed others to speak. Women and people of color expect their voices to have been heard; they expect to continue participating in the organizational conversation; and they expect that the organization will continue to change. If it does not, their original anger and frustration may deepen, and they may grow more cynical about organizational life in the United States.

Experiential Skill Building

Experiential skill building is similar pedagogically to consciousness-raising. Both training approaches are rooted in the assumption that people learn best through direct experience.[1] Rather than calling on past experience to prompt current insights, however, experiential skill building creates new situations from which participants can learn. For example, participants might be asked to take on particular roles and act out a scenario.

Business executives who are training for overseas positions often learn about the new culture that they will be encountering through role playing techniques. Role playing enables participants to see culture by bringing cultural responses into their awareness. By acting out the encounter ahead of time, executives learn what to expect and how to respond. The practice lessens the culture shock when they actually arrive overseas.

Role playing is especially helpful in diversity training because it allows participants to take on the roles of others, to walk in the proverbial "other person's shoes." For example, a popular training exercise involves placing a label on each person in the training group (e.g., CEO, up-and-comer, going-nowhere, secretary, and so forth) and then having everyone mix as if they were at a social gathering. Participants quickly learn how their own behavior is shaped both by how others act toward them and by how they feel about themselves. They also experience how their self-evaluations are shaped by how other people treat them. The person labeled "going-nowhere" soon believes that he or she is going nowhere, and begins to behave that way. Adapting this exercise for diversity training allows people to experience, albeit briefly and superficially, being African American or female—or their counterparts—in this culture. The experience often helps people develop greater empathy for others.

In addition to the concrete nature of the learning in experiential skill building, the technique is also useful because trainers can create exercises that are directly related to the workplace. A common complaint about diversity training is that too little of the training is directly related to workplace activities. Participants may learn a lot about other cultures or even the specific cultural backgrounds of coworkers, but they rarely have an opportunity to see how cultural differences affect workplace behavior. Experiential skill building can provide that opportunity.

For example, the diversity initiative for EPA Region I, described briefly in Chapter 5, included a training component. The workshops during the first year of training focused on identifying, understanding, and valuing gender and race differences. When we began talking about the programs for the second year of training, the members of the Steering Committee wanted to focus more directly on workplace interaction. They suggested developing a case study on promotion using the procedures that are actually used in the EPA when a position is being filled. A member of the Steering Committee who was familiar with the EPA screening process wrote the case, creating characters that were consistent with EPA employee profiles yet had particular experiences or characteristics that marked their cultural backgrounds.

We used the case study for a managerial workshop on promotion. The participants were asked to read the materials, assume that they were members of the selection and screening committee, and rank order the candidates for the position that was being filled in the case. Then the participants formed small groups. Each person shared his or her rankings and reasons for them, and the group had to reach a consensus on selecting a candidate for the position.

The exercise and subsequent discussion allowed the trainers to raise questions about the conclusions that the participants had drawn about the candidates, to show how cultural stereotypes and organizational expectations force us to draw certain conclusions, and to suggest how managers can avoid making stereotypic judgments and can gather additional information about candidates. Experiential skill-building exercises do not instruct as much as they help people discover how to teach themselves. They are more time-consuming than informative presentations, and trainers always risk not having the exercises work as expected. When they do work, however, the learning that takes place is both powerful and likely to result in changes in workplace behavior.

MULTICULTURAL LITERACY

Diversity trainers bring a variety of theoretical perspectives to their work. Some, such as the educational specialist at the XYZ Division, see a diverse organization as a dysfunctional family and define diversity training as a therapeutic intervention strategy. Others, such as Barbara Walker, who developed DEC's Valuing Differences Program, believe that dialogue is the key to understanding and valuing the differences between us. Others take a more political and macro-analytical approach, positing that diversity issues in the organization are simply a smaller scale version of the personal and institutional racism that pervade society generally. Those who take this position believe that if employees can deconstruct the power dynamics that support and sustain racism, then they can reconstruct the social arrangements in the workplace in more equitable ways.

My approach to workplace diversity is grounded in a cultural analysis of differences. For employees and employers to negotiate a diverse workplace in mutually productive ways, I believe that they must acquire multicultural literacy. The definitions of both terms, multicultural and literacy, are central to understanding the concept. In the various literatures on culture, being "multicultural" generally refers to the ability to move from one cultural system to another with relative ease. In this conception, a multicultural person is "a native of many homes" (Hall, 1992). The concept is an extension of a more familiar term, biculturalism, or the ability to move easily between two cultures. Businesspeople who maintain business dealings in the United States and another country are sometimes referred to as bicultural because they are comfortable doing business in both countries. When African Americans became a more visible presence in the managerial ranks of U.S. organizations, they were often described as bicultural because they were compelled to follow white organizational norms in the workplace and then switch to black cultural norms at home. Sociolinguistic research suggests that some African Americans move from speaking Black English Vernacular in their own communities or when they are with other African Americans to speaking Standard English in white institutional contexts such as school or work.

Defined as "a native of many homes," the multicultural person is a problematic concept for a diverse work force. It suggests that at any given point in time, an employee has a cultural home that has a relatively stable, enduring set of cultural assumptions. Defined this way, multiculturalism carries the same admonition as standard cross-cultural training for managers: When in Rome, do as the Romans do.

The problem is that in a diverse workplace, where is Rome? Organizations in the United States represent a microcosm of the cultural dynamics of the country as a whole. People of many different cultural backgrounds come together to recreate, on a continuing basis, our national (and organizational) culture and identity. We don't move from place to place; rather, we continually reinvent home. In this conception, being multicultural represents maintaining an attitude of openness toward expressions of different cultures while simultaneously engaging in an ongoing process of creating and recreating a multicultural culture. This resulting multicultural culture maintains the integrity of many cultures while incorporating them into a whole that is greater than the sum of its parts. It is a "superculture," as one of my students so aptly put it.[2]

Literacy is generally understood to be the ability to read and write; it is considered a sign of an educated person. Although we tend to identify people as literate or illiterate, literacy is a relative term that is culturally bound. A person may be literate in one culture and language and illiterate in another, a condition that is often true of immigrants to the United States, and is also true of the vast majority of Americans. In other words, a person who is fluent in Spanish may be able to produce sophisticated written and oral texts in Spanish, while simultaneously being unable to read, write, or speak a word of English, or vice versa.

The cultural boundaries of literacy are more sharply illuminated in a multicultural society because people confront daily the limits of their literacy as they move from encounters in which they can understand the discourse to those in which they cannot. These encounters are especially problematic when the participants share the same (or very similar) linguistic system but not the same cultural system. Because the utterances they produce appear or sound familiar, they may assume that they are capable of understanding each other when they are not. Individuals in a multicultural society are simultaneously literate and illiterate; they are "faced with an array of alternative methods and contents representing different views of literacy" (Ferdman, 1990, p. 188). In this kind of society, literacy "becomes an interactive process that is constantly redefined and renegotiated, as the individual transacts with the socioculturally fluid surroundings" (Ferdman, 1990, p. 187).

Multicultural literacy in a multicultural society is the ability to participate in a collective process of redefining and renegotiating the texts (e.g., written documents, conversations, nonverbal cues, social arrangements, organizational expectations, and so forth) that constitute the public world. Literacy, in the sense that I am using it here, has to do with the ability to read and write the different texts through which people develop, maintain, end, and recreate their relationships with each other. Because these texts are both oral and written and use verbal and nonverbal symbols, the definitions of reading and writing are expanded beyond the ability to read and write a particular language. In a multicultural society, multicultural literacy is essential for survival, and is the cornerstone of ensuring the productivity of a culturally diverse work force.

The interpretation and creation of texts requires using verbal and nonverbal symbols to create shared meanings both orally and in writing; multicultural literacy, therefore, is grounded in communication and communicative processes. It has five components, each of which is centrally related to communication: (1) The ability to recognize cultural differences, (2) a knowledge of cultural differences, (3) the ability to discover particular cultural meanings when they are unknown, (4) the ability to negotiate shared meanings, and (5) the ability to accommodate multiple meanings.

In reading and creating multicultural texts, people must acknowledge and recognize cultural differences in order to avoid the error of reading, or assuming that others will read, a text from a particular cultural vantage point. Having knowledge about cultural differences allows them to both read and create texts from other cultural perspectives. Because multicultural societies are in flux, however, people in them must also know how to learn how to read and create texts when they encounter unfamiliar cultures. Negotiating shared meanings is essential to ensuring that people understand one another. Finally, accommodating multiple meanings is the *sine qua non* of multicultural literacy, for multicultural societies, by definition, include multiple ways of thinking, acting, feeling, and interpreting.

These five components of multicultural literacy should be used to focus, frame, and develop the content and pedagogy of a diversity training program in an organization. In terms of content, for example, a training program should provide specific knowledge about several cultures so that workers will have a shared knowledge base. The program should also include training in specific skills, such as asking questions, recognizing different cultural frames, knowing how to make judgments within different cultural frames, and negotiating. Pedagogically, a diversity training program should emphasize problem solving exercises that are highly ambiguous and have no correct answers, and learning techniques that allow participants to engage in consensus building and shared decision-making.

To reiterate my earlier point, the best training programs are specifically tailored to the needs of a particular organization. If a company is based in a region of the country where its customer base is heavily Hispanic, or if its work force now has or is projected to have large numbers of Hispanic workers, then its diversity training program should include content about various Hispanic cultures. Because U.S. population and work force demographics are in flux, and will most likely remain in flux over the next century, no training program can provide knowledge about all of the cultures workers may encounter in the workplace. In developing the content of specific programs, however, trainers can emphasize those cultures that predominate in a particular organization. That information becomes the base on which employees can build their skills for learning about new cultures that they may encounter. Ultimately, the success of diversity training in developing employees' multicultural literacy depends on instilling particular attitudes about difference, ambiguity, and the willingness to ask questions rather than pretending to know answers.[3]

Cultural Sensitivity

One attitude that is fundamental to multicultural literacy is cultural sensitivity. Cultural sensitivity has three components, each of which builds developmentally on the previous component: (1) Recognition of cultural differences, (2) knowledge about cultural differences, and (3) suspension of judgment about cultural differences. The first two components are also part of multicultural literacy and were briefly discussed in the previous section.

The first component of cultural sensitivity is the recognition that cultural differences exist. For example, when I teach courses in public speaking, my students generally agree that good speakers maintain eye contact with the audience. They say that speakers who do not maintain eye contact give the impression that they are either untrustworthy or that they are not knowledgeable about their topic. Students are surprised when I tell them that eye contact is a culturally-based behavior, and that, in some cultures, direct eye contact, especially with superiors or others who are in authority, is a sign of disrespect or an invitation to conflict.

Recognizing cultural differences is often very difficult, however, because culture tends to be out of our conscious awareness. As are many other nations, the United States is highly ethnocentric. We tend to believe that the way we conduct our lives is the only way to do so. In Chapter 3 I described the disbelief of my U.S. MBA students when a Pakistani student told them that religion was the most important factor in shaping business decisions in her country. Their disbelief was based not only on their surprise that anyone would be so foolish as to allow religious beliefs to affect business decisions, but more importantly, on their inability to envision how religion could affect business decisions. Despite her insistence that religious prohibitions against usury meant that banking was not based on charging interest, the other students refused to believe her because they could not imagine how a bank that did not charge interest could be a bank.

My students further demonstrated the difficulty of seeing cultural differences when I asked them to write about their cultural backgrounds. International students and students who had recently emigrated to the United States were able to do the assignment easily. They could describe their own national or ethnic cultural backgrounds by contrasting them to U.S. culture. U.S. students, on the other hand, were generally unable to do the assignment. Recognizing difference is often a function of juxtaposing something against that which it is not.

Our inability to see cultural differences in the United States is strengthened further by our belief in equality, which is embedded in American culture. Believing that all people are equal often leads us to conclude that all people are alike; that conclusion leads us to deny differences even when they are apparent. Equating equality with sameness comes from the false assumption that quality (since equality is really a statement of equal quality) is a relative and comparative condition. In other words, something must be better than something else, and only one thing can be the best. Given that assumption, people who are equal must be the same.

The second component of cultural sensitivity is knowledge about cultural differences and the ability to read those differences. Reading cultural

differences involves knowing the meanings that others ascribe to their behaviors. For example, my colleagues often bemoan the fact that many of
their Asian students dislike participating in class discussions. They have
told me that they have given the students lots of encouragement and support, but despite their best efforts, the students still refuse to speak up. The
problem my colleagues have is based on a misreading of the students' behavior. They are assuming that the Asian students are not speaking up in
class because the students are either shy or insecure about their oral facility with English. That reading is often incorrect, however. Asian students
frequently do not participate in class discussions because speaking up in
class draws attention to themselves, making them stand out and above
other students. That behavior is culturally inappropriate for them.

The last component of cultural sensitivity is the willingness to suspend
judgment about culturally different behavior. The willingness to suspend
judgment is based on the recognition that different does not equal deficient, and that things that are equal do not need to be the same. People can
achieve the same ends in entirely different ways. Culturally sensitive managers recognize that employees may have culturally different ways of accomplishing their work. These managers nurture and encourage the best
work in all employees, not just those who conform to the managers' expectations of how work should be accomplished.

PEDAGOGICAL CONCERNS

Diversity training programs that focus on acquiring multicultural literacy
in the workplace are risky for both the organization and the people who
participate in the training. Both invest heavily in the process. Organizations commit financial resources in terms of the cost of developing and
implementing the training, employee time in training, and possible organizational changes that grow out of the training. Employees invest their
time, their identities, and their relationships with one another. As with any
risky investment, investors need to be aware of the dangers, and of the
strategies for minimizing them.

Creating Trust

Examining cultural differences often gives rise to serious and deep cultural and personal conflicts, which must be voiced, acknowledged, and
explored. That exploration is often painful for those who share their stories
about past and present injustices, and can be hurtful to those who feel im-
plicated, rightly or wrongly, in those stories. Discussions about gender, race,
class, and ethnic differences are frightening to many people. They often
bring to the surface anger, guilt, and mistrust, and lead to verbal conflicts
that many participants feel unable to handle. Asian Americans and some

ethnic whites, for example, dislike public conflict and either smooth over differences or avoid them entirely. Also, the fear of being labeled racist or sexist can create a chilling effect in these discussions that precludes any real exploration of the issues.

For all of these reasons, it is imperative that employees who participate in diversity training feel safe. Everyone, regardless of cultural background or organizational status, must feel safe to speak. Participants need assurance that anything they say will remain within the room, that their feelings will not be denied by others, and that they will not be punished for what they say, either professionally or personally.

The trainer (or facilitator or discussion leader) must acknowledge the importance of trust to the success of the training from the outset of the session, and should pledge that he or she will maintain the confidentiality of the discussions. Using a trainer who is not involved in employee evaluation is especially helpful in demonstrating that what gets said in the workshop will not affect an employee's performance evaluation or promotional opportunities. Outside consultants may provide the clearest signal of safety to employees, although consultants are sometimes too closely identified with management.

It is also helpful to establish a set of ground rules to govern all discussions. For example, Estelle Disch (Sept. 28, 1993), a sociology professor who teaches courses that focus on issues of gender and race, distributes the following list of discussion guidelines to her students at the beginning of each semester:

1. All comments are welcomed and encouraged.
2. Use "I" statements to describe your own beliefs and opinions.
3. Listen respectfully to each other.
4. Maintain confidentiality.
5. Do not assign blame to others; we are all products of learned socialization.

This list is a useful compendium of behaviors that will help create and maintain trust among participants in diversity training workshops. Using this list also gives the trainer an opportunity to explain each of the behaviors and how they function to create an environment in which people can safely confront their conflicts with each other.

The guidelines encourage full and open discussion while setting parameters within which the discussion can take place. For example, asking people to use "I statements" to describe their own beliefs and opinions ensures that the participants will always know if someone recognizes that he or she is expressing a personal belief or believes that he or she is stating a fact. The difference is critical. We are entitled both to hold our own opinions and to expect others to hear them respectfully. We are not entitled, however, to state personal opinions as universal truths, or to assume that beliefs and opinions are necessarily factual or based on factual data. For example, I may believe that religious training is essential to the formation of positive values, but my believing it doesn't make it true. Ideas that I present as truths are open to challenge.

Using "I statements" also forces people to take ownership of their ideas rather than escaping confrontation on difficult ideas by attributing them to others or asserting that they are factual claims. People often use statements that they attribute to others to express their own beliefs when they feel those beliefs will be ridiculed or denied. Discussions about racism are especially likely to evoke comments such as, "Many of my friends believe . . . ," or "I don't feel this way, but many people I know . . . ." Having people acknowledge their own feelings and beliefs is fundamental to multicultural literacy. Each of us needs to understand the self and to be willing to engage in self-critique before we are open to studying and understanding others.

A variation of the "I statement" guideline that I have used in workshops is that participants may not in any way attempt to deny the experiences or feelings of another person. In other words, I may disagree that the words that I spoke to you were intended to hurt you, but I cannot deny that you felt hurt when I said them. Acknowledging people's feelings validates their experience, and empowers them to join the discussion without fear of being dismissed or ignored.

Avoiding Misperceptions

Diversity training programs that include an analysis of cultural differences create the possibility that people will misperceive or misunderstand the examples that are presented in the workshop, or that stereotypic comments will be taken personally. Those misperceptions can lead to serious consequences outside of the workshop and the organization. For example, a worker filed a discrimination lawsuit against a west coast supermarket chain, Lucky Stores, Inc., charging that a supervisor had made stereotypic comments during a diversity training workshop. More likely, however, misperceptions will create additional conflict and ill-will among the participants. Although some conflict is both natural and necessary in diversity training, conflict created by misperceptions that are created within the training program is not productive for the individuals or the organization.

Avoiding these misperceptions is very difficult. There is a very fine line between describing cultural differences and perpetuating stereotypes. I was especially self-conscious as I wrote Chapter 3 because I feared that readers might easily accuse me of unfairly generalizing about individuals. That is why I included disclaimers about the generalizability of the characteristics that I described and continually reminded readers that particular individuals that they knew might not conform to the cultural descriptions.

In describing cultural differences, however, one is forced to generalize about all members of a cultural group, ascribing to all the characteristics of some. That process is identical to stereotyping. There are important differences, however, between stereotyping and describing cultural differences. In stereotyping, the generalization is from the group to the individual; it is fixed; and it is simplistic. Stereotyping reduces the complexity of human identity and behavior. Descriptions of cultural differences, on the other hand, begin deductively. Cultural attributes are deduced across a wide range of members, they are assumed to vary in degree among group members and by situation, and they are placed within a complex matrix of factors that shape identity and behavior.

The individuals who lead diversity training workshops should have the training and skills to defuse situations in which individuals confuse stereotyping with descriptions of cultural behaviors and become offended by the descriptions, or misunderstand the difference and see the discussion as an opportunity to express, with approval, their stereotypes. Trainers must be able to clarify the differences between common stereotypes, cultural characteristics, and real people. In addition, they need to model appropriate behavior when they hear participants expressing ideas that are grounded in stereotypes. The difficult moments that occur when participants misperceive the material or when noxious stereotypes are used to describe and evaluate individuals can be used to educate participants. Disch (Sept. 28, 1993) calls these "teachable moments."

White Male Bashing

White male bashing, or placing the blame for all of society's evils on the backs of white men, is directly related to stereotyping, and sometimes to misperceptions about examples. A common complaint about diversity training, especially from white males, is that it is nothing more than an opportunity to dump on white men.

The content of diversity training can easily be understood within a context of blame. Any analysis that is culturally grounded will examine both how minority group cultures in the United States have been shaped by the experience of oppression, and how they have been suppressed and denied by the majority culture, which, in organizational life, is white and male. That analysis is necessary for understanding the behaviors and beliefs of different cultural groups in the workplace. As I said in Chapter 3, for example, African American culture is the product of the African heritage of most blacks in the United States and their experience of slavery in the United States. Further, the behavior of many African Americans in the workplace is affected by the tension and fear created by the suppression of African American culture in organizational life.

In addition to blaming white men as a cultural group, diversity training sessions also may include blaming of individual white men. As people of color and white women tell their stories, they may identify specific individuals as responsible for oppressing them. Individualizing the oppressor in this way heightens the sense that white male participants may have that they are being accused of oppressing others.

To some extent, blaming is a matter of perception that is culturally based. For example, African Americans believe that assigning guilt is the responsibility of the accused rather than the accuser. If an African American accuses whites of racism, he or she expects only those whites who are guilty of racism to feel guilty. On the other hand, the responsibility for assigning guilt rests with the accuser in white culture. Whites, therefore, expect that any accusation made generically about a group refers specifically to all members of that group. When an African American accuses whites of racism, therefore, the whites who are present take offense and usually try to deny the charge. Since African Americans believe that only individuals who are guilty will feel guilty, protestations of innocence by whites only convince blacks that these whites are guilty. This cultural misunderstanding about assigning and accepting or denying guilt sets up a downward spiral in the discourse and the relationships between blacks and whites, with each set of accusations and protestations deepening the anger between them.

This discussion of cultural misperceptions about accusations of racism is not meant to minimize the reality of individual racism or to suggest that all accusations of racism in an organizational workshop are intended generically. Trainers must be prepared to deal with the anger and conflict that can emerge when members of historically oppressed cultural groups are encouraged to have genuine conversations with majority group members. The anger of many people of color and women is real and it is based on real injustices that they have experienced. To deny it or to refuse to hear it, regardless of how painful it is for others, effectively precludes any chance for honest dialogue, personal healing, and productive working relationships in the future.

On the other hand, it is important to recognize that the mutterings from the men's room are also real. White men are often confused and hurt by accusations of racism, especially when they cannot identify instances in which they overtly or knowingly discriminated against people of color. They also feel confused and vulnerable in conversations on subjects such as oppression, patriarchy, ethnocentrism, or multiculturalism. Their vulnerability sometimes reveals itself in anger, sullenness, derision, laughter, and braggadocio.[4]

For many white men, accusations that they are privileged ring hollow.

As members of religious or ethnic minorities, they, too, feel constrained within the values and norms of what they would call WASP organizational culture. For some of them, their social class is a constant reminder of privileges they neither have nor can ever imagine having. Despite cultural myths to the contrary, class is a fundamental cultural category in the United States, with serious economic, social, and political consequences. Further, even men who are privileged by virtue of their ethnicity and social class sometimes feel the burdens of a culture that continues to expect men to provide for their families.

Trainers need to understand the range of possible explanations for the behaviors of the white males in a training group and to defuse the potential problems they may create. One way to do so is to acknowledge at the outset that diversity discussions make people uncomfortable. If participants feel sufficiently safe, they can share their own feelings about being in such a training program. If not, the trainer can have people share possible feelings without any self-attribution. The group can then explore the reasons why diversity training might make people experience those feelings. Trainers should also be explicit about the content of the program, letting participants know what to expect in terms of both the issues that will be discussed and people's possible responses to those issues.

The rhetoric of oppression is difficult to avoid in diversity training, and it is often a necessary part of the discourse. But it should not be the entire discourse. The rhetoric of oppression is a rhetoric of victimization, a drama with victim and victimizers as the central characters. It is a discourse that polarizes it participants, pitting victim again victimizer, and empowers some at the cost of disempowering others. Victimizers are by definition more powerful than their victims, and victims, by definition, are powerless to defend themselves.

Diversity training that is aimed at creating multicultural literacy must embrace a discourse that brings people together in a way that is inclusive and empowering for everyone. Disch's last ground rule, that participants should not assign blame to each other because we are all products of learned socialization, is very helpful in laying the foundation for such a discourse. At the same time, it is important to remember that an inclusive and empowering discourse must go beyond feel-good rhetoric. Celebration of differences without following through and incorporating those differences into organizational life provides empty promises to women and people of color and only perpetuates the majority suppression of other cultures.

Workplace Relevance

One of the most often heard criticisms of diversity training is that it has little relevance to actual workplace interaction. Participants either complain that it is a waste of time to share personal stories about their cultural roots or they say that they enjoy the personal stories but don't see how they explain anything about workplace behavior. Neither response is surprising.

First, dichotomy is a central organizing principle of the western, white male culture that permeates organizational life in the United States. Separating one's personal life from life at the office is a hallmark of male culture, and a pervasive expectation of organizational culture in the United States. In fact, a frequent criticism of women in the workplace is that they have a hard time setting boundaries between work and home (e.g., bringing personal problems such as sick children into the workplace) or separating personal feelings about coworkers from conclusions about their professional competence. Since organizational culture separates the personal and the public, employees have a hard time seeing the relationship between them.

Diversity training, whether it focuses on cultural differences or individual differences per se, assumes a direct and significant relationship between the personal life and the public. Diversity training, therefore, begins by violating a central premise of organizational life, which is almost certain to evoke tremendous skepticism about the efficacy of the training. The perceived dichotomy between personal life and work life also leads some employees to resist becoming engaged in the training. By minimizing or even denying the relevance of discussions about their own and others' cultural backgrounds, these employees disengage themselves from the training and undermine its chances for success.

A second reason why some participants do not see the relevance of sharing personal stories is that even when people acknowledge their cultural differences, they generally fail to see those differences in the workplace. One consequence of the systematic suppression of minority cultures in the workplace is the denial of differences, not simply as a strategy for sustaining the majority culture, but also as a learned and genuine understanding of the workplace environment. Words provide a map of the world around us. We can actually see the objects and events that we experience only by naming them. If differences are unnamed, they remain unseen. Because cultural differences in the workplace have been denied for so long, employees have a hard time recognizing and acknowledging them even when they are identified and named.

Denying cultural differences in workplace behavior is not unique to white males.[5] Women and people of color are sometimes unwilling to acknowledge that their cultural differences make any difference at work. I recently participated in a training retreat for employees of a small, nonprofit organization. The staff was racially and culturally diverse; whites, in fact, were a minority in the organization. Despite their numerical majority, however, people of color in the organization felt that they did not have the same degree of power as did white employees. The staff members were split along racial lines, and the conflicts were so intense that the white staff and staff of color often held separate meetings.

The purpose of the retreat was to talk about the ways that cultural differences shape how we accomplish our work. As I described earlier in the chapter, we began by having each person share his or her life story. The stories were remarkable, and, for the first time, people in the organization began to open up to each other. Unlike previous sessions in which I had participated with this group, people talked, laughed, cried, and genuinely seemed to listen to each other, even across racial lines. When we shifted the discussion to the ways in which our cultural backgrounds affect how we do our work, however, communication again became strained. The group either remained silent or argued vehemently, not with each other, but with the consultants.

To initiate the discussion of the relationship between our cultural backgrounds and how we accomplish our work, we had grouped staff members by their cultural and racial backgrounds and asked the groups to draw their conceptions of time, rhythm, communication, leadership, community, and team. The drawings were markedly different, and suggested important cultural differences among the groups. As soon as we began to explore those differences, however, the groups began to disavow their drawings. The staff members appeared to want to deny differences, to be able to claim, instead, that their work styles were similar.

Despite years of frustration about not having their visions acknowledged and validated, people of color in the organization refused to acknowledge the ways that their visions differed when they were directly compared to each other and to white cultural styles. Even though the discussion contained no explicit evaluative comments, I believe that the fear that such a hidden agenda might exist and the pervasive belief or suspicion that white male work styles are better kept the groups from recognizing and acknowledging their differences.

Trainers need to understand that many employees, regardless of cultural background, may resist acknowledging differences in work behavior. Trainers need to move beyond that resistance, however, in order to demonstrate the relevance of cultural differences in the workplace. One approach to getting beyond the resistance is to depersonalize the discussions by using case studies. Employees can then discuss the ways that culture influences values, attitudes, and behavior in the workplace without worrying about possible evaluations of their own behavior.

The advantage of case studies, however, is also their greatest pedagogical shortcoming. Although depersonalizing the discussion enables participants to see differences, they see them in relation to other people, not to themselves or even necessarily to their coworkers. People often find it difficult to generalize from the experience of others to their own experience.

It is much easier to move in the reverse direction and gain greater understanding of others by generalizing from your own experience.

Experiential activities that are based on real workplace activities provide a means of using people's own experience to help people see how their own and others' cultural backgrounds affect workplace beliefs and behaviors. The case study on promotion that I described earlier is an example of an experiential exercise. Workshop participants undertook the task of choosing the person in the case who should be promoted. The details in the case were designed to provoke culturally specific assessments of each of the candidates for promotion. Similar exercises can be developed for any organization and can be designed to tap a variety of cultural responses, both attitudinal and behavioral.

In addition to overcoming resistance to diversity training by demonstrating its relevance, experiential exercises have another benefit. By creating situations in which individuals from different cultural backgrounds have to work together to solve problems, the exercises become exemplars of the kind of multicultural negotiating that needs to go on in a culturally diverse workplace. Trainers can help people model the attitudes and behaviors that are necessary for achieving multicultural literacy.

The road to multicultural literacy, both in the workplace and throughout U.S. culture generally, is difficult and, most likely, never ending. We will remain a culture in flux for many decades, continually creating and recreating ourselves. Diversity training that helps employees improve their interpersonal relationships with each other is one step along the road. Chapter 7 explores additional steps that organizations can take to make the workplace more welcoming and accommodating to all employees, regardless of cultural background.

NOTES

1. Most teachers and trainers use some form of experiential learning. Early childhood education has always relied on direct experience as the primary mode of learning. Young children, for example, learn about numbers and numeric relationships by counting actual objects. More recently, educators have recognized that older children and adults are often better able to understand and apply concepts in different situations if they discover the concepts experientially. Interestingly, research suggests that women tend to learn best through experience (inductive reasoning through concrete examples) rather than through traditional linear conceptualizing (Belenky et al., 1986).

2. I am using "super" here in its double meanings of (1) extra or additional, and (2) excellent. In other words, a multicultural culture is a superculture in that it is larger than the individual cultures it encompasses and it is a terrific culture. I am *not* using super to mean superiority or placement above the individual cultures. My intent is not to recreate the ethnocentric assumption of the superiority of U.S.

culture within the concept of multiculturalism. The term superculture is meant to identify the inclusivity and positive attributes of multiculturalism.

3. Pretending to know the answers is a macho attitude that presently pervades organizational life, especially among managers and executives. Many managers appear to believe that asking questions is a sign of weakness, that if they don't know the answers to everything, other people will perceive them as incompetent. In fact, the pretense of knowledge in the absence of knowledge is more likely to lead to incompetent behavior. At the very least, it leads to unproductive behavior.

4. It is both ironic and yet unsurprising that white males often accuse women and people of color in organizations of displaying these same attitudes and behaviors. In a workshop discussion on the oppression of women and people of color, the roles of minority and majority group members in the organizational conversation are reversed. Members of minority cultures are the ones who understand the terms and the rules; white males (as individuals, not as a social group) are marginalized in the discussion. Trainers can sometimes call attention to the reversal, allowing people to discover and acknowledge their own feelings when the roles are reversed, hopefully gaining greater empathy with others. These are the kinds of "teachable moments" Disch (Sept. 28, 1993) describes. It is the rare teacher, however, who can seize upon them.

5. In fact, when white males perceive that it is to their advantage, they are quick to point out differences in workplace behavior, arguing, for example, that women are unfit for managerial positions because they are too emotional. Generally, however, white males have a vested interest in denying differences and thus maintaining the myth that white male ways of organizing are the only ways.

7

ORGANIZATIONAL STRATEGIES: POLICIES AND PRACTICES FOR MULTICULTURAL ORGANIZATIONS

The previous chapter detailed various interpersonal approaches to creating a productive multicultural work force. This chapter looks at ways that organizations, through various policies and practices, can nurture and support that work force.

CREATING A MULTICULTURAL ORGANIZATIONAL CULTURE

Policies and practices intended to support a multicultural work force cannot fully succeed unless they are grounded in an organizational culture that embraces multiculturalism. Such a culture is open to new ideas and ways of doing things, supportive of differences among employees, and flexible in responding to employee needs and concerns. Communication is central to creating and maintaining this kind of organizational culture: Employees and managers must communicate with each other. Management must be willing to listen to employees, to value what they say, and to respond seriously to employee concerns and ideas. Employees must take responsibility for communicating their concerns and ideas, rather than waiting passively for others to speak for them. They must also, however, be assured that they are safe when they speak.

Assess Employee Needs

Continuously monitoring employee needs and concerns is one way to begin creating a multicultural organizational culture. Assessment is a critical first step. All too often, organizations presume to know what employ-ees need or want. Organizations can take a proactive stance by surveying employees, either through written questionnaires or oral interviews, using focus groups, establishing open discussion groups, making suggestion boxes available, and/or creating opportunities for employee dialogue in departmental newsletters and other internal organizational communica-tions. Regardless of the method, however, several principles should guide the assessment.

Continuous Assessment

First, assessing employee needs and concerns must be continuous. The one characteristic of the work force of the future that is certain is that it will be changing. The cultural mix in any organization may vary dramatically within a relatively short time span. Employee concerns may also change as the work force and the workplace change. For example, an organization with only a few Asian employees may discover that Asians in the organi-zation feel isolated and want the company both to hire more Asian work-ers and to create an informal support group. Over time, as more Asians are hired, Asian employees may develop concerns about their career paths. Asians are often pigeon-holed into technical and scientific positions that hold little promise for long-term advancement. Although the company may have been successful in recruiting Asians, it may not have worked as hard at ensuring that the new hires will have challenges and opportunities in the company over time. Asians working in the organization may now want the company to shift its emphasis from recruiting and hiring to training and development. Employees may also feel that the informal support group now needs greater structure and a more formal endorsement from man-agement.

Employee-Set Agendas

The second principle that should guide assessments of employee needs is that employees should set their own agendas for professional develop-ment and explain their own needs. Management should not establish em-ployee needs from the top down. Creating a culture in which employees take responsibility for communicating their needs requires that employees be asked to identify those needs themselves.

It is also very important not to have preconceived ideas about what employees need or want. A number of years ago, the CEO of a large public utility asked two colleagues and me to investigate what he perceived to be high turnover among professional women in his company. His own anec-dotal evidence suggested that the company was hiring professional women and investing a lot of money in their careers, and then the women were quitting their jobs in order to have children. As part of our investigation, we interviewed both men and women professionals in the company (Fine, Morrow, & Quaglieri, 1990). We discovered that the men were significantly more satisfied with their jobs than were the women. Conventional wisdom in management would suggest that the women felt that they were not being treated equally with the men and that they were unhappy because they saw fewer opportunities for promotion. The CEO believed that they were unhappy because they had to juggle work and family responsibilities.

In this case, both conventional wisdom and the CEO were wrong. The women did not think they had fewer opportunities than the men. Nor did they want help in easing their work responsibilities so that they could devote more time to their families. They were unhappy because they were not sufficiently challenged at work, and they thought that no one, male or female, had much of a future with the company. The men believed that they would replace their superiors in about five years, a time line that they thought was reasonable. The women, on the other hand, wanted to be promoted much sooner than that, and most of them indicated that they would be willing to move to another company if they were not promoted quickly. These women had succeeded in both engineering school and a male-dominated industry; they were in a hurry to move on to the next career challenge. Neither statistics comparing the promotional experiences of women and men nor organizational policies intended to give working mothers greater flexibility would make and keep them happy.

Although the company could probably do little to speed up the promotional opportunities available to professional women (public utilities typically have low turnover and long tenure), knowing why professional women were unhappy with their working conditions was a necessary first step for the company in developing policies and practices to help retain their professional women for a longer time. If a promotion to the next level was not possible, perhaps a lateral move with the opportunity to develop a set of new managerial or technical skills could be accomplished instead. The important point here is to recognize that these professional women wanted new challenges, additional responsibilities, and personal recognition—not a Mommy track. The CEO's preconceived stereotypes about women led him to assume he was losing his professional women to babies rather than boredom.

Open Discussion and Consideration of Options

Exploring new options for employees brings me to the third principle. Allowing employees to set their own agendas assumes that employers are open to discussing the items on the agenda. If employees are to feel safe when they speak, they must believe that they are free to name their own issues in their own terms, without any threat of reprisal for naming difficult issues or any fear that their voices will be ignored or silenced. The freedom to name issues does not carry the assumption that an organization will necessarily do what employees ask. It does, however, demand that the organization hear and recognize employee concerns, and that the organization make a good faith effort to meet employee needs.

Just as managers often presume to know what employees want, they also presume that particular policies or practices cannot be implemented. For example, when we were developing the needs assessment questionnaire for EPA Region I, several employees whom we interviewed voiced concerns about the availability and cost of child care. We included a question about child care, therefore, that listed several different options, including on-site daycare facilities. When senior management reviewed the questionnaire, we were asked to remove the question. I asked why and was told that the agency could not afford on-site daycare; senior management, therefore, did not want to raise employee expectations by including a question that suggested that on-site daycare was a viable option.

My colleagues and I argued that if a significant number of employees wanted on-site daycare, it was better for management to know that and to explain why on-site daycare was not viable than not to let employees name their needs. Silencing any discussion undermines an organization's efforts to create a culture of openness. If employees and managers know that certain topics are not open for discussion, then they will always question whether other topics may be similarly banned. This kind of uncertainty almost always leads to fearfulness about what is appropriate to talk about and what is not, and eventually chills all discussion in the organization.

In this particular instance, management's concern was unnecessary. Although a significant number of employees, both female and male, voiced personal concerns about child care arrangements, few indicated that they wanted the agency to have on-site daycare available for them. If a significant number had said that they wanted on-site daycare, however, management's response should have been to explore the option rather than to assume that it would be too expensive.

Just as management's assumptions about employee concerns can be incorrect, so can its assumptions about the viability of policies and practices to address those concerns. A major U.S. university recently agreed to extend health care benefits to unmarried domestic partners. The new policy was created in response to repeated requests from several gay and lesbian employees. The employees had requested the benefits several years before, but the university had refused to discuss the issue, saying that its health care insurers would not agree to implement such a policy. The university took that position, however, without actually investigating whether the insurers would agree to extend the benefits to unmarried partners, or, if they would not, what strategies might help the insurers change their minds. When university officials eventually did investigate, they discovered that the insurers were willing to extend health benefits to unmarried domestic partners.

All too often, organizational cultures incorporate an attitude that certain things cannot be done, especially about things that affect human resources. Flextime, working at home, not wearing suits or skirts, providing benefits to parttime workers—these issues are matters of organizations saying "we/you can't do/allow this" when, in fact, the organization is saying, "we won't do/allow this." Creating a multicultural organizational culture requires a new attitude, one that says all things *might* be possible. Just as employees who have multicultural literacy must be open to different modes of thinking, feeling, acting, and interpreting, multicultural organizations must be open to exploring all options and trying new ways of operating.

Create and Maintain a Code of Conduct

A multicultural organizational culture is one in which all employees feel free to be themselves. That freedom is grounded in a fundamental respect for all people. Having employees participate in training to increase their interpersonal sensitivity and multicultural literacy is important in creating respect for all people. Equally important, however, is an organizational commitment to a code of conduct that guarantees each individual's right to work in an environment that is respectful, supportive, and free from harassment.

At Lotus, for example, all employees received an electronic mail message about the unacceptability of offensive jokes. Although the message did not include a description of possible punishments, it served to make people think before telling an offensive joke. More importantly, it legitimized every individual's right to tell other employees that particular jokes are offensive. The public statement that the company would not tolerate jokes grounded in disrespect for different cultural groups and their members helped establish an organizational culture that is respectful of cultural differences.

As part of its diversity initiative, Morgan Memorial Goodwill Industries, Inc., published an Equal Opportunity Code of Behavior that was sent to all employees by the president of the organization. The Code helps employees understand "the expectations for appropriate behavior for Morgan Memorial Goodwill Industries' employees" (*Equal Opportunity Code of Behavior*, Morgan Memorial Goodwill Industries, Inc., July 10, 1991, p. 1). The Code comprises 15 statements about employee and organizational rights, responsibilities, and behavior, ranging from a statement on nondiscrimination in hiring and promotion, to an affirmation of the individual's right to speak a language other than English as long as speaking in another language does not affect his or her job performance, to a guarantee that employees may complain of unequal treatment without fear of retribution. In addition to clarifying what the organization expects of its employees, the Code also clarifies what employees can expect of the organization. Senior managers, department heads, managers, and supervisors also received a memorandum detailing a Supervisory Code of Behavior, which set out the organization's expectations for supervisors (*Equal Opportunity Code of Behavior*, Morgan Memorial Goodwill Industries, Inc., June 26, 1991). In addition to reminding supervisors that inquiries about an applicant's race, age, physical disability, religion, and so forth were not allowed, the Code affirmed the organization's commitment to providing employees a workplace that is free from harassment, and the supervisor's responsibility in meeting that commitment.

An organizational code of conduct serves as a public affirmation of the organization's culture. It tells people both inside and outside the organization what behavior is appropriate within the organization, and serves as a contract between the organization and its employees, setting out the rights and responsibilities of each. A code of conduct is a guarantee for employees of their right to be treated with respect and their responsibility to treat others with respect. It is also an enforceable document that holds the organization and its employees accountable for their behavior.

Some codes of conduct have come under public scrutiny in recent years, and many have fallen victim to charges of political correctness. Critics of conduct codes often voice concerns about the constitutionality of such codes, especially when they limit what one person can say to or about other people and their cultural groups. They also charge that codes of conduct have a chilling effect in the workplace, making people fearful of disagreeing with or criticizing others because their comments might be perceived as racist, sexist, or homophobic.

Codes of conduct, however, have long existed in organizations, although they have generally been unwritten and often unstated. People who liberally use obscenities in their workplace discourse are usually asked to control their speech; sometimes they are asked to leave the company. Employees who behave in ways that U.S. culture deems uncivil (e.g., name calling, obscene language, laughing at other people's physical characteristics, and so forth) are often reprimanded by those in positions above them. A written code of conduct makes explicit the values that are tacit in the organization or the values that the organization hopes to create. It sets the organization's standards; affirms that everyone, regardless of position in the organization, is expected to maintain those standards; and ensures that the organization and its employees are accountable for maintaining them.

Celebrate Diversity

In many ways, celebrating diversity is the easiest initiative for organizations to undertake. Having ethnic food festivals, playing the music of different cultures in the company cafeteria, sponsoring a lecture series on different cultures or an artists series that features performers from different cultures are examples of ways that companies can celebrate diversity. These celebratory efforts can represent a major investment of company funds and time (e.g., a major performance series) or they can involve very little money and effort (e.g., having employees share and display holiday greetings from around the world). Regardless of the scope of the initiative, such celebrations of diversity serve both to inform employees about cultural differences and to make them feel good about differences, including their own. Celebrating cultural diversity helps an organization create a culture of acceptance and understanding of cultural difference.

It is important, however, that organizations not focus on celebrating cultural diversity as the sole, or even primary, means of creating a multicultural organization. Celebrations of diversity are an excellent way to help people feel good about themselves and others. But feeling good about each other is not powerful or creative enough to transform organizations. Organizations need to move beyond appreciating cultural differences to incorporating those differences into organizational life. Appreciating and valuing difference is a necessary but not sufficient characteristic of multicultural organizations.

Focusing on celebrations of difference can, in fact, divert an organization's attention away from multicultural transformation. Celebrating difference can easily become a substitute for incorporating difference. Employees are led to believe that their cultural differences are appreciated because those differences are publicly acknowledged, and organizations believe that they have demonstrated their commitment to diversity for the same reason. The celebration of diversity turns into a celebration of self, and self-congratulation hides the need for self-assessment. It is relatively easy for me to tell another person that I appreciate the ways in which they differ from me. It is, perhaps, even easier for me to appreciate and enjoy the music, dance, food, and other cultural displays that represent those differences. It is quite another step for me to appreciate and value the fact that my African American coworker insists on being "in time" as we work on a project together, while I am panicking because I am certain we will not produce our final report "on time." And it is yet another step for me and the organization for which we work to respect my coworker's need to be "in time," and to value and encourage the creativity that results from doing activities that are in harmony with the rhythms of the universe.[1]

Practice What You Preach

Employee disillusionment with organizational efforts to create a culture that is accessible to everyone can quickly and powerfully undermine all personal and organizational diversity initiatives. Employees must believe that the organization is truly committed to diversity issues. Without that belief, they will develop little loyalty to the organization, and they will lack the personal will and commitment that are needed to make diversity initiatives work.

The belief that organizations are truly committed to making organizational life accessible to everyone is also central in encouraging new workers to move into careers and particular organizations in which they have been underrepresented or not represented at all. The recent exodus of women students from schools of business provides a case in point. Despite the gains realized by women in business over the past two decades, women still perceive that the business world is hostile toward them. Men still get paid more than women for the same or comparable work; sexual harassment is frequent, and sometimes tolerated by organizations as an expected part of a male and female work force; and, despite the male perception that reverse discrimination is the norm, men continue to get hired for and promoted to senior positions in far greater proportion than women.[2] Throughout the 1970s and 1980s, women enrolled in record numbers in business schools throughout the United States; in some undergraduate programs, women accounted for half of the total enrollment, and the graduate school numbers were not far behind. As young women began to realize, however, that businesses are not making a good faith effort to be more hospitable to them, they began leaving business degree programs and turning to majors in more traditional occupations, such as teaching, health care, and social services. In a recent survey, women who decided against pursuing a career in business cited a continuing pattern of discrimination in business as the primary reason why they were not enrolled in a management curriculum (Dembner, July 5, 1993).

For employees to believe that an organization is committed to diversity issues, the organization must not only preach diversity, but also practice it. On the surface that seems an obvious point. But it is one that organizations all too often overlook or ignore. Many organizations believe that a few affirmative action hires, a one-time training program, and a written statement affirming a commitment to diversity are all that is needed to fulfill their responsibilities to diversity. Although each of these is important and valuable, they are not, even together, proof of a continuing commitment to diversity.

Organizations must conduct themselves in ways that are ethically consistent with the values of a multicultural culture. They must demonstrate, both internally and externally, that they are committed to diversity issues. Internally, organizations need to hire and promote people of different cultural backgrounds, and they need to allow and encourage people to retain their differences. Employees need to see evidence of the organization's commitment to diversity. Hiring people of different backgrounds is not enough if those individuals are forced to conform to a pre-existing set of organizational norms of how work gets done. Employees also need to see that the organization rewards different ways of accomplishing work.

It is especially important that the upper echelons of an organization model what is expected of everyone else. For example, organizations can show that they are open to difference internally by appointing women and people of color to their boards of directors or other governing boards, and by making a genuine commitment to hiring women and people of color for senior positions. When the Board of Directors of Morgan Memorial Goodwill explicitly decided that the next head of the organization would be a person of color, they continued their search until they found a candidate whose qualifications and skills were exactly what the organization needed. Morgan Memorial Goodwill achieved an internal cultural transformation by appointing an African American woman to head the organization. That transformation was only possible, however, because the Board was genuinely committed to changing the organization, and the members were willing to continue their search until they had found the right person to achieve that change.

Externally, there is much that organizations can do to demonstrate their commitment to diversity. As a first step, organizations must get involved in the community. Community involvement is essential, especially involvement in activities and issues that are critical to the communities of their employees. Good citizenship is not a new business concept. Senior officials of corporations have always served on the boards of directors of nonprofit agencies and cultural organizations. U.S. corporations generally donate large amounts of money to support the arts, to provide college scholarships, or to match the charitable donations of their employees. Some companies have a long history of civic responsibility and close community ties. Demonstrating a commitment to diversity simply requires broadening the definition of civic responsibility and creating ties with multiple communities. In addition to supporting the arts and other projects that traditionally serve middle- and upper middle-class white communities, companies need to support projects, programs, and issues that focus on the concerns and needs of other communities (e.g., adult literacy programs, public schools, anticrime and violence initiatives, bilingual education efforts, drug education for school children, environmental projects, antiracism efforts, and so forth).

Broad community involvement serves multiple purposes for organizations. First, it is another public affirmation of an organization's values, especially its commitment to diversity. When an organization gives money to develop an antiracism curriculum in the public schools or sends its employees into the inner city to teach adult literacy courses, it states publicly its commitment to communities that have historically been excluded or disadvantaged in the United States. This public affirmation confirms and strengthens the multicultural culture within the organization.

Second, community involvement makes the organization and its employees visible in communities of color, thus enhancing the organization's recruiting and hiring efforts. Having an active, visible, and positive presence in the community tells community members that the organization has a genuine commitment to communities of color. That commitment is a necessary adjunct to any recruiting efforts.

Third, community involvement demonstrates that the organization recognizes the interdependence of the organization and the communities it serves. That interdependence is clearly evident as businesses determine consumer needs and desires and identify the available labor pool. It is more subtly evident, however, in the relationship between the values, attitudes, and beliefs of the organization and the values, attitudes, and beliefs of the larger community in which it is situated. Organizations cannot hope to create organizational cultures that embrace multicultural values if their employees return home each day to live in communities that embrace values that are antithetical to multiculturalism.

Beyond involvement in community activities generally, organizations can also participate with external communities to create a multicultural culture outside of the organization. Although an individual organization or business cannot eliminate racism per se in the United States, it can get involved in community projects that undermine the roots of racism. By supporting antiracism projects, education, anticrime and violence initiatives, drug education and rehabilitation projects, antipoverty programs, and a host of other activities that are aimed at allowing all Americans access to decent education, jobs, housing, and health care, organizations work toward eliminating the historical roots and current consequences of racism.

Organizations can also refuse to participate in racist practices in the community. They can drop their own memberships and request that senior managers drop their individual memberships (if the company pays for them) in country clubs and other private organizations that discriminate, either officially or in a de facto manner, against particular peoples. Or they can act assertively to change those practices. I know of one organization that successfully lobbied the membership of a private, men only club to admit women after the organization was faced with denying its first female vice president the same organizational perks that its male executives received.

Most analyses of organizations look at the organization as a closed system, and assume that organizational transformation is possible through internal change alone.[3] Such analyses ignore the historical and structural components of racism, and assume that prejudice within the organization can be eliminated without attention to the racism in the larger society, and the historical roots of that racism. Unless we pay serious attention, however, to the root causes and consequences of racism, we will never be able to transform our organizations into multicultural communities. Establishing a multicultural culture within the organization requires that organizations work to establish the same culture in the external environment.

MULTICULTURAL POLICIES AND PRACTICES

An organizational culture that is open, supportive, and flexible should give rise to organizational policies and practices that also are open, supportive, and flexible. Multicultural policies and practices are open to new people and their cultures are supportive and nurturing to all employees, and are sufficiently flexible to accommodate the needs of all employees. Multicultural policies and practices should pervade all aspects of the organization, from marketing through operations, not just human resource management. Human resources must be the starting point, however, in developing multicultural policies and practices because a multicultural work force that is multiculturally literate provides the foundation for multicultural organizational policies and practices.

Recruiting and Hiring a Multicultural Work Force

Proactive Recruiting

Organizations that want to develop a multicultural work force should continue (or implement, if they have not already done so) their proactive recruiting efforts. Although issues of cultural diversity have supplanted affirmative action concerns in organizations, the concept of proactive recruiting, which is inherent in affirmative action, is still very important. Although the population demographics in the United States have already changed dramatically, and a significant number of organizations are now reporting substantial increases in the representation of minorities in their work forces, many organizations remain primarily white and male, especially in the managerial and/or professional ranks. Women and people of color rarely hold executive positions and often are not represented in middle management. Asians tend to hold scientific or technical positions, but have difficulty being hired for or promoted to managerial positions. African Americans and Hispanics, on the other hand, have difficulty getting technical positions.

Proactive recruiting can take a variety of forms. Companies can expand their employment advertising beyond traditional outlets. In many areas of the country, for example, minority communities have their own newspapers and television stations. In Boston, many companies routinely advertise employment opportunities in the *Bay State Banner*, a local newspaper that has wide readership in communities of color. Organizations can also recruit through the networks that are most influential in particular minority communities. Organizations that are serious about recruiting African Americans, for example, need to make connections in local African American churches and community youth programs. In some instances, companies need to recruit out of their geographical location. GrandMet, for example, expanded its recruiting out of its primarily white midwestern location in order to create a pool of applicants of color.

Printing advertisements in traditional newspapers or professional journals that say "EEO/Equal Opportunity Employer" or "Women and Minorities Invited to Apply" is not enough. Proactive recruiting involves positive action, going to others rather than waiting for them to come to you.

The Boston Law Firm Group provides a good example of proactive recruiting. Boston has long had a reputation as a racist city that is inhospitable to minorities. Few professionals of color are visible in the city, and business leaders frequently complain about the difficulty of attracting minorities to jobs in Boston. Several widely publicized racial incidents in the mid-1980s worsened the prospects for recruiting minorities even more. The Law Firm Group, which is a consortium of 24 law firms in Boston, was formed in 1986 in an attempt to increase the number of minority lawyers working in Boston law firms. The group recruits minority law students, offers assistance with resume writing and interviewing, and has a mentoring program that matches Boston lawyers with first year law students. In 1985, the year before the Law Firm Group began, minorities accepted 5.8 percent of all offers made by Boston firms; in 1992, minorities accepted more than 15 percent of all offers (Kennedy, June 27, 1993).

Sometimes organizations or industries have to be even more proactive. Often the lack of representation of particular cultural groups within a profession or industry is the result of that group's lack of representation in educational programs that provide the necessary training or credentials for positions in the profession or industry. For example, colleges and universities have difficulty hiring minority faculty in many disciplines. Although the reasons for the difficulty are varied and generally complex, one fundamental reason is that there is not a sufficiently large pool of minority candidates with Ph.D.s from which to recruit. To eliminate that problem, institutions of higher education need to find ways to place more minority candidates in the academic pipeline. They could, for example, hire talented minority students who have a Master's degree, sponsor their doctoral work, and guarantee them a tenure-track position if they satisfactorily complete their doctoral degrees. Some universities have formed consortia to offer scholarships to women and/or students of color that want to pursue doctoral degrees in academic fields in which women or people of color are underrepresented. Although these programs do not provide a guarantee to the sponsoring institutions that the students will join their faculties when their degrees are completed, they do increase the pool of available candidates, thus improving recruiting efforts at all colleges and universities.

Several years ago, the Boston hotels developed an innovative program for developing minority managers, in which each member hotel identified employees of color who it believed had management potential. These employees came from the ranks of chambermaids and other jobs that are generally not considered for management positions because they lack the necessary education and training. The employees were offered management training, paid for by all the participating hotels. When they completed the training, they could be hired by any hotel in the group that had an appropriate management position available.

An important cultural issue is embedded in proactive recruiting. Members of minority cultures that have been historically excluded from traditionally white institutions are understandably suspicious of the genuineness of the invitation to apply for employment. Simply telling them that they are welcome to apply is insufficient to overcome their suspicions. In fact, the verbal invitation, whether written or oral, is often viewed as just another lie, given to meet the letter but not the spirit of the law. Companies that do not back up their words with actions to match them often find themselves having difficulty recruiting people of color.

Particular cultural groups also have expectations about how invitations are extended. For example, inviting African American students to drop by to talk with me during my office hours usually is insufficient to make them feel comfortable coming to see me. Instead, if I want them to know that I am serious about helping them, I need to set up an appointment, and when they come to see me, I need to spend a lot of time talking with them about topics that may seem very distant from their work in my course. They will not open up and talk with me about school problems until I have proven that I know something about their cultural expectations and that I am trustworthy.

Successful recruiting involves knowing and understanding the cultural expectations of the communities in which you plan to recruit. Several years ago, I attended a senior level meeting at a federal agency in which senior managers were reporting that they were not having any success recruiting young African American college graduates to the agency. They said that they were losing the young graduates to industry, where they could command significantly higher salaries than they could working for the government. The Equal Employment Opportunity officer, an older African American male, listened to the conversation for a while, then told the managers that they were using the wrong strategy. He suggested that recruiters stress the agency's mission and the contribution that the agency makes to the public good, rather than apologizing for the lower salary. African Americans have a long history of government employment, both because government positions were open to blacks long before corporate America opened its doors, and because African American culture highly values community service.

Proactive recruiting is essential for organizations that are still primarily white and male. Some organizations may believe that they do not need to recruit now because their work force will change naturally as the demographics change. Others may believe that they will be immune from the changes in the population. Both assumptions are incorrect. As the number of available workers in the United States shrinks, organizations will place a premium on talented workers of all cultural backgrounds. Workers, however, will place a premium on organizations that they perceive as open and accessible to them. Those organizations that have already hired and promoted significant numbers of culturally diverse employees and have created a multicultural environment will be more likely to recruit the best workers. Organizations that think that they can wait for change to happen may discover, when it is far too late, that the new workers don't want to work for them.

Redefining Qualifications

Redefining job qualifications can take a variety of forms, from recognizing the organizational skills inherent in raising a family and maintaining a household to reconceptualizing the job itself. Whatever form it takes, however, redefining job qualifications does not mean hiring less qualified employees; it means, instead, hiring differently qualified employees.

The most common form of redefining qualifications is recognizing nontraditional ways of acquiring particular skills. Most positions in organizations require a particular set of skills, and individual organizations and professions tend to have a fixed idea about how people acquire those skills. For example, management schools have traditionally shunned hiring faculty with either Ph.D.s outside of traditional management disciplines or Ed.D.s. The reason that is typically given is that faculty with degrees outside of management are not knowledgeable about management, even if they have studied the relevant material, have done research on management issues, or have managerial experience. Management faculty hold tightly to this requirement even though there appears to be no relationship between type of doctorate and teaching effectiveness. The issue is simply one of credentials.

Fixed concepts of appropriate education, training, or experience can both severely limit the pool of qualified applicants and exclude women and people of color. For example, companies based in one part of the country often recruit heavily at colleges and universities in their region, and, in some instances, firms show a marked preference for graduates of local schools. In Boston, for example, where higher education is one of the city's biggest businesses, firms have a tendency to recruit locally because so many college graduates are available. And given the New England elitism that favors private over public schools, graduates of private schools are generally preferred. Statistically, however, limiting recruiting to people who have degrees from Boston, or even New England, schools severely restricts the number of African Americans, Hispanics, and American Indians who will be hired. If Boston companies want to increase the pool of applicants, they need to recruit and be willing to hire people with degrees from schools outside of New England. For example, a major source of highly educated and skilled African Americans is historically black colleges that are located in the South. The issue here is not simply the ease or the cost of recruiting and hiring local graduates; local residents who have degrees from colleges and universities outside of New England also have difficulty being hired. The primary issue is the belief that New England colleges and universities are better, and graduates of those schools, therefore, are better qualified than graduates of other schools.

Expanding the definition of the education and experience that fit a particular job also should include a willingness to consider unusual qualifications. Many women who are returning to or just entering the work force after spending a number of years at home raising children argue quite convincingly that their experience at home has given them excellent organizational and interpersonal skills. Historically, women have also filled the vast majority of volunteer positions in the United States, and have been active in community, school, and religious activities. In these positions, they have acquired numerous business skills, such as fundraising, organizing events, developing and overseeing large budgets, mobilizing resources, and negotiating with different constituencies.

During the 1980s, when many Ph.D.s could not find teaching positions and elementary and secondary school teachers wanted to improve their salaries, some of them tried to get jobs in business. Many businesspeople refused to hire them, saying that teachers lacked specific management training, and telling the old joke, "Those that can, do; those that can't, teach." Yet teachers usually have excellent communication skills and are highly independent and motivated workers who are capable of taking on new and complex tasks without needing much direction. Also, individuals who have completed doctoral degrees generally have strong research, critical thinking, and decision-making skills. Businesspeople often talk about the need for workers with these skills, but fall back on preconceived ideas about the education and experience required for a job.

This tendency to adhere to rigid definitions of appropriate qualifications is especially true of people in middle management, who are typically responsible for hiring new employees. Senior executives are often more willing to be flexible about qualifications because they have broader perspectives on the skills necessary to do the actual work and they feel less constrained by organizational rules. Senior executives, however, rarely oversee hiring decisions.

This same sort of thinking also restricts employees' mobility within an organization. For example, human resource departments are known as female-friendly departments, and they are often staffed by women. Most senior women in organizations, in fact, are from the human resource function. Because human resources is a support function, however, and one that is often considered less central than other support areas in organizations, women are rarely able to make a lateral move to a central area. The typical line of succession promotes people with experience in operations, who have line authority, or people in staff positions in the financial end of the business. The conventional wisdom is that experience in human resources does not give managers a sufficient background in understanding the company and what it does. That conventional wisdom frequently limits women's promotional opportunities.

African Americans face similar promotional barriers. For example, African American males are often tapped to be the Equal Employment Opportunity or affirmative action officers in organizations, positions that carry important titles and admission to senior management meetings, but rarely include any line authority. As are positions in human resources, these positions are often an organizational deadend for the people in them.

To find senior women and people of color to appoint, organizations need to look beyond traditional career paths, ignore conventional wisdom, and promote people based on unconventional aspects of their experience, education, or training. Organizations can look at employees' activities and achievements in the community; at the skills required to do the work in their current positions, even if the work itself is not similar to the work in the position for which they are being considered; or at personal characteristics that suggest the person will be able to learn new concepts and take on new responsibilities. These individuals are no less qualified—they are just differently qualified. And, in some cases, people with different qualifications can bring new visions of how to accomplish work creatively and productively.

Redefining qualifications, however, can go well beyond recognizing nontraditional ways of acquiring the requisite skills. For some positions, organizations need to reconceptualize the qualifications and skills that are actually needed to accomplish the work. Often such reconceptualizations are based on reorganizing departments or functions; sometimes they are based on redefining or refocusing the organization's mission, objectives, or strategies. For example, if a manufacturing firm seeks to increase its market share by developing a new market among Hispanic consumers, it will need employees working in new product development and marketing who are knowledgeable about Hispanic culture. Once that strategy has been set by the company, the qualifications for some positions in product management or marketing must change. I am not suggesting that certain positions be reserved for members of particular cultural groups, or that, in this example, a non-Hispanic would be incapable of doing the work. I am suggesting, rather, that knowledge of Hispanic culture is necessary to accomplish the work. All things being equal, an Hispanic applicant may be more qualified for the position than a non-Hispanic.[4]

Certain types of positions traditionally have been envisioned in terms of a set of behaviors, skills, and expertise that are within the domain of white male culture. Several years ago I worked with a nonprofit agency that sought to improve the quality of life of public housing residents by making economic and social services available to them. The agency had just undergone a major organizational restructuring in response to the loss of state funding, dividing the staff into teams that worked with all developments instead of assigning individual field staff to each public housing development. Each team was assigned a particular function, such as education and training. The reorganization moved the staff from a working environment in which staff members were autonomous in their day to day activities and accountable directly to the residents of the development in which they were assigned, to one in which team members had to coordinate their own work and their team's activities with the activities of the other teams.

The shift to a team model of organizing proved problematic for the agency, primarily because everyone in the organization (board members, the director, managers, and staff) had difficulty revising employee work roles. Several months after the reorganization, the agency's fund raiser resigned. Prior to the reorganization, the agency had decided to expand its fund-raising activities. Because virtually all of the agency's funding came from either state and local government contracts or public and private grants, the Board wanted to add an individual donor component to the agency's fund-raising strategy. To strengthen the fund-raising efforts, the Board also decided to add a second fund-raising position. The resignation of the current fund-raiser created an opportunity for the staff to re-vision the fund-raising function in light of the new organizational structure, and to develop job descriptions for the two fund-raising positions.

I worked with the staff to help them articulate their expectations for a development team, a position description for the senior member of the team, and their vision of the kind of person who would best fit the organization and the position. The primarily female staff was racially mixed, about half white and half African American, with one Latina and one Asian American. The group began by describing its image of a traditional development person: A white male with a college degree, wearing a suit and tie, who met with corporate executives who looked just like him. That image was rooted in a set of expectations about the work that needed to be done and how it should be done. For example, the staff envisioned the development person working closely with corporations or wealthy individuals to solicit donations. The group assumed that the senior person would work on establishing the individual donor program and the second person, when the position was authorized, would be responsible for writing grants and contracts. In the interim, of course, the senior person would do both. The staff members believed that people in the corporate world would only meet with individuals who fit into that world, people who wore suits, spoke proper English, and maintained a properly reserved demeanor. They also described the development function in the organization as independent, with the senior development person reporting directly to the director and the board, the second person reporting to the senior person, and the development team having no direct lines of authority or responsibility to the other teams or the public housing residents.

We then talked about how well that model of a development team and its personnel would fit the agency's mission and structure. They all agreed that it did not. The agency's mission is to empower public housing residents to improve the quality of their own lives, and the agency is committed to meeting that mission by ensuring that residents define their own needs and set their own agendas for action. The new development function in the agency needed to be coordinated with that mission and commitment, so that all fund-raising efforts would be guided by the residents' agendas. The development staff, then, would need to spend a lot of time with the residents, and would, therefore, need to be able to talk their talk, understand and identify with their concerns, and then make those concerns vivid and real for potential donors. In addition, since the agency was now organized into teams that worked to support each other's efforts, the development function would need to be integrated into that structure. Clear lines of responsibility and accountability had to be established between the development staff, the other teams, the residents, and the director and board members.

Although the development person the agency hired would be required to have access to the oral and written discourse of the white corporate world, she or he also needed access to the discourse and experience of public housing residents and to potential donors and businesses in minority communities. That person also needed to work as part of a team, and to have the skills and personal characteristics that put teamwork and accountability to others ahead of competitiveness and individual performance. Once the staff understood the requirements of the work that the agency needed to accomplish, it was able to put aside its assumptions about how fund raisers look and act, and to imagine hiring someone who looked and acted quite differently.

Supervision and Evaluation

As I stated previously, having a culturally diverse work force does not guarantee that an organization will have a multicultural culture. Creating that culture also requires supervision and evaluation practices and policies that accommodate and nurture cultural differences.

Culturally Appropriate Supervision

All employees need supervision, but the degree and kind of attention they need varies by the individual. Supervisors who provide culturally appropriate supervision are able to both motivate individual employees by using culturally specific incentives and create cohesive and productive teamwork among culturally diverse employees.

Culturally appropriate supervision bears little resemblance to the traditional concept of supervision, which is defined as directing and inspecting the work of employees. In culturally appropriate supervision, the supervisor's role is neither to ensure rigid conformance to established modes of doing work nor to create employees in the supervisor's image. Instead, the supervisor's task is to provide the environment and resources that all of his or her employees need to be fully productive members of the organization. Culturally appropriate supervision empowers employees, enlarging instead of constraining their modes of working. Managers serve rather than supervise their employees:[5] They are used by or are of use to their employees rather than vice versa.

Providing culturally appropriate supervision requires training in both multicultural literacy and management as service. To create culturally diverse work teams, managers must recognize and value diverse work styles, problem-solving strategies, ways of learning and knowing, and opinions about problems and solutions. To learn how to recognize and value diversity, managers need to learn about different cultures and how to ask questions when they encounter new cultures or behaviors they do not know how to interpret. They also need to explore the implications of viewing supervision as service rather than direction.

Asking questions, serving others, and being sensitive to nuances of difference in the behavior and demeanor of others are all part of a process of decentering the self and making others the central focus. That process dramatically alters the task of managing, and suggests a new and very different picture of the skills and personal characteristics of good managers. Traditionally, organizations have valued and rewarded individual initiative and individual achievement. Individuals who are identified as "comers" in the organization are promoted to managerial positions; they stand out because they combine technical expertise with personal drive and motivation. Those qualities, however, make them self-centered and focused on their own achievements, characteristics that undermine their ability to manage a culturally diverse work force. Managers, therefore, need to learn how to readjust their lenses and focus on others rather than themselves.

In addition to ensuring that managers receive appropriate training, organizations also need to develop reward systems that reward managers for their new roles. Performance appraisals should include an evaluation of a manager's ability to create culturally diverse teams and to motivate culturally diverse employees. In making that evaluation, evaluators need to gather information from team members. The productivity of the team as a whole and the job satisfaction of individual team members are important indicators of how well a manager is serving the team.

Culturally Specific Assessments of Behavior

Successful reward systems in organizations depend, to a large extent, on fair and appropriate assessments of behavior. In a culturally diverse organization, fair assessments of an employee's behavior must be culturally specific; in other words, the assessments should be based on interpretations of the behavior that are within the employee's cultural frame. For example, an Asian worker who speaks softly should not be identified as shy or lacking in leadership qualities. Asians are usually soft spoken, but that vocal quality reflects their cultural upbringing rather than their sociability or leadership abilities.

Culturally specific assessments of behavior are not only based on identifying the appropriate cultural frame for interpreting the behavior, they also depend on identifying and defining the required behaviors. Managers need to define clearly the attributes they value in workers, and to question their tacit assumptions about those attributes. For example, good communication skills are almost always at the top of the list of requisite skills for managers. When I ask managers what they mean by good communication skills, they usually say they mean the ability to speak or write well, or to talk to other people one-on-one. Those definitions, however, are circular; they do not specify the particular communicative behaviors that make up good communication. Without a clear definition of the specific behaviors involved in good communication, the assessment category can become an excuse to screen out people who are different.

Several years ago, in a organizational training session with managers on communicating across gender and race, I asked the participants to describe the communication skills of good managers. Later in the session, participants were asked to describe how men and women communicate. When the individual lists were combined to create a composite sketch of male and female communication characteristics, the participants were surprised to discover that the list of female characteristics was virtually identical to the earlier list they had created describing the communication skills of good managers. The group was quiet for a moment, until a male manager asked, "If women have better communication skills, then why do we promote so few women to management positions?"

One part of the answer to that question is that managers often do not specify the behavioral characteristics of good communicators. Instead, evaluation forms usually include the global category, "communication skills," and the assessment of "good" communication skills generally gets attached to white males. Having evaluators deconstruct the global category and define clearly the specific behaviors that compose the category often causes them to question tacit assumptions about who performs well and who does not.

Another way to raise questions about tacit assumptions about job performance is to ask a wider range of people to evaluate an individual's performance. A multicultural team is likely to bring together different understandings of an employee's performance, creating a fuller and more accurate assessment.

Outcome-based Evaluation

Americans expect performance appraisal systems and other evaluation measures to be unbiased. Unbiased in this context means that the evaluation is based on an objective definition of the skill that is being measured, and an objective description of the actual behavior that is being observed. Objective definitions and descriptions should lead to the same performance evaluation regardless of the person's gender or race. We are all familiar, however, with examples of evaluations that are not unbiased. The woman who asks for a raise after six months on the job is aggressive; her male counterpart is assertive. Identifying the gender bias in such evaluations is both admirable and necessary.

Unbiased evaluations, while often necessary, are not sufficient to ensure appropriate evaluation systems in a multicultural organization. In fact, such evaluations can undermine efforts to create a multicultural organizational culture if people in the organization always focus on valuing behavioral similarities rather than differences.

One method for developing objective performance evaluations that respect cultural differences among employees is to evaluate outcomes rather than the means that were used to achieve the outcomes. Different work styles can lead to the same outcomes. For example, an Asian executive in a Fortune 500 company was faulted by his superiors for setting vague performance objectives for his employees. At the end of the year, however, his division had achieved better than expected production. Although the performance objectives that he set with his employees were not as specific as management textbooks suggest they should be, they did not impair his division's productivity. It is impossible to know if the employees were productive as a consequence of having more amorphous objectives or in spite of them. Regardless, productivity was high and the employees were happy. Both superiors and subordinates gave the executive high marks based on outcomes.

A culturally diverse work force will include employees with a wide variety of work styles. The multicultural organization values that diversity and uses evaluation procedures that recognize, validate, and reward differences in work styles. At the same time, the multicultural organization refuses to tolerate evaluations that reflect unquestioned biases about gender and race rather than objective definitions and measurements of behavior.

Development and Support

Organizations need to develop and support a multicultural work force, providing both career development opportunities and social and emotional support for employees. I have put career development and social/emotional support together because they are interdependent activities. The psychological well-being of employees is often affected by whether they believe that they can develop professionally in the organization. Employees who believe that they are at a professional deadend in an organization generally lose interest in and commitment to their jobs. Conversely, their professional success depends on their ability to cope with the social and emotional stresses of organizational life.

While this interdependence of professional development and social/emotional support is true for all employees, it is especially significant for employees who have historically been excluded from organizational life. Traditional professional development opportunities in organizations favor white males, and women and people of color face additional stress in the workplace based on their cultural differences. The combination of the lack of professional opportunities and the additional job stress intensifies the pressures on women and people of color, often deadening their creativity and diminishing their productivity, and sometimes driving them out of organizational life.[6]

Career Development

Most organizations provide little support in the area of career development for any employees. Career development opportunities usually comprise a few management training courses and some general or technical skills courses (e.g., public speaking, writing, computer applications, sales, new accounting procedures). A few large organizations have succession planning programs in place, but these provide opportunities for only a few senior personnel in the organization. A full range of career development offerings might include providing information about careers in general and specific jobs that are available in the company, offering employees different career tracks and opportunities to move to new jobs, access to mentoring relationships, support for education and training generally, and special training programs.

Although all employees, regardless of gender or race, should have access to career development programs and can benefit significantly from them, women and people of color have particular needs and can reap particular benefits from them.

Support for career development begins with providing information about careers, both generically and more specifically within the organization. Most people have a fairly narrow range of vision about the career opportunities they have, and they rarely think beyond their next move, which is usually seen as a step up the organizational ladder from their current position. All employees need to be able to expand their vision, and to think more broadly about the possibilities they have based on their skills and interests.

Being able to envision one's self in a different job or a new career path depends in large part on an individual's knowledge of the new job. Many people gain that knowledge through the people we know personally: Through families, friends, communities, and work. Women and people of color often lack access to that knowledge because either they encounter few professionals or business people in their families and communities, or they have been socialized into particular career and job expectations. Organizations can expand the opportunities available to women and people of color simply by developing a resource library with information about particular jobs and careers. Having human resource staff available who can provide advice about preparation for particular jobs or careers, resume writing, interviewing, and other career skills would be even more helpful.

In addition to providing information and advice, organizations can expand the career opportunities of women and people of color by developing new career paths within the organization that include lateral moves and different career tracks. Traditional career paths in organizations tend to mirror the hierarchical assumptions of male patterns of thinking and organizing. Success is defined in terms of moving up the organizational ladder. The next step on the ladder is usually occupied by the person above you on the organizational chart, and at some point in the ascent, the steps shift from technical to managerial.

Other organizational moves are necessary, however, to ensure that women and people of color have adequate opportunities for professional growth and personal success. Just as women are often socialized into particular careers (e.g., teaching, social work, and nursing), women and people of color are often pigeonholed into particular places in organizations. Human resources, as was mentioned, is sometimes characterized as an organizational ghetto for women. Breaking out of the ghetto requires that women develop expertise in other areas of the organization, especially functional rather than support areas. A lateral move to a different department could be helpful in gaining the necessary knowledge and experience to fashion a new and more rewarding career path.

Other alternative career paths are also helpful in attracting and retaining diverse workers. I mentioned in Chapter 4 that Felice Schwartz (Jan./Feb. 1989) created a furor several years ago when she recommended that organizations develop a Mommy track for women who wanted to put their careers on hold while their children were young. Acknowledging that organizations demanded and deserved the fulltime attention and work of fast-track employees, Schwartz suggested that women who wanted to devote time to their children and families could choose to get off the fast-track and onto the Mommy track. Such a move would most likely take them out of the running for senior positions in the organization, but would keep the women professionally productive and protect the company's investment in them.

Schwartz's critics argued that a Mommy track was sexist because it both singled out women as responsible for child-rearing and relegated them to subordinate positions in organizations. Although the criticisms are valid, the concept has merit. Rather than a Mommy track, however, organizations might consider offering employees a variety of career tracks as options. For example, women or men could choose more flexible job configurations that would give them more time at home with young children or ill family members or to devote to community service. Although assuming that women should be responsible for raising children is sexist, recognizing the reality that women usually take on that responsibility (along with the responsibility of caring for elderly parents) is pragmatic. Organizations that offer women options such as flextime, job sharing, and shorter work weeks enhance their ability to attract and retain women employees.

The Mommy track concept also opens the door to other career tracks. For example, not all employees who have technical expertise in their professional fields (e.g., accounting, engineering, science, information systems) want to move into managerial positions. Yet unless they do, their careers tend to stall out, leaving them with no opportunities to receive organizational rewards and no incentives to improve their skills. Professional/technical career tracks would give employees who want to continue to specialize in their technical areas the opportunity to advance their careers without taking on managerial responsibilities.

I am not suggesting that all women and people of color need or want alternative career tracks, nor am I suggesting that employees who choose these options will always have the same opportunities to showcase their talents that employees in more conventional positions generally have. I am only saying that organizations that offer a variety of career tracks will be better able to support a diverse work force, including white males.

Special training programs offer organizations another way to improve the career opportunities for women and people of color. Training is an essential part of any organization's efforts to develop its human resources. All employees need to improve and update the skills required to do their jobs and to develop new skills that will allow them to take on different responsibilities. Training programs also carry symbolic importance. Because training costs money, both in terms of the cost of training per se and the opportunity cost of lost time on the job, employees view training as a sign that the organization values them. That symbolism can have dramatic pay-offs in improved productivity and job satisfaction.

Training plays a special role, however, in career development for women and people of color. Training programs offer organizations an ideal way to develop and promote talented women and people of color from within the organization. For example, although more and more women are entering organizations in the middle ranks, women still are clustered in lower-level positions, especially in the clerical ranks. By offering special training programs designed to help clerical workers develop managerial or other technical skills, organizations can create a new pool of skilled, loyal, and committed workers. Linking the training to a new job enhances its effectiveness in encouraging women (and men) to move up in the organization.

Special training programs can also be used to meet the unique career development needs of different cultural groups, such as improving the oral and written English skills of workers for whom English is a second language, many of whom are people of color, or to accommodate people with different learning styles. Women, for example, often do better in classes and workshops that are restricted to women. Women's public voices have been silenced for so long that few women feel sufficiently empowered or safe to speak up in mixed gender groups. Women's reluctance to speak in front of men is particularly powerful for those women, such as secretaries, who were socialized into traditional gender roles. Studies show that women and men have different learning styles. Women tend to learn best in environments that are cooperative and collaborative, rather than competitive, and that emphasize experiential learning (Belenky et al., 1986).

The purpose of tailoring training to the unique needs of particular cultural groups is not to protect people from interacting with others who are unlike themselves, nor is it to encourage the segregation and isolation of particular groups. Its purpose is to create spaces where people can do their best learning, so that when they enter (or re-enter) a more diverse environment where they will have to cooperate and compete with men and women who are different from themselves, they will have the confidence and skills to do so.

Mentoring is another aspect of career development that is important for the success of women and people of color. A mentor is an experienced manager who relates well to a less experienced employee and facilitates the personal development of that employee (Kram, 1985). Mentoring relationships usually develop informally in organizations, most often between individuals who are drawn together because they share a common background or interests. Mentors serve a variety of functions for their protégés, both aiding them in their career development and supporting them interpersonally (Noe, 1988). Mentors may sponsor their protégés for new positions or assignments, give them visibility in the organization, coach them on their managerial skills, protect them from organizational politics, or just be available for informal discussions about their work or personal lives. Mentors also serve as role models, helping less experienced employees learn how to negotiate organizational life.

Although all employees benefit from mentoring, women and people of color often need mentoring to a greater extent than do white men. They especially need mentors who can serve as role models. Some women, for example, need mentors who will help them overcome sex-role stereotypes. People of color, particularly African Americans, need mentors who can show them how to deal with the subtle (and sometimes not so subtle) racism that pervades most organizations in the United States.

Despite their greater need, women and people of color often have difficulty finding mentors. Organizational studies show that people generally feel most comfortable with members of their own sex and/or race. Since most mentoring relationships develop spontaneously between people who feel a natural affinity toward each other, they are usually same-sex or same-race relationships. The paucity of women and people of color in senior positions substantially decreases the likelihood that women and people of color will informally find mentors.

Even when women and people of color try to cross gender and racial boundaries in establishing mentoring relationships, several other factors decrease the chances that they will be mentored. First, they tend to be outside of the informal organizational networks where mentors are available. They are not likely to be playing golf, tennis, or squash at the same clubs as more senior white males, nor are they likely to be asked to have drinks with a group of senior managers after working hours. Second, women and people of color are less likely to be identified as a "rising star" in the organization. Just as protégés seek mentors who have access to power and organizational resources, mentors look for protégés who have the potential to make the mentor's star shine even brighter.

Finally, women and people of color are less likely to ask senior managers to help them, yet implicit in a mentoring relationship is a call for help—and one for which there is generally no quid pro quo. African Americans are unlikely to reveal any professional or personal vulnerabilities to whites. Many Asians are reserved in their relationships with coworkers, and highly deferential toward senior managers. They also tend to avoid engaging in self-promotion. Many women also dislike self-promotion, and find it difficult to ask for personal favors, especially from men. Many years ago, a male mentor told me that, in his experience in organizations, men tended to be more successful than women because they were willing to ask even total strangers for favors. He said that women did not seem to understand the "ethics" of asking for favors. Rather than expecting some sort of quid pro quo, men do not expect the other person to return the favor, at least not directly to them. Instead, they assume that the person who asked for and received the favor would someday extend the same courtesy to someone else. While his analysis does not fully account for the disparities between men and women in organizations, his characterization of women's reluctance to ask for favors is consonant with my own experience and that of other women who have discussed this issue with me.

Organizations can create opportunities for women and people of color to find mentors through formal mentoring programs. Although the concept of a *formal* mentoring program is somewhat of an oxymoron (since mentoring relationships are usually spontaneous and informal), formal mentoring programs can work. For such programs to be successful, however, organizations must adequately prepare participants and must create structural changes that encourage mentoring (Burke & McKeen, 1988). First, both mentors and their protégés need to participate in training programs that allow them to learn about mentoring and to explore their respective roles as mentors and protégés. Second, the reward system needs to be changed to include rewards for successfully mentoring less experienced employees; concomitantly, the performance appraisal system should be revised to include evaluations of an employee's performance as either (or both) mentor and protégé. Third, organizations need to create new job designs that encourage more frequent and meaningful interaction among junior and senior employees. In addition to these structural changes, companies need to develop a pool of qualified and trained mentors and to match mentors and protégés carefully. In some cases, organizations may need to look externally for suitable mentors.

Social/Emotional Support

Having a social support network is fundamental to the psychological health of most individuals. Although our closest interpersonal relationships are usually with family members or friends outside of the workplace, most of us enjoy personal friendships with at least a few coworkers and friendly acquaintanceships with others. These relationships give us places to go at work where we can be ourselves without being afraid that a moment of vulnerability, or a comment made in anger or jest, will be used against us.

Many women and people of color either do not have the opportunity to establish such friendships or cannot afford the luxury of trusting others in the organization, although the stress created by their numerical isolation and cultural differences heightens their need for interpersonal support. Women and people of color need to have opportunities at work to be with others who are like themselves and who will allow them to be themselves. They need to talk with other people who can help them do some reality testing so that they can distinguish discrimination and racism from the ordinary hurdles everyone in an organization encounters and endures.

Organizations can help women and people of color cope with the stress of being different by encouraging and supporting both informal and formal social networking. Networks can range from informal lunchtime groups to more structured, formal bodies, such as a women's caucus that carries the imprimatur of the company. Both kinds of network provide needed social and emotional support for women and people of color. More formal structures can also give them a voice in the organization and provide management a way to gather information about their needs and concerns.

Social networks that include only members of a particular cultural group can, however, create tensions within the organization. Employees who are not part of these networks often view them with ridicule or suspicion, and, in some cases, fear. This reaction is often the strongest in response to informal networking. Whites often complain that African Americans sit together for meals in the cafeteria; I have heard my white students say that it's not right that black students won't invite others to join them, or U.S. students accuse foreign students of being cliquey. Male faculty members in my college became very angry when women faculty decided to hold an informal potluck supper for women only. The men demanded to know what we were plotting.

One way to dissipate these tensions is to create safe places, or sanctuaries, where employees of different racial and cultural backgrounds can come together and work out their conflicts. Cultural conflict is a natural part of any interaction among culturally different people, and it must be acknowledged and confronted in organizations. As long as the conflict remains unvoiced, it will fester underneath the surface, creating tension among employees and making it difficult for people to work together productively. Although some of the tension arises out of real conflicts over values, attitudes, or behaviors, much of it is the result of a lack of knowledge and understanding about other people. The more opportunities people have to get together with people who are different, the more knowledgeable they will become about each other, and the more sensitive they will become about others. Understanding some differences helps people recognize the importance of questioning their assumptions about everyone and asking questions before they make judgments.

Digital's original Core Groups serve as a model of such sanctuaries. The Core Groups comprise employees of varied cultural backgrounds who meet on a continuing basis to explore their cultural differences. The groups are formed voluntarily, and over time, as the members discover more about and learn to trust each other, they become safe havens where people are free to work out their personal conflicts.

THE POLITICS OF INCLUSION

Although the purpose of the organizational strategies that I have outlined in this chapter is to create organizations that respect and nurture differences among employees and are inclusive of all employees, implementing these strategies can lead to charges of reverse discrimination. Sometimes those charges are justified. Maternity leave policies that do not recognize that fathers, too, need time at home with newly born or newly adopted children discriminate against men. The Mommy track concept assumes that only women need or want to cut back on their work hours in order to spend more time at home raising their children. Policies and practices that extend privileges to some employees but not others who also need or want them are discriminatory. More often, however, charges of reverse discrimination are the product of white male fears—fear of loss of power and privilege, fear of being marginalized, fear of exclusion.

Those fears are not irrational. They are based on the perception that organizations have a fixed number of resources (e.g., positions, promotions, salary increases) at any given time, and that as the workplace becomes more diverse, fewer of those resources will go to white men. That perception is generally accurate. With fewer white men and more white women and people of color in the work force as a whole, the mathematics suggest that white women and people of color will begin to receive more of the resources than they have in the past. That is the reality of diversity.

All things being equal, however, an individual white male has the same statistical probability of receiving a particular set of resources in the diverse work force as he did in the homogeneous work force. What has changed is not the opportunity for resources, but the color and gender of those who are competing for the resources. The change in the color and gender of the competition is significant, however, not because it changes the odds, but because it changes the perceptual frame in which the participants give meaning to the odds.

When people compete, they need to account for their successes and failures. Those accounts are socially constructed explanations of the situation that are considered reasonable and acceptable, both to ourselves and to others. When we fail, we tend to look for something in the situation or in other people that led to our failure, rather than identifying the cause within ourselves (at least in our public accounts). When a white male competes with another white male for a promotion, and the other man is promoted, he can say that the other man had "friends in the right places" and no one will raise an eyebrow. When a white male competes with an African American male for a promotion, however, and the African American is promoted, the public accounting that he "had friends in the right places" is not likely to be considered a reasonable explanation. On the other hand, the white male's public accounting that he was the victim of affirmative action is socially reasonable and acceptable, at least among other white men. In this instance, the charge of reverse discrimination is not irrational, but it is unwarranted.

The claim of being victimized by affirmative action gains greater credence through a complex web of associations. The stereotypes of African Americans in the United States that result from the "different equals deficient" perspective help to perpetuate the myth that African Americans who are hired and promoted are inferior to the white candidates who were not. The stereotypes are often accorded false credibility based on culturally biased measures of evaluation, such as standardized tests or traditional concepts of appropriate training and experience. Newspapers and magazines are replete with stories about firefighters, police, college applicants, or others who are outraged that an African American (or other minority candidate) was selected over them, even though they had higher test scores. That the scores reflect a bias in favor of members of the majority culture is usually left out of the stories, as is the reminder that such tests usually have a range of scores that are acceptable for demonstrating competence.

The stereotypes also get reinforced when organizations do hire less qualified affirmative action candidates (something that happens infrequently, organizational mythology to the contrary). Sometimes organizations hire less qualified candidates because they genuinely misunderstand affirmative action policies; other times it is an attempt to undermine the policies by creating a self-fulfilling prophecy. Some people felt that former President Bush did this when he nominated Clarence Thomas to the Supreme Court. And sometimes organizations hire affirmative action candidates who are less qualified than their white male competitors, but are nonetheless fully qualified to do the job. The fact that they are less qualified, however, usually is translated as *un*qualified.

Further complicating the charge of reverse discrimination, of course, is that all things are not equal, and when they are not, white male fears are more difficult to allay. If some new job descriptions include knowledge, skills, or personal characteristics generally outside of the domain of white males, white men will be at a disadvantage in competing for those jobs. If groups that historically have been marginalized in the workplace are now given space in the center, white men need not be marginalized, but they will have to share their space with others. Sharing once exclusive privileges can feel very much like being marginalized.

The sense of loss that white males feel and their fears about their lack of opportunities in the new workplace are very real. One of my colleagues recounted a conversation with a talented male associate who was genuinely reluctant to apply for positions that would move him to the next level of responsibility. He felt certain that these jobs would go to women and people of color, even though he was aware that the recent hiring statistics in his field showed that 75 percent of the positions had gone to white males.

Although it is important to ensure that white males have accurate information about work force diversity and the ways organizations are changing to incorporate that diversity, it is equally important to acknowledge their feelings and give them opportunities to voice them. A multicultural perspective is open to all ways of understanding the world, and a multicultural organization attempts to be inclusive of all peoples. To include new voices in the workplace by marginalizing others violates the ethical principles of multiculturalism.

It is also important to avoid white male bashing. As noted in Chapter 6, the discourse of oppression that tends to permeate discussions of multiculturalism is replete with examples of the horrors done to women and people of color by white men. Those horrors are very real, and I do not mean to trivialize them, but the social, economic, political, and cultural causes of oppression are far too complex to reduce to the evil intentions of white men. Further, conclusions about white men in general have little to do with the particular white men in an organization.

As organizations develop and implement diversity initiatives, they need to frame their discourses in terms of the ways in which new organizational policies and practices improve the workplace for everyone. White men have paid an enormous personal price for organizational success. They have had to suppress their ethnic identities, put their work ahead of their families, and maintain rigid control over expressing their emotions. Organizations can recognize and validate the experiences of white males, just as they recognize and validate the experiences of women and people of color.

As organizations practice the politics of inclusion, however, it is important that the fears of white men not dominate the discourse or control the agenda for change. Many women have attended all-female gatherings designed to ensure that they be heard, only to discover that the lone male in attendance set the agenda and dominated the discussion. The centering of white male experience so pervades and dominates the culture that it is often difficult for white men to move away from the center and for white women and people of color to move into it. Organizations need to guard against having their concerns about charges of reverse discrimination and white male bashing become the focus of their diversity initiatives, while at the same time fully acknowledging the legitimacy of those concerns. Practicing the politics of inclusion is a difficult balancing act, but one that is critical to the success of any organizational efforts to develop and nurture a multicultural work force.

NOTES

1. I do not mean to ignore or trivialize the tension that exists in this example between the concepts of "being in time" and "being on time." Organizations are pragmatic, goal-oriented entities. Unquestionably, much of the United States' economic success has been the product of our understanding the importance of and our adherence to certain values embedded in the Protestant work ethic, including doing our work "on time." But our respect for and commitment to certain values have caused us to ignore, and even deny, the worth of other values and other modes

of being. The very values that have allowed us to lead the industrialized world through most of the twentieth century have blinded us to the possibilities for change that are needed to sustain our economy in the twenty-first century. There is no easy answer to resolving the tensions inherent in "being in time" and "being on time." Although difficult, looking at those tensions may open our eyes to new possibilities.

2. The white male argument that affirmative action policies have led to reverse discrimination is an interesting case of the credence of perception over reality. Although there are individual instances in which a white woman or person of color has been hired or promoted instead of a white man, the overall statistics on hiring and promotion suggest that white men are still favored. The individual instances of preference for affirmative action candidates (even when the woman or person of color is *more* qualified than the white male) coupled with the pervasive talk about affirmative action policies, both public and private, have created a perception of reverse discrimination that has become embedded as reality in the public consciousness. The power of that perception became strikingly apparent to me several years ago when I was interviewing a group of white male managers in a large organization about affirmative action. When I asked them if they thought that women and people of color had equal opportunities with white men for promotion to management, the male managers said that women and people of color had more opportunities. They told me that all of the promotions to manager in the past year had gone to women and people of color. When I checked their perception against the actual promotions, I was surprised to discover that the majority of managerial promotions had gone to white men. Even more surprising, the organization had no managers of color.

3. For example, Cox (1991) offers one of the most fully articulated descriptions of a multicultural organization and suggests an extensive taxonomy of tools for creating it. The tools include a wide variety of training programs and seminars, changes in human resources policies and practices, the inclusion of diversity as part of the company's mission statement, and diverse representation on key organizational committees. None of these tools is external to the organization. Yet Cox defines a multicultural organization as having no prejudice or discrimination against minority group members. His model is comforting, but very misleading. People's lives are not completely circumscribed by work and their activities in the workplace. Eliminating prejudice and discrimination requires more than internal organizational efforts. Fernandez (1975) takes what I believe is a more realistic perspective than Cox. Fernandez studied black managers and concluded that racism is the primary factor hindering black managers from full participation in corporations. Although Fernandez provides an extensive analysis of the varied forms of corporate racism, he cautions that all problems cannot be solved in the corporate context, and he says that society as a whole has to deal with its racial problems.

4. Not all individuals who have Hispanic backgrounds and who are legally considered Hispanic in the United States are knowledgeable about Hispanic cultures. Cultural identity is complex, and not determined solely, or even primarily, by one's racial, ethnic, or national origins. Cultural groups, in fact, have unflattering names for members who do not identify culturally with the group. African Americans refer to blacks who identify culturally with whites as "Oreos" (black on the outside but white inside), while Asian Americans use the term "banana" to

describe Asians who are yellow on the outside and white inside. Both terms are intended to be derogatory. I do not mean to suggest anything derogatory about individuals who are not culturally knowledgeable about their racial, ethnic, or national origins. My point is only that being Hispanic (or African American or Asian) does not ensure that an individual is knowledgeable about the culture, and, therefore, more qualified for jobs requiring that knowledge.

5. I am grateful to Linda Putnam for suggesting the use of service in this context. Although we were discussing leadership in organizations rather than supervision of employees, the metaphor works well to define both the relationship between supervisor and employee and the role of the supervisor.

6. Numerous articles have been written about the number of women who have abandoned corporate careers in order to start their own small businesses (see, for example, Taylor, Aug. 18, 1986). In recent years, the growth in small businesses owned by women has been phenomenal, far surpassing the growth in male-owned businesses. From 1982 to 1987, the number of women-owned firms increased 57 percent, from 2.6 million to 4.1 million. The growth in sales and receipts was even more dramatic, increasing 183 percent, from $98 million to $278 million (U.S. Bureau of the Census, 1992, p. 527). Women who go into business for themselves tend to start home-based businesses, in which they offer professional services or manufacture and/or sell specialized products, such as cosmetics or handmade clothing. These women generally have a litany of complaints about life in the corporate world: Job discrimination, sexual harassment, few opportunities for job advancement, rigid corporate policies, and long working hours away from their families. Unlike many male entrepreneurs, who seem to thrive on the uncertainty, riskiness, and potential financial rewards of new business ventures, many women who start small businesses are seeking greater control over their lives and more modest lifestyles.

Large numbers of Asian immigrants, especially Koreans, also choose to start their own small businesses rather than attempt to get jobs in large organizations. While minority ownership of businesses increased 64 percent and sales increased 126 percent among all minorities in the United States from 1982 to 1987, the increases were substantially larger among Asians (89 percent and 162 percent respectively)(*Survey of Minority-Owned Business Enterprises*, 1991, p. 2). Immigrants who have gone into business for themselves frequently cite prejudice and discrimination in organizations as the primary reasons for starting their own businesses. Small neighborhood businesses, such as grocery stores, dry cleaning shops, and household cleaning services, allow immigrant families to work together and provide goods and services for other immigrants in their neighborhoods, effectively shielding them from the prejudice in the larger community. Of course, localized racial and ethnic rivalries still flare up, such as the conflicts between Hasidic Jews and African Americans in Brooklyn, New York, and Korean merchants and African Americans in South Central Los Angeles. Even working for yourself is no guarantee that prejudice won't rear its ugly head.

EPILOGUE:
THE PARADOX OF
DIFFERENCE

We end where we began: Envisioning and re-visioning organizations in a culturally diverse society. In Chapter 2, I characterized multicultural organizations as ones that:

1. Value, encourage, and affirm diverse cultural modes of being and interacting;
2. create an organizational dialogue in which no one cultural perspective is presumed to be more valid than other perspectives; and
3. empower all cultural voices to participate fully in setting goals and making decisions.

A truly multicultural organization must do all of these things. As Kochman (1981) says, cultural pluralism is an *impotent* concept in American society if it only acknowledges cultural differences without also incorporating those differences into the social and political system (p. 62). Cultural diversity is equally impotent in organizations unless diverse voices and perspectives can share equally in organizational decision-making and are represented in organizational policies and practices.

Envisioning organizations that both acknowledge and incorporate differences is difficult. Much of what defines such organizations is attitude. Multicultural organizations require an attitude of openness and flexibility, within both workers and the organization itself. The key personal and organizational characteristics that guide multicultural organizations are adaptability, fluidity, and open-mindedness. Achieving these characteristics requires the following two things, at a minimum.

First, individuals need to develop multicultural literacy. They must be willing to learn about cultures other than their own, and in their discourse and work with each other, they need to check for the cultural biases in their responses to each other and to ask questions to ensure that they are correctly interpreting the other person's words or actions. Managers need to be sensitive to cultural differences among employees. They need to learn how to encourage multiple ways of analyzing problems and accomplishing work.

Second, organizations need to develop flexible policies and systems that can respond quickly to differences among employees. The organizational perspective must shift from objectivity to subjectivity, recognizing the integrity of different cultural perspectives rather than trying to standardize and mechanize all policies and practices in an effort to ensure that employees are treated equally. Equality in the workplace must be based on valuing employees equally rather than treating them identically.

If this vision of multicultural organizations sounds somewhat familiar, it is because many management gurus offer similar visions of organizations that will successfully make the transition to the twenty-first century. Organizations possessing the flexibility and openness that are the prerequisites for creating multicultural organizations will have an opportunity to meet not only the imperative of adapting to a changing work force but also the challenges created by rapid changes in technology, the marketplace, international politics, and myriad other internal and external factors that affect doing business. Individuals who possess the flexibility and open-mindedness that are the prerequisites for multicultural literacy will have tools for successfully adapting to the workplace demands of the twenty-first century.

Creating multicultural organizations, however, is not simple. It is difficult enough to imagine them, let alone to create them. A current television advertisement for Oreo cookies shows two little boys sitting in an airport waiting area. One child is Anglo, the other Asian. The Anglo child offers the Asian boy an Oreo. When the Asian child begins to eat it, the Anglo child says "no," and shows him how to take the Oreo apart, lick off the inside icing, put the two pieces of the cookie back together, and then eat it. Both children smile, delighted with their cookies and each other. Part of the appeal of the advertisement comes from its assumption that, despite their different nationalities, these children share more than just a cookie. They share the delights of childhood, the pleasures that make children the world over smile. Bringing culturally diverse people together, however, requires more than an Oreo cookie.

Human beings tend to stick with their own kind. Whether we have an innate tendency to seek out people who are similar, or we have to be "carefully taught" to hate others, as Oscar Hammerstein poignantly wrote in the lyrics to *South Pacific*, the signs are everywhere that we prefer people who look and act as we do. In college classrooms and school cafeterias, students segregate themselves by color, country of origin, and sometimes by ethnicity. In small towns and large urban centers, Polish American, Italian American, and other ethnic clubs are gathering spots for people who share the same ethnic background. Cross-gender friendships are rare; cross-race friendships even rarer. In large organizations, the tendency to group with similar people has served to exclude women and people of color. Moore (1962) called attention to the importance of social similarity for individual success in the organization by defining the corporation metaphorically as a "bureaucratic kinship system" based on "homosexual reproduction," in which the men who populate the organization bond together and recreate themselves (p. 109). Even when organizations have a diverse work force, employees are more likely to seek out others who are like themselves to discuss both work-related and personal issues (Fine, Johnson, & Ryan, 1990).

This human tendency to seek out people who are similar works against the personal openness that is necessary to become multiculturally literate. Achieving multiculturalism within organizations is even more difficult because there are additional pressures exerted against change. Organizations appear to have a natural tendency to resist change and maintain the status quo. What is known appears better than what is unknown. That tendency is often expressed in fears about organizational change. For example, in discussions about diversity, managers and executives often say that programs aimed at developing and encouraging cultural diversity will cost too much money, will decrease productivity, or are too "soft" to be really worthwhile.

U.S. organizations are wont to bury their heads in the sand, to refuse to acknowledge and prepare for a future that is vastly different from what exists now. A typical response to a predicted crisis is to argue that conditions will change or trends will shift, making any organizational changes unnecessary. Those arguments are beginning to emerge now in response to the demographic predictions about the U.S. work force. An illustration of this appeared in a recent article in *Working Woman* (Crittenden, Aug. 1994), which reports on "where *Workforce 2000* went wrong" (p. 18). The author reports that the Hudson Institute study on work force trends mistakenly identified black women rather than Hispanics as the group responsible for the largest increase in the labor market during the 1990s. She also faults the study for omitting the word "net" in describing the percentage of white males added to the work force between 1985 and 1990. The article serves to caution companies about moving too quickly to prepare for a culturally diverse work force because the demographic changes are happening more slowly and are different from those predicted in *Workforce 2000*. The author loses sight of the larger picture, however. The 1990 U.S. Census confirmed the demographic trends toward a more culturally diverse population and work force. Conservative estimates indicate that the United States will no longer be a majority-white country shortly after the middle of the next century. Given the powerful pressures against change, both interpersonally and organizationally, organizations need to start now to initiate programs to adapt to the changing work force. Waiting until the trends are realities will be waiting too long. Quibbling over the exact year when whites will no longer be the majority or which racial or ethnic group will be the largest only diverts attention from the hard work that needs to begin now.

There are some hopeful signs, however, that organizations are developing strategies for meeting the changes. The same issue of *Working Woman* includes a description of flextime options that are available for parents who work in some departments at Aetna Life & Casualty ("Zoë goes public," Aug. 1994). I recently received a marketing letter from Dell Computer targeting me not as a potential buyer of a new computer but as a potential employee. The sales pitch was based on Dell's reputation as an organization that treats women well.

As cultural diversity initiatives have been adopted in a variety of contexts (e.g., corporations, government agencies, universities, and so forth), they have begun to encounter intense criticism for allegedly undermining American unity. Critics on both the right and the left argue that focusing on the differences between people drives a wedge between them. These critics say we need to look for and celebrate our commonalities instead of our differences.

Americans like to believe that underneath it all, people are alike because we share a set of common characteristics that make us human. The United States was founded on that belief. The Declaration of Independence states that people share certain inalienable rights (although, until relatively recently, only white men could claim those rights). Although this book has emphasized the differences among us, people do share some uniquely human qualities. One of those qualities is our desire to be recognized and valued for ourselves, to be known to others and respected by them. In that desire lies a paradox that is inherent in multiculturalism. Because cultural identity is a fundamental part of who people are as individuals, being known and respected includes having one's cultural background acknowledged and respected. What draws us together as Americans is also precisely what separates us.

Over the last several decades, ethnic pride has enjoyed a resurgence in the United States. The Black Power movement in the late 1960s gave us the slogan "Black is beautiful," which told African Americans to be proud of their racial and cultural heritage. African American pride led the way for numerous other cultural groups to express their own sense of pride in themselves. Manifestations of cultural pride can now be found throughout U.S. culture, ranging from fashion, to music, to college courses in a variety of racial and ethnic studies, to ethnic cultural festivals, to the annual Gay Pride marches held in major U.S. cities.

Ethnic pride is a source of both great joy and deep sorrow, for it has historically been, and continues to be, the cause of hatred, conflict, and war among people of different cultural backgrounds throughout the world. Group pride can easily move from self-respect to self-importance to a shared belief in the superiority of the group. Hitler's belief in the superiority of German Aryans fueled his hatred of Jews, gypsies, homosexuals, and numerous others in the 1930s and 1940s. Group pride continues to fuel racial, ethnic, and religious strife around the world, in the Middle East, Northern Ireland, Bosnia, India, Rwanda, and numerous other places. Numerous critics of multiculturalism point to these ethnic divisions and hatred and conclude that the focus on cultural diversity in the United States is dangerous because it fuels the conflicts among us and draws us further apart from one another.

Racial and ethnic conflicts have long been with us, however, sometimes rumbling just below the surface and other times erupting into riots in the street. Avoiding our differences has not served to bring us any closer together or to ensure equal opportunities and rights for all our citizens. It is time for a bold new experiment. Rather than denying our differences, we need to embrace them, to find our common values in the recognition of our cultural differences and the individual respect such recognition accords each of us. The tension inherent in the conflicts contained in the paradox of difference generates the creative energy to allow us to transform and recreate ourselves in the image we began with as a nation.

The process of creating multicultural organizations is difficult, filled with conflict, and never ending. The process itself, however, *is* our final goal. What is important is not a stable vision of the multicultural organization, but a genuine process of change that invites and includes the full participation of all of us.

Diversity initiatives in organizations are an important part of that process of change. But they are not sufficient. Real employment opportunity and full organizational participation requires a sound education. Business, government, and each of us individually must become involved in a coordinated effort to improve the educational attainment of *all* young people in the United States. We all share equally in the responsibility of ensuring that tomorrow's workers have sufficient skills to be productive members of the work force. Disproportionate numbers of African American and Hispanic youth fail to complete high school and college. Women are frequently discouraged from pursuing the study of math and science, while Asians are discouraged from studying anything else. We need to create educational environments in which all students are valued and encouraged. A few urban school systems are making great strides in teaching multiple literacies and cultural understanding, but this pedagogy is still developing.

An educated citizenry goes hand in hand with efforts to create multicultural organizations. The economic well-being of all of us is dependent upon our success in both of these efforts.

REFERENCES

Asante, M.K. (1987). *The Afrocentric idea*. Philadelphia, PA: Temple University Press.

Asante, M.K., & Davis, A. (1989). Encounters in the interracial workplace. In M.K. Asante & W.B. Gudykunst (Eds.), *Handbook of international and intercultural communication* (pp. 374–391). Newbury Park, CA: Sage.

Basil, D.C. (1972). *Women in management*. Cambridge, MA: Dunnellen.

Belenky, M.F., Clinchy, B.M., Goldberger, N.R., & Tarule, J.M. (1986). *Women's ways of knowing: The development of self, voice, and mind*. New York: Basic Books.

Bell, E.L. (1990). The bicultural life experience of career-oriented black women. *Journal of Organizational Behavior, 11*, 459–477.

Bennett, C.E. (1992a). *The Asian and Pacific Islander population in the United States: March 1991 and 1990* (U.S. Bureau of the Census, Current Population Reports, P20-459). Washington, DC: U.S. Government Printing Office.

Bennett, C.E. (1992b). *The Black population in the United States: March 1991* (U.S. Bureau of the Census, Current Population Reports, P20-464). Washington, DC: U.S. Government Printing Office.

Berger, P.L., & Luckmann, T. (1967). *The social construction of reality*. Garden City, NY: Anchor Books.

Bly, R. (1990). *Iron John: A book about men*. Reading, MA: Addison-Wesley.

Bowman, G. W., Worthy, N.B., & Greyser, S.A. (1965, Jul./Aug.). Are women executives people? *Harvard Business Review*, pp. 15–28, 164–178.

Bowman, P.J. (1991). Work life. In J.S. Jackson (Ed.), *Life in black America* (pp. 124–155). Newbury Park, CA: Sage.

Brislin, R.W. (1989). Intercultural communication training. In M.K. Asante & W.B. Gudykunst (Eds.), *Handbook of international and intercultural communication* (pp. 441–457). Newbury Park, CA: Sage.

Burke, R.J., & McKeen, C.A. (1988). *Developing formal mentoring programs in organizations* (Working Paper Series No. NC 88-29). London, Ontario: University of Western Ontario School of Business Administration.

Carbaugh, D. (Ed.). (1990). *Cultural communication and intercultural contact.* Hillsdale, NJ: Lawrence Erlbaum Associates.

Case, S.S. (1993, Summer). The collaborative advantage: The usefulness of women's language to contemporary business problems. *Business and the Contemporary World*, pp. 81–105.

Catalyst Staff. (1981). *Upward mobility.* New York: Warner Books.

Census reform: Early outreach and decisions needed on race and ethnic questions. (1993, Jan.). Report to the Chairman, Subcommittee on Census, Statistics, and Postal Personnel, Committee on Post Office and Civil Service, House of Representatives (GAO/GGD-93-36). Washington, DC: Government Accounting Office.

Cianni, M., & Romberger, B. (1991). Belonging in the corporation: Oral histories of male and female, white, black, and Hispanic managers. *Academy of Management Best Paper Proceedings*, 358–362.

Commission on the Skills of the American Workforce. (1990). *America's choice: High skills or low wages!* Rochester, NY: National Center on Education and the Economy.

Condon, J.C. (1985). *Good neighbors: Communicating with the Mexicans.* Yarmouth, ME: Intercultural Press.

Cox, T., Jr. (1991). The multicultural organization. *The Executive, 5*(2), 34–47.

Cox, T., Jr., & Blake, S. (1991). Managing cultural diversity: implications for organizational competitiveness. *The Executive, 5*(3), 45–56.

Crichton, M. (1993). *Disclosure: A novel.* New York: Random House.

Crittenden, A. (1994, Aug.). Where *Workforce 2000* went wrong. *Working Woman*, p. 18.

Daly, M. (1987). *Webster's first new intergalactic wickedary of the English language* (with J. Caputi). Boston: Beacon Press.

Daniel, J.L., & Smitherman, G. (1976). How I got over: Communication dynamics in the black community. *Quarterly Journal of Speech, 62*, 26–39.

Davis, G., & Watson, G. (1982). *Black life in corporate America.* Garden City, NY: Anchor Press.

Davis, O. (1976). The English language is my enemy. In C.D. Eckhardt, J.F. Holahan, & D.H. Stewart (Eds.), *The Wiley Reader* (pp. 312–313). New York: John Wiley & Sons.

Day, J.C. (1993). *Population projections of the United States, by age, sex, race, and Hispanic origin: 1993–2050* (U.S. Bureau of the Census, Current Population Reports, P25-1104). Washington, DC: U.S. Government Printing Office.

Deal, T.E., & Kennedy, A.A. (1982). *Corporate cultures.* Reading, MA: Addison-Wesley.

DeFreitas, G. (1991). *Inequality at work: Hispanics in the U.S. labor force.* New York: Oxford University Press.

Dembner, A. (1993, July 5). Women, business schools crossing paths less. *Boston Globe*, pp. 1, 12.

Dickens, F., Jr., & Dickens, J.B. (1982). *The black manager: Making it in the corporate world.* New York: AMACOM.

Disch, E. (1993, Sept. 28). *Classroom strategies for responding to incidents of intolerance and insensitivity*. Workshop presented at the University of Massachusetts on the Building of a Pluralistic System of Higher Education: Strategies for Combating Racism and Promoting Civility, UMass/Amherst.

Epstein, C.F. (1975). Institutional barriers: What keeps women out of the executive suite? In F.E. Gordon & M.H. Strober (Eds.), *Bringing women into management* (pp. 7–21). New York: McGraw Hill.

Equal opportunity code of behavior. (1991, June 26). Roxbury, MA: Morgan Memorial Goodwill Industries, Inc.

Equal opportunity code of behavior (1991, July 10). Roxbury, MA: Morgan Memorial Goodwill Industries, Inc.

Fairhurst, G.T., & Snavely, B.K. (1983a). Majority and token minority group relationships: Power acquisition and communication. *Academy of Management Review, 8*, 292–300.

Fairhurst, G.T., & Snavely, B.K. (1983b). A test of the social isolation of male tokens. *Academy of Management Journal, 26*, 353–361.

Farney, D. (1992, Dec. 2). Mosaic of hope. *Wall Street Journal* (eastern ed.), pp. A1, A4.

Federal data collection: Agencies' use of consistent race and ethnic definitions. (1992, Dec.). Report to the Chairman, Committee on Government Operations, House of Representatives (GAO/GGD-93-25). Washington, DC: Government Accounting Office.

Ferdman, B.M. (1990). Literacy and cultural identity. *Harvard Educational Review, 60*, 181–204.

Ferdman, B.M., & Cortes, A.C. (1992). Culture and identity among Hispanic managers in an Anglo business. In S.B. Knouse, P. Rosenfeld, & A.L. Culbertson (Eds.), *Hispanics in the workplace* (pp. 246–277). Newbury Park, CA: Sage.

Ferguson, K.E. (1984). *The feminist case against bureaucracy*. Philadelphia, PA: Temple University Press.

Fernandez, J.P. (1975). *Black managers in white corporations*. New York: John Wiley & Sons.

Fernandez, J.P. (1981). *Racism and sexism in corporate life*. Lexington, MA: D.C. Heath.

Fieg, J.P. (1989). *A common core: Thais and Americans* (rev. ed. by E. Mortlock). Yarmouth, ME: Intercultural Press.

Fierman, J. (1990, July 30). Why women still don't hit the top. *Fortune*, pp. 40–42, 46, 50, 54, 58, 62.

Fine, M.G., & Johnson, F.L. (1984). Female and male motives for using obscenity. *Journal of Language and Social Psychology, 3*(1), 59–74.

Fine, M.G., Johnson, F.L., & Foss, K.A. (1991). Student perceptions of gender in managerial communication. *Women's Studies in Communication, 19*(1), 24–48.

Fine, M.G., Johnson, F.L., & Ryan, M.S. (1990). Cultural diversity in the workplace. *Public Personnel Management, 19*, 305–319.

Fine, M.G., Morrow, A.A., & Quaglieri, P.L. (1990). Professional women in a male-dominated industry: What do they want and where are they going? *HR Horizons, 1*(1), 54–60.

Foeman, A.K., & Pressley, G. (1987). Ethnic culture and corporate culture: Using black styles in organizations. *Communication Quarterly, 35*, 293–307.

Friedan, B. (1963). *The feminine mystique*. New York: Dell.

Frost, P.J., Moore, L.F., Louis, M.R., Lundberg, C.C., & Martin, J. (Eds.). (1985). *Organizational culture*. Beverly Hills, CA: Sage.

Garcia, J.M., & Montgomery, P.A. (1991a). *The Hispanic population in the United States: March 1990* (U.S. Bureau of the Census, Current Population Reports, P20-449). Washington, DC: U.S. Government Printing Office.

Garcia, J.M., & Montgomery, P.A. (1991b). *The Hispanic population in the United States: March 1991* (U.S. Bureau of the Census, Current Population Reports, P20-455). Washington, DC: U.S. Government Printing Office.

Gilligan, C. (1982). *In a different voice*. Cambridge, MA: Harvard University Press.

Ginorio, A.B. (1987). Puerto Rican ethnicity and conflict. In J. Boucher, D. Landis, & K.A. Clark (Eds.), *Ethnic conflict: International perspectives* (pp. 182–206). Newbury Park, CA: Sage.

Gochenour, T. (1990). *Considering Filipinos*. Yarmouth, ME: Intercultural Press.

Gordon, F.E., & Strober, M.H. (Eds.). (1975). *Bringing women into management*. New York: McGraw Hill.

Greenhaus, J.H., Parasuraman, S., & Wormley, W.M. (1990). Effects of race on organizational experiences, job performance evaluations, and career outcomes. *Academy of Management Journal, 33*, 64–86.

Gudykunst, W.B. (1991). *Bridging differences: Effective intergroup communication*. Newbury Park, CA: Sage.

Gudykunst, W.B., Nishida, T., & Morisaki, S. (1992, May). *The influence of personal and social identity on expectations for interpersonal and intergroup encounters in Japan and the United States*. Paper presented at the annual meeting of the International Communication Association, Miami, FL.

Hall, B.J. (1992). Theories of culture and communication. *Communication Theory, 2*, 50–70.

Harragan, B.L. (1977). *Games mother never taught you: Corporate gamesmanship for women*. New York: Warner Books.

Harré, R., & Secord, P.F. (1973). *The explanation of social behavior*. Totowa, NJ: Littlefield, Adams.

Hatchett, S.J. (1991). Women and men. In J.S. Jackson (Ed.), *Life in black America* (pp. 84–104). Newbury Park, CA: Sage.

Hatchett, S.J., Cochran, D.L., & Jackson, J.S. (1991). Work life. In J.S. Jackson (Ed.), *Life in black America* (pp. 46–83). Newbury Park, CA: Sage.

Hatfield, J.D., & Huseman, R.C. (1982). Perceptual congruence about communication as related to satisfaction: Moderating effects of individual characteristics. *Academy of Management Journal, 25*, 349–358.

Hecht, M.L., Collier, M.J., & Ribeau, S.A. (1993). *African American communication: Ethnic identity and cultural interpretation*. Newbury Park, CA: Sage.

Hecht, M.L., Ribeau, S., & Alberts, J.K. (1989). An Afro-American perspective on interethnic communication. *Communication Monographs, 56*, 385–410.

Hennig, M., & Jardim, A. (1976). *The managerial woman: The survival manual for women in business*. New York: Pocket Books.

Hoffman, E. (1989). *Lost in translation: A life in a new language*. New York: Penguin.

Hofstede, G. (1984). *Culture's consequences: International differences in work-related values* (abridged ed.). Newbury Park, CA: Sage.

Hull, G.T., Scott, P.B., & Smith, B. (1982). *All the women are white, all the blacks are men, but some of us are brave*. Old Westbury, NY: Feminist Press.

Inoue, K. (1979). Japanese: A story of language and people. In T. Shopen (Ed.), *Languages and their speakers* (pp. 241–300). Cambridge, MA: Winthrop Publishers.

Jacklin, C.N., & Maccoby, E.E. (1975). Sex differences and their implications for management. In F.E. Gordon & M.H. Strober (Eds.), *Bringing women into management* (pp. 23–28). New York: McGraw Hill.

Jackson, S.E., & Associates. (1992). *Diversity in the workplace: Human resources initiatives*. New York: Guilford.

Johnson, F.L. (1983). Political and pedagogical implications of attitudes toward women's language. *Communication Quarterly, 31*, 133–138.

Johnson, F.L. (1989). Women's culture and communication: An analytical perspective. In C.M. Lont & S.A. Friedley (Eds.), *Beyond boundaries: Sex and gender diversity in communication* (pp. 301–316). Fairfax, VA: George Mason University Press.

Johnson, F.L., & Aries, E.J. (1983). The talk of women friends. *Women's Studies International Forum, 6*, 353–361.

Johnson, F.L., & Fine, M.G. (1985). Sex differences in uses and perceptions of obscenity. *Women's Studies in Communication, 8*(1), 11–24.

Johnson, J., & Arneson, P. (1991). Women expressing anger to women in the workplace: Perceptions of conflict resolution styles. *Women's Studies in Communication, 14*(2), 24–41.

Johnston, W.B., & Packer, A.E. (1987). *Workforce 2000: Work and workers for the 21st century*. Indianapolis, IN: Hudson Institute.

Kanter, R.M. (1977). *Men and women of the corporation*. New York: Basic Books.

Keller, E.F. (1985). *Reflections on gender and science*. New Haven, CT: Yale University Press.

Kennedy, J.H. (1993, June 27). Overcoming a racist image. *Boston Globe*, pp. 51, 52.

Kerlinger, F.N. (1964). *Foundations of behavioral research*. New York: Holt, Rinehart, and Winston.

Kochman, T. (1981). *Black and white: Styles in conflict*. Chicago: University of Chicago Press.

Kondo, D. (1990). *Crafting selves: Power, gender, and discourses of identity in a Japanese workplace*. Chicago: University of Chicago Press.

Knouse, S.B., Rosenfeld, P., & Culbertson, A.L. (Eds.) (1992). *Hispanics in the workplace*. Newbury Park, CA: Sage.

Kram, K. (1985). *Mentoring at work: Developmental relationships in organizational life*. Glenview, IL: Scott, Foresman.

Krone, K.J., Jablin, F.M., & Putnam, L.L. (1987). Communication theory and organizational communication: Multiple perspectives. In F.M. Jablin, L.L. Putnam, K.H. Roberts, & L.W. Porter (Eds.), *Handbook of organizational communication: An interdisciplinary perspective* (pp. 18–40). Newbury Park, CA: Sage.

Lakoff, R. (1975). *Language and woman's place*. New York: Harper & Row.

Larwood, L., & Wood, M.M. (1977). *Women in management*. Lexington, MA: D.C. Heath.

Loden, M. (1985). *Feminine leadership or how to succeed in business without being one of the boys*. New York: Times Books.

Loden, M., & Rosener, J.B. (1991). *Workforce America! Managing employee diversity as a vital resource*. Homewood, IL: Business One Irwin.

Louis, M.R. (1983). Organizations as culture-bearing milieux. In L.R. Pondy, P.J. Frost, G. Morgan, & T. Dandridge (Eds.), *Organizational symbolism* (pp. 39–54). Greenwich, CT: JAI Press.

Mamet, D. (1993). *Oleanna*. New York: Random House.

Moore, W. (1962). *The conduct of the corporation*. New York: Random House Vintage.

Mumby, D.K. (1987). The political function of narrative in organizations. *Communication Monographs, 54*, 113–127.

Noe, R. (1988). Women and mentoring: A review and research agenda. *Academy of Management Review, 13*, 65–78.

Pearce, W.B., & Cronen, V.E. (1980). *Communication, action, and meaning: The creation of social realities*. New York: Praeger.

Peters, T., & Waterman, R.H. (1982). *In search of excellence*. New York: Harper & Row.

Peterson, R.A. (1979). Revitalizing the culture concept. *American Review of Sociology, 5*, 137–166.

Powell, G.N. (1990). One more time: Do female and male managers differ? *The Executive, 4*(3), 68–75.

Putnam, L.L. (1983). The interpretive perspective: An alternative to functionalism. In L.L. Putnam & M.E. Pacanowsky (Eds.), *Communication and organizations: An interpretive approach* (pp. 31–54). Beverly Hills, CA: Sage.

"Race and Hispanic origin." (1991, June). *1990 Census profile* (No. 2). Washington, DC: U.S. Bureau of the Census.

Raymond, J.G. (1979). *The transsexual empire: The making of the she-male*. Boston: Beacon Press.

Redding, S.G., & Ng, M. (1982). The role of "face" in the organizational perceptions of Chinese managers. *Organization Studies, 3*(3), 201–219.

Rodriguez, R. (1982). *Hunger of memory*. Toronto, Ontario: Bantam Books.

Rosener, J.B. (1990, Nov./Dec.). Ways women lead. *Harvard Business Review*, pp. 119–125.

Schein, E.H. (1987). Defining organizational culture. In J.M. Shafritz & J.S. Ott (Eds.), *Classics of organization theory* (2nd ed.) (pp. 381–395). Chicago: Dorsey Press. (Reprinted from *Organizational culture and leadership*, 1985, San Francisco, CA: Jossey-Bass.)

Schiffrin, D. (1984). Jewish argument as sociability. *Language and Society, 13*, 311–335.

Schwartz, F.N. (1989, Jan./Feb.). Management women and the new facts of life. *Harvard Business Review*, pp. 65–76.

Sehgal, R. (1991, Aug. 9). Firms restricting women, minorities. *Boston Globe*, pp. 1, 10.

Servaes, J. (1988). Cultural identity in east and west. *Howard Journal of Communications, 1*(2), 58–71.

Shafritz, J.M., & J.S. Ott (Eds.). (1987). *Classics of organization theory* (2nd ed.). Chicago: Dorsey Press.

Smircich, L., & Calas, M.B. (1987). Organizational culture: A critical assessment. In F.M. Jablin, L.L. Putnam, K.H. Roberts, & L.W. Porter (Eds.), *Handbook of organizational communication: An interdisciplinary perspective* (pp. 228–263). Newbury Park, CA: Sage.

Smitherman, G. (1977). *Talkin and testifyin: The language of black America*. Boston: Houghton Mifflin.

Snavely, B.K., & Fairhurst, G.T. (1984). An examination of the male nursing student as a token. *Research in Nursing and Health, 7*, 287–294.

Sternlieb, G., & Hughes, J.W. (1988). The demographic long wave: Population trends and economic growth. In G. Sternlieb & J.W. Hughes (Eds.), *America's new market geography* (pp. 19–42). New Brunswick, NJ: Center for Urban Policy Research.

Storti, C. (1990). *The art of crossing cultures*. Yarmouth, ME: Intercultural Press.

Survey of minority-owned business enterprises: Asian Americans, American Indians, and other minorities (1991). Washington, DC: U.S. Bureau of the Census.

Sutton, C.D., & Moore, K.K. (1985, Sept./Oct.). Executive women—20 years later. *Harvard Business Review*, pp. 42–44, 48, 50, 52, 56, 58, 60, 62, 66.

Swenson, C.A. (1990, Feb.). How to speak to Hispanics. *American Demographics*, pp. 40–41.

Swidler, A. (1986). Culture in action. *American Sociological Review, 51*, 273–286.

Tannen, D. (1990). *You just don't understand: Women and men in conversation*. New York: William Morrow.

Taylor, A. (1986, Aug. 18). Why women managers are bailing out. *Fortune*, pp. 16–23.

Taylor, R.J., & Chatters, L.M. (1991). Religious life. In J.S. Jackson (Ed.), *Life in black America* (pp. 105–123). Newbury Park, CA: Sage.

Ting-Toomey, S. (1985). Toward a theory of conflict and culture. In W.B. Gudykunst, L.P. Stewart, & S. Ting-Toomey (Eds.), *Communication, culture, and organizational processes* (pp. 71–86). Beverly Hills, CA: Sage.

Towers Perrin & Hudson Institute. (1990). *Workforce 2000: Competing in a seller's market: Is corporate America prepared?* New York: Towers Perrin.

Tucker, R.K., Weaver, R.L., Jr., & Berryman-Fink, C. (1981). *Research in speech communication*. Englewood Cliffs, NJ: Prentice-Hall.

Tung-Sun, C. (1970). A Chinese philosopher's theory of knowledge. In G.P. Stone & H.A. Farberman (Eds.), *Social psychology through symbolic interaction* (pp. 121–139). Waltham, MA: Xerox College Publishing.

U.S. Bureau of the Census. (1991). *Statistical Abstract of the United States: 1991*. Washington, DC: U.S. Government Printing Office.

U.S. Bureau of the Census. (1992). *Statistical Abstract of the United States: 1992*. Washington, DC: U.S. Government Printing Office.

Walker, B.A., & Hanson, W.C. (1992). Valuing differences at Digital Equipment Corporation. In S.E. Jackson & Associates (Eds.), *Diversity in the workplace: Human resources initiatives* (pp. 119–137). New York: Guilford.

Weber, S.N. (1991). The need to be: The sociocultural significance of black language. In L.A. Samovar & R.E. Porter (Eds.), *Intercultural communication: A reader* (6th ed.) (pp. 277–282). Belmont, CA: Wadsworth.

Wenzhong, H., & Grove, C.L. (1991). *Encountering the Chinese: A guide for Americans*. Yarmouth, ME: Intercultural Press.

Will, G. (1991, Feb. 11). The military meritocracy. *Newsweek*, p. 70.

Winkler, K.J. (1992, July 8). A scholar's provocative query: Was Huckleberry Finn black? *Chronicle of Higher Education*, pp. A6, A7, A8.

Wood, J.T. (1994). *Gendered lives: Communication, gender, and culture.* Belmont, CA: Wadsworth.

Wyatt, N. (1984). Power and decision making. In G.M. Phillips & J.T. Wood (Eds.), *Women communicating: Studies of women's talk* (pp. 147–176). Norwood, NJ: Ablex.

"Zoë goes public" (1994, Aug.). *Working Woman,* pp. 47–48, 51.

INDEX

ABOUT THE AUTHOR

MARLENE G. FINE is Chair and Associate Professor in the Department of Marketing and Communication at the University of Massachusetts, Boston. With numerous articles in the scholarly and professional journals, Fine lectures widely on cultural diversity in organizations, with particular emphasis on gender and race issues.